Exploring
Strategic Groups

Exploring
Strategic Groups

James Rafferty

The University of Buckingham Press

First published by Europrime Publishing 2008
Second Edition Published by Buckingham University Press 2017

British Library Cataloguing in Publication Data
A catalogue record for this book is available from the British Library

ISBN 978-1-908684-67-7

Printed and bound in Great Britain by Marston Book Services Ltd, Oxfordshire

To my grandson, George

CONTENTS

Contents

Contents

LIST OF FIGURES

LIST OF TABLES

Contents

PREFACE TO THE SECOND EDITION

For more than a quarter of a century, the concept of strategic groups has established itself in the literature on strategy and strategic management. At the most familiar level it is presented as either a fairly rudimentary form of analysis involving two dimensional characteristics to map firms in competitive space, or as a bionomics perspective that emphasises strategic group identity through managerial cognition. In the former there is a subliminal tendency to assume that strategic decision-makers share the same perceptions about strategic dimensions and in turn, that this is reflected in the nature and extent of their firms' commitment to particular strategic choices. In the latter case, the assumption of homogeneity is less pronounced and more cautious. However, while it presents strategic group effects that may be negative as well as positive, it nevertheless affirms a strong commitment to the existence of strategic group identity through the development of cognitive groups. Importantly, strategic group identity is held to be significantly meaningful at the level of the frim and to provide strategic coherence in decision-making.

Initially this book was a response to the rudimentary mapping perspective, but with the output of scholarship in this field it became a more engaging and longitudinal task. On the one hand, this seemed necessary because of the very thin layer of empirical research that seemed to be supporting so much of this output; and on the other hand, it presented an opportunity to conduct empirical research that attempted to provide a more stalwart view of the realities of cognitive groups and strategic group identity.

The endeavour was rewarding. Not only did it reveal the frailties of relying on the assumption of homogeneity among strategic decision-makers in firms, but it provided gainful evidence of significant weaknesses in the strategic group identity thesis. Indeed, it suggested that far from the emergence of strategic group identities at the level of the firm, there were very weak ties among managers in relation to their cognitions at this level. However, of significance was the existence of strong managerial cognitions about hybrid generic strategy at the level of the industry.

This strategy was informed by the scope, scale and concentration along historical lines in the industry and offered the opportunity to test the meaningfulness of the research by taking a longitudinal view to establish if the hybrid generic strategy would indeed continue to be pursued in the industry. I believe the wait was worthwhile and the updates to the first edition will hopefully elucidate that at the level of the industry there is indeed evidence that managerial cognitions in a group sense, do coalesce to provide strategic continuity.

For his enduring patience throughout this 'wait' I am very grateful to Christopher M Woodhead of University of Buckingham Press.

PREFACE TO THE FIRST EDITION

This book reflects the outcome of research I first began in the late 1980's and early 1990's and which, at that time, culminated in the submission of my doctoral thesis. As with many forms of critical inquiry, the dialectical process infuses the researcher with a longitudinal perspective that, from time to time, stimulates reflections and reviews of notions and ideas that result in the re-evaluation of the material. This often leads to the adoption of a fresh approach and new insights, or the reaffirmation of the original ideas based on a more extensive history of the opinions under scrutiny. This book, therefore, represents an exploration, which began some time ago, and attempts to encompass the audible observations that, with the passage of time, have enhanced the discussion and the disputation of the theme of strategic groups.

The revisions from the original work represent less of a change of emphasis than an attempt to expand certain issues and provide greater clarity that may be of interest to a wider audience. In this sense the key disputation within the theme of strategic groups, namely, the existence of cognitive strategic groups is the central focus of exploration in this book. The popularised concept of strategic groups is of firms in an industry following similar strategies along particular strategic dimensions. These dimensions provide examples of prototypically similar firms who can then be clustered as a strategic group. This clustering enables analysts, including managers within the industry, to identify specific prototypes as a means of disaggregating industry complexity and consequently to examine the extent and depth of industry competition.

Implicit in the prescriptive notion of strategic groups is the assumption that managers' perceptions of strategic dimensions are homogenous. Indeed this assumption may extend to the existence of the homogeneity of managerial perceptions of strategic dimensions of the individual firms within a strategic group. This assumption links the individual's cognition of strategic dimensions in a way that suggests that the closeness and similarity of manager's perceptions of these dimensions results in a group cognition, which leads to collective agreement and action. The independence of specific prototypes of firm clusters in turn is presumed to underpin the robustness of this assumption.

The main aim of the exploration of strategic groups in this book is to examine the above assumption from an empirical perspective rather than to theorize about issues of group cognition. In this way it is intended to elucidate the realities of managerial cognition in relation to strategic dimensions and to link these to the operational characteristics of firm strategies. The cognitive mapping of core constructs is facilitated by the use of repertory grid methodology and the hypothesis that managers' perceptions of key strategic dimensions are homogenous within strategic groups is tested utilising cluster analysis to identify "cognitive" groupings across firms in the UK Brewing industry. Principle components analysis and factor analysis are used to validate the cluster solutions.

The UK Brewing industry provides the backcloth for the empirical evidence and analysis of "cognitive groups" and is based on the original research thesis, with recent developments in the sector being incorporated to bring the case up-to-date. The Brewing industry has historical significance in the UK, dating back to the Middle Ages. In more recent times it has provided an example of an industry that experienced substantial turbulence emanating from government regulation that went straight to the heart of competition policy in the industry. This period witnessed acute strategic instability and as such provided a particularly interesting setting for an exploration of managerial perceptions of strategic dimensions.

While the literature on strategic groups is comprehensive, at least in terms of articles in academic journals, there is persistent controversy about the notion and existence of cognitive strategic groups within the realms of strategic group analysis as a disaggregating tool for analysing industry structure. My purpose here is to provide a robust exploration of this dichotomy based on the traditional approach of empirical evidence. For some my findings may be controversial, since they detract from what has become a fairly habitual point of view and may cut across a convenient academic concept. However, the findings reflect a reality of managerial perceptions that, while not corroborating the phenomenon of homogeneity, enables us to appreciate that managers do not necessarily need to share common perceptions about key strategic dimensions in order to formulate and implement strategies aimed at sustaining competitive advantages in their industry. In this respect I hope both scholars and practitioners of strategic analysis and management will find this book persuasive.

*   *   *

This book is the result of the positive influences I have experienced over many years from scholars in the academic community and from practitioners in the real world, both wittingly and unwittingly. In the late 1970's, whilst studying at the University of Strathclyde Graduate Business School, I was fortunate to get to know the late Professor Neil Hood, who planted the initial seeds of enthusiasm about strategy in my mind. Later this interest found challenging contexts in the business world with General Motors Corporation and the Granada Group, prior to periods as managing director with firms in the electronics, financial services and precision engineering industries. These managerial settings provided a rich mixture of strategic analysis and decision– making and I am grateful to all of those who contributed to my understanding of strategy along the way.

Managers in the UK brewing industry made the original research possible and I am very grateful for the time and cooperation they extended to me.

Others who have conversed with me and stimulated my interest in strategy, economics and industrial policy include Michael Best, Robin Murray, and Tom

Payton.

Finally, I would like to thank my children who are a constant source of encouragement and to whom this book is dedicated.

Every effort has been made to cite sources accurately and acknowledge copyright and the publisher will be glad to hear from any copyright holders whom it has not been possible to contact. Any errors, omissions and shortcomings of the text are naturally my responsibility.

James Rafferty
Olney, 2008

Chapter 1 Setting Out The Background

Introduction

The genesis of this book is the trial of experience. Like many who share an interest in the concept of business strategy, my initial perspective on the subject emanated from a fairly narrow economic base, extending from the Traditional Theory of the Firm. However, having spent a number of years operating at a strategic level in business, these insights were informed by the processes of strategic management. This fostered the conviction that the cognition of managers about competition was shaped by their perceptions of specific strategic aspects of their industry and the importance of these to competitiveness.

Little has been written in the popular literature on strategy of how managers' thinking shapes strategy or how strategy shapes managerial thinking. This is perhaps explained, not surprisingly, by the fact that many writers on strategic management have tended to concentrate on the economic structure/strategy issue to the detriment of perhaps this most important link in strategic analysis and formulation; the extent to which shared group cognition actually reflects the strategic outcomes of firms. This in turn begs the question, is the group cognitive component of strategic management the key component, or is it really a non-issue?

In the economic literature, the classification of firms into particular industries is a fairly broad method of categorisation. Firms are grouped into industries on the basis of product categories (e.g. the insurance industry) and these in turn are grouped into industry sectors (e.g. the manufacturing sector; agriculture and fisheries; transport; defence; construction; and financial services). While these groupings assist us in analysing the growth and decline of sectors in an economy, in competitive terms they tells us little about changes in industry structure based on the strategic moves of particular groups. To analyse firms in the same industry that are competitors to each other on the basis of particular strategies, we need to subdivide industrial groupings into more comprehensive clusters. The method of analysing industries to produce clusters of firms, who follow the same strategic dimensions, is the essence of the strategic group concept.

Implicit in this concept is the notion that competitive strategies are the manifestation of the homogeneity of managerial cognitions about the strategic dimensions to be implemented. However, while managerial cognition of strategic dimensions informs the business policies and corporate strategies of firms, it is not clear that these strategic outcomes represent and reflect the collective agreement of managers. The assumption of homogeneity is a normative prescription which, while fitting neatly with the dissagregative concept of strategic groups, does not provide any significant insights into the nature of the shared group cognition process that is suggested is the underlying characteristic of the outcome of firms following the same strategic dimensions. The aim of this book is to explore the presumption that strategic development is synonymous with group mental models about strategy that are shared among decision-makers in the strategy process.

The Traditional Theory of the Firm

The Traditional Theory of the Firm equated the actions of the business entity with profit maximisation. In essence, the theory made predictions about the behaviour of firms faced with choices a relatively simple matter. In the Theory, the firm was synonymous with a "black box" upon which environmental stimuli impinged in the form of market variables, with the business entity responding in what was viewed as essentially an input/output relationship. This view undoubtedly influenced the theoretical constructs that characterised the early development of business strategy as a rational process. The notion of a firm's strategy being the embodiment of a rational and intrinsically logical set of policies imbued policy makers with a rather blinkered economic determinism - arguably a characteristic most pronounced throughout the 1960's and 1970's.

Consequently, strategy in its early application to business management, initially mirrored a rather sharp contrast between planning and doing. The planning was to be done by firms' senior executives, the Managing Director, the CEO and the Board, while the doing was to be delegated through the ranks of the firm. In this sense strategic decisions were seen as somehow distinct from the actual process whereby they were to be implemented.

In the academic literature, this view corresponded with economists understanding that the objective of the firm was to maximise profits and the strategy employed to achieve this was to ensure that marginal cost was equal to marginal revenue. This basic strategy of the firm excluded any behavioural assumptions and represented a simple mathematical model, which linked the objective of profit maximisation with the strategy of how this was achieved. In this sense, the traditional theory of the firm was the first normative model adopted by economists to inform firms of strategic action.

The purpose of the theory of the firm is to predict the prices which firms will charge for their products or services and the quantity they will produce or supply in a given period. The predictive model developed from these aims to ensure that the objective of profit maximisation is always met and can be illustrated as follows:

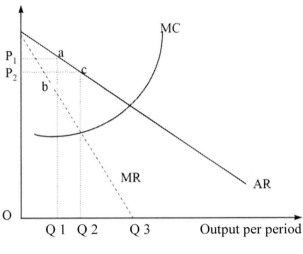

Where: AR = Average Revenue
        MR = Marginal Revenue
        MC = Marginal Cost
        P = Price
        Q = Quantity

Figure 1. Marginal Revenue and Marginal Costs

Figure 1 summarises the logic behind the objective of MC=MR. It can be seen that output OQ_2, where MC=MR, is the point at which profits are maximised. The strategic actions which follow from this model dictate that, by necessity, firms must be output orientated whereby they must seek the output at which MC=MR. There is also a focus on price. That is, from the demand curve AR, firms will engage in finding the price at which this quantity will be bought.

Equilibrium

The theory of the firm and the notion of equilibrium in traditional economics is underpinned by the assumption of perfect information, a notion which evokes the concept of perception in relation to external stimuli. In classical economics the idea that supernormal profits (i.e. profits which exceed the industry norm) will accrue to firms primarily as a result of first mover advantages is utilised to explain why some firms do better than others in the short-term. However, the assumption of perfect information nullifies this advantage, as firms in an industry level-out at equilibrium and normal profits characterise the success of firms.

Equilibrium explains the short-term phenomenon of firm and market interaction, *ceteris paribus*. Since the idea of theorising is to abstract the essential characteristics of the interplay of variables and to examine the general implications of these, the traditional theory provides a relevant useful point of departure for strategic analysis. However, while perfect information provides an explanation of how firms reach equilibrium in the short-term, where normal profits accrue to firms and the price level reflects the demand of the market, it does not reveal why some firms consistently out-perform others over the longer-term.

This is because short-term profit maximisation is not the principal objective of the firm. The long-term strategic behaviour of firms suggests that firms and the managers who run them are prepared to forego short-term profit maximisation in order to gain longer-term supernormal profits, which can be consistently defended and sustained over time.

Accommodating Uncertainty

Financial economics has attempted to modify the theory of the firm by emphasising the maximisation of the value of the firm over time. This recognises that firms are prepared to defer higher returns in the short-term for longer-term value. Firms' actions, which forego short-term profit maximisation, are explained by two additional tenets of economics, namely, liquidity preference and the time value of money. Financial economics attempts to accommodate the long-term disequilibrium of firms by encompassing uncertainty and the time value of money in a model which reflects the present value of expected profit maximisation. In order to explain the dynamic of long-term disequilibrium, but remain within the realms of economic rationality, the economic model is adjusted to reflect "expected profit maximisation" through discounting at an appropriate interest rate.

Profit maximisation is "expected" in this model because the future course of events may alter the outcome, as this affects profit maximisation. Therefore, future events must be factored down to take account of this. In short, there is a cost of waiting and this cost is reflected in the level of interest rates. Interest rates represent a broad proxy of an entity to forego current consumption (profits) now (i.e. liquidity preference) in favour of a greater level of consumption in the future. The model deals with the problem of short-term maximisation and presents a rationality to explain the possibility of disequilibrium both in the short and long-term. This model and its refinement of the traditional theory of the firm can be summarised as follows: -

$$Value\ of\ the\ firm = \frac{\pi_1}{(1+i)^1} + \frac{\pi_2}{(1+i)^2} + \cdots + \frac{\pi_N}{(1+i)^N} = \sum_{t=1}^{N} \frac{\pi_t}{(1+i)^t}$$

The model reflects that profits are equal to revenues minus costs, viz: -

$$Value = \sum_{t=1}^{N} \frac{TR_t - TC_t}{(1+i)^t}$$

where: TR = Total Revenue
TC = Total Costs
i = Interest Rate
N = Number of periods
π = Profit

Figure 2. The Expected Value Model

The key feature of this model, in line with traditional theory, is its rationality and its implicit capability as a predictive or normative model. However, while the model characterises the rational interplay of variables to help explain the theoretical underpinnings of value maximisation, it does not deal with the nature or essence of strategic management in explaining how these economic interplays came about. In short, it ignores the process that takes place within the firm and, in this sense, its prescriptive nature mirrors the "black box" approach to economic organisation, where inputs and outputs are dealt with in an essentially rational manner.

The Optimisation Model

The orthodox economic model emanating from the theory of the firm also has its refinement in linear programming models that attempt to explain the economic interplay, which determines value and its maximisation within the firm. Linear programming models however reflect market constraints and deal with the criticism that maximisation is flawed because no one can tell what a firm's maximisation will be. Another price and another output may increase profits, and the firm cannot know this for sure unless it tries these other price and output levels. By introducing market constraints (and shadow variables), linear programming models enable maximisation objectives to be tested. The basic model is characterised as follows: -

$$Z = X_1 + X_2 + X_3 \ldots + X_n$$

where: Z = Profit optimisation
X = Product contribution

Figure 3. The Linear Programming Technique

However, how managers arrive at decisions concerning the inputs to achieve their profit (or contribution using accounting terminology in linear programming) is a consequence of their cognitive constructs about the dimensions and aspects of the competitive situation which they perceive to be important. This cognitive lens perspective views managerial action against a backcloth whereby knowledge, beliefs, cultures and structure cannot be objectively de-coupled from decisions concerned with strategy. In this sense, even if we consider strategic decisions to be mirrored in a game model such as that offered in game theory, the basic idea that we attempt to look at a competitive situation from all sides at once ("he knows we know he knows we know"), we are compelled to assume a common rationality and shared perception of the importance of some strategic dimensions over others, even when we know these dimensions may become random variables. In reality, it is clear that the data upon which we make decisions is not necessarily independent of those decisions. For example, in a competitive situation, if we base our selling price on our competitor's selling price, this may well result in our competitor changing his/her selling price.

The perception of which dimensions are strategically important to competition may be shared by decision-makers within and across firms and on these cognitive constructions, strategic actions and plans may follow. In this sense we could say that within an industry there may exist strategic groupings of firms along strategic dimensions, which will reflect the managerial perception of their decision-makers. Indeed, we may hypothesise that strategic groups exist because of the cognition of managers and their construction of cognitive frameworks that guide their strategic positioning in competitive space.

The Concept of Strategy

Orthodox economic theory is based on a plan/market dichotomy where firms are envisaged as "...... islands of conscious power in an ocean of unconscious co-operation like lumps of butter coagulating in a pail of buttermilk" (Robertson, 1928:85). Traditional theories of the firm treat both business and industrial organisation as exogenously and independently determined. A firm's actions and organisation are determined by the "laws" of supply and demand and industrial organisation is independent of both intra and interfirm organisation. This orthodox account depends upon the assumption that competition over price is the only form of competition. However, if, instead, firms can choose the form of competition, then the implications for economic analysis are far reaching. Managers are no longer passive responders to external constraints, but strategic agents capable of developing actions designed to relax constraints on their future actions or to impose constraints on the actions of actual or potential competitors. The way a business is organised can itself become a competitive weapon and strategic action and struggles can shape industrial organisation (Best, 1990).

Strategy is a word with a military history. In military terminology we could define strategy as the marshalling of one's forces in such a way as to impose upon the enemy the place, time and conditions for competing, advantageous to oneself. It thus involves, in the military context, assessing the contours of the terrain, assessing the strengths and weaknesses of the enemy relative to one's own, and framing a plan of action in the light of these judgements and, most importantly, of the military objectives.

In his seminal work on strategy and structure, Chandler (1962) presented what is perhaps the first, and arguably the most, enduring definition of business strategy. He defined strategy as the determination of, and courses of actions and allocation of resources that lead to, the achievement of long-term objectives and goals. Chandler saw the long-term objectives as the raison d'être of companies and the courses of action and allocations of resources as the decision-making areas for managers in achieving these goals and objectives. Reflecting the classical notion of rationality as defined by Weber (1964), Chandler argued that the complexity of the business environment, both internally and externally to the firm, produced a hierarchy of decisions. This notion also reflected the existence of a hierarchy of objectives (Payton, 1986). This hierarchy in turn related to different levels of managerial decision-making and to the different implementation times associated with the actions of the firm. While Chandler's work broke with the economic orthodoxy of the firm, it promoted the vision of strategy-making as essentially a top down phenomenon.

Corporate Strategy

The hierarchical implications of strategy development have been expanded by Schendel (1985) to inform an identification of different levels of strategy making. Following Uyterhoven et al (1977), Schendel identifies the question of what business a company is in, as a corporate strategic level decision. This question reflects considerations of long-term investment commitments, their timing and the criteria for accepting or rejecting proposals. The second strategic decision-making level concerns the individual business unit and decisions about achieving and maintaining competitive advantage. Finally, functional level decisions concerned with marketing, production, personnel and so on, reflect strategic decision-making at an operational level aimed at achieving the objectives of the business unit.

Within the literature on strategic groups by far the majority of studies (Hunt, 1972; Newman, 1978; Porter, 1980; Galbraith and Schendel, 1983) have identified groups from decisions made at the corporate strategic level. In the main these studies have used strategic investment decisions to classify strategic groups. Porter in his work on corporate strategy developed the notion of strategic groups. He defined them as a "group of firms in an industry following the same or a similar strategy along the [same] strategic dimensions" (Porter, 1980: 129). One difficulty with this approach is that it neglects the competitive advantage level decision making process within individual firms. Indeed, it assumes that corporate level decisions in an industry share the same level of support from the other strategic levels of the firm. The result is that these equilibrium studies are really concerned with the creation and height of entry barriers or at best with the establishment of long-term mobility barriers, rather than the competitive dimensions which form the basis of seeking competitive advantage. The problem with these corporate level studies is that firms are grouped on a structural basis that fails to capture the extent to which firm rivalry differs in the actual competitive situation. The essence of competitive actions is to be found in the emphasis on particular competitive dimensions, and corporate level strategic decisions obscure the existence of strategic actions at the competitive level.

The vision of the plan/market dichotomy in orthodox economic theory projects an image of a sector as a multitude of identical firms each replicated from the same blueprint. In this vision, firms are either in a sector within which they each produce products that can be substituted one for the other or in a distinct sector. The possibilities of distinctive strategic groups of firms within a sector or of non-market, interfirm relations are ruled out by definition.

An alternative vision of a sector projects an image of collections of heterogeneous firms, which can be interrelated in a variety of ways. In this vision, no firm is an island. Instead, each firm is sustained by access to a variety of resources provided by other firms and interfirm institutions that in themselves are the embodiments of cognitive frameworks of managerial perceptions of strategic dimensions. Economic viability demands that each firm establishes a distinctive competence within a specific process, activity or function that will give it a competitive advantage in what it does over potential competitors. It does so by developing an organisation and management structure in which the shared experience of human productive resources is a basis for a competitive edge. Firms such as this are interrelated sometimes by spontaneous, impersonal market relationships, but at other times by carefully nurtured, consultative, quasi-administrative relationships. To better understand this vision within an industry sector, we have to replace the market/plan dichotomy with a conceptual framework that can account for such non-market, non-plan forms of co-ordination (Best, 1990). The homogeneity of strategic groups based on strategic dimensions provides this conceptual framework. Strategic groups are therefore not equivalent to market niches or, for that matter, to strategic business units, but rather clusters of firms following almost homogeneous strategies within an industry based on managerial cognitions of key dimensions.

These specific forms underpin the issue of managerial cognition in strategic groups. The strategic group concept, therefore, begs the question: is there a causal relationship between managerial cognition and homogeneous strategic groups within industry sectors, given the vision that strategic groups are characterised by clusters of firms following similar (if not identical) business strategies? However, before addressing the issue of managerial cognition in more detail, it is necessary to specify the problem being explored more comprehensively.

The Central Question

The economic organisation perspective (Hunt, 1972; et al) has stressed the value of exploring performance differences within industry sectors as a means of challenging Bain's (1956) proposition that barriers to entry lead to the symmetrical distribution of economic benefits among firms. Bain's (1956) study represents a continuum of the orthodox approach in that the theory of perfect information and equilibrium underpins his concept of barriers to entry. He defined barriers to entry as "the extent to which, in the long run, established firms can elevate the selling prices above the minimal average cost of production and distribution without inducing potential entrants to enter the industry" (Bain, 1956:5). In this sense, early definitions of strategic groups focused on the industry dynamics rather than the individual firms.

The economic organisation perspective (Porter, 1980, et al) redefines this view by arguing that strategic groups are groupings within industries which have made major asset commitments, but who are not necessarily competing along the lines portrayed by the industry dynamics. Within the main body of literature on strategy (Porter; Schendel; McGee and Thomas; Mascarenhas and Aaker; Hatten and Hatten: et al), the shift in defining strategic groups has argued that strategic groups are competing along strategic dimensions and therefore should be identifiable where firms' actions can be seen to be homogeneous. However, this view does not give an entirely satisfactory answer to the question of what defines a strategic group. It is possible that firms' actions in terms of their asset commitments may be seen to be homogeneous, and if so, this presents a difficulty in differentiating the Bainsian dynamics argument from the strategic dimensions viewpoint. They are not mutually exclusive and, if anything, tend to blur the definitive edges of what constitutes a strategic group.

Competitive Advantage

It can be argued that the essence of competitive strategy lies in the concept of competitive advantage (Ohmae, 1982; Porter 1985). On this basis, we could advance the proposition that every firm in an industry could have at least one unique mobility barrier in the form of its particular competitive advantage. If this proposition were true, then we might conclude that the notion of strategic groups was redundant.

However, it could also be argued that it is the shared groupings of such mobility barriers which distinguishes one particular strategic group from another. There is, therefore, an *a priori* basis for identifying strategic groups, which may well not correspond with the industry dynamics nor with the homogeneity of firms' actions. For example, a firm's strategy may reflect the pursuit of a competitive advantage that does not correspond with the conventions of size, which may only reflect efficiency. Seeking competitive advantage may be a function of scope, resources, competencies and synergy (Galbraith and Schendel, 1983). Scope refers to the particular segments a firm wishes to reach with its products and to the geographical extent of its position. Resources refer to the level of commitment and specific distribution of factors to key areas of the business.

The webbing binding the effectiveness of these variables will be a function of the firms' competencies and the extent of its synergistic efficiency at an operational level. The precise nature of these variables may well be industry specific, but what is important in relation to strategic groupings is what firms competing within an industry identify in terms of scope and resource commitments with competencies to achieve advantage in competitive space. Crucial to strategic group identification, therefore, is the perception of managers of the importance of competitive dimensions and the cognitive frameworks that inform their strategic behaviour in terms of their choice of strategy.

The objective of this book is to empirically explore the hypothesis that strategic groups can be identified from a managerial perception perspective and that it is the cognitive frameworks of managers which guide firm's positioning in competitive space. In this respect, the basic research question addressed is: can strategic groups be identified from the cognitive frameworks existing among decision-makers within firms? The study, therefore, is concerned with managerial perceptions of key strategic dimensions and how, if shared, these relate to firm's strategic postures within industries in terms of Porter's (1980) proposition that firms can be characterised along these dimensions as strategic groups. In other words, are "strategic groups" in the Porteresque sense synonymous with "cognitive groups" in the managerial sense?

Porter's contention that strategic groups compete "along the same strategic dimensions" (Porter, 1980:129) is based on his view that, "industries must be segmented for competitive strategy formulation" and that this segmentation differentiates firms' "intrinsic attractiveness" in terms of their offerings and through which they gain competitive advantage. Porter's argument that "differences in structural attractiveness and in [the] requirements for competitive advantage among an industry's products and buyers create industry segments", (Porter 1985:234), explicitly emphasises strategic dimensions as the basis of his strategic group formations.

These structural requirements imply homogeneity among decision-makers in relation to these dimensions. Indeed, Porter goes on to add that, "industry segmentation..., which flows from the intrinsic characteristics of an industry's products and buyers…, is a building block for analysing strategic groups" (Porter 1985:234). This exploration will examine whether strategic groups, based on Porter's notion of strategic dimensions, also reflects managerial homogeneity at the competitive advantage decision-making level. At this level the establishment of distinctive competencies in specific dimensions should be seen as shared by decision-makers within firms leading to rivalry across groups and firms in a sector.

With a few exceptions, the literature on strategic groups treats the notion of groups as a mere analytical convenience for empirical researchers. Secondary research dimensions concerned with firm size and performance account for the majority of group classifications. However, these classifications have not encouraged a confidence level that leads researchers to predict industry evolution. The reality of the complexity of business activity and its dynamics does not lend itself to an appropriate subvention in terms of a classification system. What is appropriate, however, is the identification of strategic groups on the basis of primary research that reflects the complexity of strategic conduct across an industry. In this respect longitudinal analysis reflecting the evolution of strategy and structure in industry development, is an important missing link in strategic group research. This aspect, emanating from research in the UK Brewing industry, will also be addressed in this book.

Having introduced the setting of this exploration through its historical context in relation to orthodox economic theory and the theory of the firm, chapter 2 will outline the contributions of management scholars to the literature on this subject. Chapter 3 will address the important issues of perception from the point of view of providing an understanding of what is meant by shared cognition. The industry from which the empirical evidence was drawn will be detailed in Chapter 4. Chapter 5 will present the research methodology, and Chapter 6 will discuss the findings and analysis of the results and the conclusions and implications to be drawn from the research. Finally, chapter 7 will conclude with an epilogue that attempts to explain how managers, lacking the shared cognitions implicit in strategic group theory, nevertheless interact through experience to reach consensus about strategic dimensions.

Summary

This book is concerned with cognition in strategic management and how this shapes managers' perception of the importance of competitive dimensions. The traditional "rational" models of prescriptive studies are contrasted with the view that strategy and strategic decisions are formed through a cognitive lens perspective whereby knowledge, beliefs, culture and learning cannot be de-coupled from decisions concerned with strategy. And in some industries the historical development of industry structure is compelled by a dominant strategy that continues to cloak this cognitive lens perspective.

The theory of strategic groups epitomises the prescriptive view of strategic management through the assertion that strategic groups in an industry are groups of firms following the same or similar strategy along the same strategic dimensions. In this sense, the essence of competitive actions is to be found in the emphasis on particular competitive dimensions. Strategic groups are, therefore, homogeneous through their pursuit of strategies based on these key competitive dimensions.

Strategic groups beg the question of whether a causal relationship exists between actual shared managerial cognition and clusters of firms following the same business strategy. Crucial to the theory of strategic groups, therefore, is the perception of managers of the importance of competitive dimensions and the cognitive frameworks that inform their strategic behaviour. In this respect, this book addresses the basic question: can strategic groups, as defined in the prescriptive sense, be identified from the shared group cognition process?

PART I STRATEGIC GROUPS

Chapter 2 Defining Strategic Groups: Characteristics and Implications

It is generally argued in the literature on strategic groups that the characteristics that distinguish groups differ from industry to industry and that some of these characteristics, in turn, may have particular importance, which manifest themselves in the distinctiveness between high performance and low performance groups. However, there is little evidence presented to substantiate this view. While analysing industries on the basis of particular dimensions such as scope and resource commitments, enables us to cluster different firms into groups, it does not *per se* distinguish groups in relation to performance. Many dimensions reflect asset configurations and the scale of resources, but it does not follow that there is a linear relationship between scale and scope in a performance sense. Undoubtedly, in some industries there exists a relationship between financial returns and the scale and scope of firms. However, caution should be exercised in regarding this as a homogenous correlation across all industries. In this respect research has indicated that profitability and financial returns within strategic groups are no less different than differences between strategic groups (Cool and Dierickx, 1993).

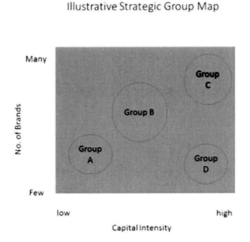

Illustrative Strategic Group Map

Figure 4. Mapping Strategic Groups

Conventionally, strategic groups are clustered in stylised two-dimensional illustrations. These dimensions cover a range of competitive factors (see

Appendix 1) and present a spatial map of the positioning of firms in an industry along particular dimensions. The diagram above illustrates this method of grouping in a typically stylised fashion.

Porter (1980) has argued that the first step in conducting a structural analysis of an industry is the mapping of the industry into strategic groups based on the characterisation of key strategic dimensions. In this respect, Porter makes a distinctive break with orthodox economic theory and traditional theories of the firm.

Hunt (1972) first used the term "strategic groups" in his thesis on the U.S. home appliance industry. The concept was subsequently formalised by Newman (1978) in his study of chemical industries. Porter (1980) popularised the notion of strategic groups and defined them as a "group of firms in an industry following the same or a similar strategy along the [same] strategic dimensions" (Porter, 1980:129). Porter further developed this definition to suggest that "an industry could have only one strategic group if all the firms followed essentially the same strategy. At the other extreme, each firm could be a different strategic group. Usually, however, there are a small number of strategic groups which capture the essential strategic differences among firms in the industry" (Porter, 1980:129). Moreover, Porter suggested that there is homogeneity within strategic groups in that "firms within strategic groups generally resemble one another closely and, therefore, are likely to respond in the same way to disturbances, to recognise their mutual dependence quite closely, and to be able to anticipate each other's reactions quite accurately" (Porter, 1980:130). Porter's work is seminal in that the meaning of an industry sector appeals to a new vision of the economy in which competitiveness is analysed using the competitive advantage paradigm and comparative advantage, in the traditional sense, is increasingly less important.

However, while Porter, by definition, departs from the orthodox economic view of the firm, he appears to ignore the managerial corollary of this view; that is, of rational choice and utility maximising managers. Implicit in the strategic group concept must be a challenge to the traditional economic assumption that managers conform to rational choice and utility maximisation in the way that a firm's actions and organisation are determined by the "laws" of supply and demand.

Characteristics

Chandler defined strategy as "the determination of the basic long term goals and objectives of an enterprise, and the adoption of courses of action and the allocation of resources necessary for the carrying out of these goals." (1962:11). Chandler also gave a simpler definition of strategy as "the plan for the allocation of resources to anticipate demand." Galbraith and Schendel (1983) suggested that strategies are built around four components; scope, resource deployment, competitive advantage and synergy. From these components, they identified six strategy types for consumer goods producers and four for industrial goods producers. Chrisman et al (1988) generalised this to three major components in a business strategy; scope, segment differentiation, and types of competitive weapons. Cool and Schendel (1987 and 1988) built on Galbraith and Schendel's analysis, applying it to strategic groups. They concluded that groups depended on two sets of variables: scope and resource commitments. Scope commitments refer to what segments, with what products, and in what geographical reach, a business positions itself, while resource commitments are regarded as commitments of resources to key functional areas.

Industry Groupings

This poses the question of why all firms in an industry do not always follow the same strategy, i.e. the most successful that can be identified in the industry. Newman (1978) proposes two main reasons why firms do not choose the same strategies for achieving the same goal, and hence are unlikely to do so. The first is that a firm may possess specific assets special to that firm. Second, the different firms' products may differ in non-price dimensions in response to the preferences of heterogeneous buyers. If there are differences in strategies among the firms in an industry, which are persistent and significant, Newman argues, strategic groups will exist (pursuing dissimilar strategies).

Porter (1980) suggests a further three explanations of why groups would form. First, the fact that firms are likely to have differing risk postures. Secondly, that firms are likely to have different goals, and thirdly, due to the historical development of the industry. McGee and Thomas (1985, 1986a, 1986b and 1989) point out a fourth explanation: exogenous reasons, such as technological change, may also cause strategic group formation.

Hallagan and Joerding (1983) drew conclusions from biologists' ethological research on polymorphic equilibriums to provide an explanation of why firms pursue different strategies. They argue that, even if there were no mobility barriers, strategic groups would form due to heterogenic demand. Mascarenhas and Aaker (1989), on the other hand, defined strategic groups as "a grouping of businesses within an industry that is separated from other groups of businesses by mobility barriers" (Mascarenhas and Aaker, 1989:480). Important to note here is Mascarenhas and Aaker's emphasis on the word grouping. They point out the importance of not looking at a strategic group as a unified force, but rather as a grouping of firms with similar strategies.

The differences in the definition of strategic groups are subtle but important. Some of the more important differences centre on the notions of barriers to entry and mobility barriers.

Barriers to Entry

The concept of mobility barriers emanates from the structure-conduct-performance studies originated by Bain (1956). The structure-conduct-performance studies cover the relationship between the basic conditions of demand, market structure, industry conduct and firm performance.

Market structure is defined by variables such as concentration, diversification, and, the main concern here, barriers to entry. The conduct of the industry is analysed in terms of competitive practices and the business strategies pursued, leading to an analysis of performance measures such as profitability. However, the main interest of this field of industrial organisation economics has been to look at what the social consequences of different forms of conduct and structure are, an issue touched on in the strategic group literature (Porter 1974 and 1979).

Barriers to entry imply factors operating to restrict the number of firms in an industry. As previously noted, Bain (1956) defined barriers to entry as "the extent to which, in the long run, established firms can elevate the selling prices above the minimal average cost of production and distribution...without inducing potential entrants to enter the industry". (Bain, *op cit*) Bain's main concern was to measure the height of barriers, and how effective they were in different industries. He saw three main sources of barriers: absolute cost advantages, product differentiation advantages, and scale economies advantages.

Types of Barriers

Advantages, such as absolute cost advantages, refers to the incumbent firms having access to cheaper raw materials, such as companies owning the only sources of a certain raw material. Product differentiation barriers are raised when, for instance, brand names are created and cannot be acquired by new entrant firms without substantial investments. Scale economies create a barrier when large-scale production is necessary to be able to compete at the same price levels as the incumbent firms.

The height of a barrier is measured, and this was the main concern of Bain, by the difference between the competitive price and the actual (or minimal long-run average cost with actual price). The entry-forestalling price is the highest price incumbent firms can set without encouraging entry. Briefly explained, it means that the firms in the industry set their output at such a level, that if a new firm entered the industry and prices fell to the competitive level, the demand left for the new firm would force it to produce at a level where its average cost would lie above average income. This assumes that the incumbent firms maintain the same level of output. Bain's findings suggested that high barriers to entry implied high concentration, which in turn led to higher profitability. Mann (1966) argued that the cost of obtaining capital related to high concentration was a further barrier to entry.

Stigler (1968) defined barriers to entry as the "cost of producing (at some or every rate of output) which must be borne by a firm which seeks to enter an industry but is not borne by firms already in the industry". He did not recognise Bain's scale economics, arguing that an entrant can adopt the same level of output as the incumbent. The main criticism of the research related to barriers to entry and the structure-conduct-performance model has come from Demsetz (1973 & 1982), who suggests that Bain and Stigler's differing definitions of what is and what is not a barrier to entry makes the concept and its applications questionable. Advertising, Demsetz argued, must be a barrier for Bain as it is correlated with high profit rates, but not for Stigler, as long as advertising is available on equal terms for all who wish to use it.

Demsetz further criticised Bain on his assumption that barriers always create profits, as even a secure monopolist can fail to cover his costs. Demsetz also points out that advertising is an important tool for signalling, and, consequently, it is information costs which create barriers to entry. His main conclusion was that barriers to entry are only a sign of efficient firms being in the industry and inefficient ones being unable to enter. Oster (1982) has also argued that mobility barriers are a function of efficiency, with levels of efficiency being correlated with size. Demsetz also concluded that the only time when barriers are harmful to society, an issue which he claims has been overlooked by research, is the case of artificially imposed barriers through government intervention.

Entry Barriers and Concentration

Industry concentration per se, like barriers to entry in general, is a relevant issue in strategic group analysis based on the structure-conduct- performance paradigm. Concentration ratio measures (Clarke 1985, Utton 1970 and Georski 1981) have been used to determine the concentration of an industry by looking at the strategic group market shares of the largest four or eight firms in an industry. However, the problem with concentration ratios is that the result is not always clear and unambiguous. The Herfindahl index, H (first proposed by Hirschman), is a widely used measure of concentration. The measure sums the squares of all the firms' market shares in a particular industry. The minimum value of H is 0, which reflects the perfectly competitive nature of the industry. The maximum value is 1, which indicates a monopoly situation.

The formula for the concentration ratio is,

$$H = \sum_{i=1}^{n} Si^2$$

where, n is the total number of firms and S_i is the market share of the nth firm.

The number of firms $n = \frac{1}{H}$

The weakness of the measure is that it tends to over-represent the larger firms to the detriment of the identification of possible strategic groups. As an indicator of concentration the measure has advantages. However, it fails to indicate the competitive dynamics at work in the industry as these relate to strategic group competitive dimensions.

Mobility Barriers

Caves and Porter (1977) introduced mobility barriers into the literature. They are defined on the same basis as barriers to entry, with the adjustment that they surround strategic groups within an industry, rather than the whole industry. Barriers that protect the industry as a whole must, by definition, protect all incumbent firms, with the benefits distributed symmetrically.

However, it should be noted that the mobility barrier concept does not make the concept of barriers to entry redundant. Both are relevant to firms that seek to enter an industry, but only mobility barriers affect or take account of movements within industries.

Mobility Barriers and Strategic Groups

The idea of group barriers has been suggested to provide an explanation for the differing results of the various structure-conduct-performance studies. Empirical studies have found differing degrees of barriers to entry effects, from Bain's positive results to Brozen's (1971) conclusion that the effects are insignificant. If, however, one looks at barriers in a mobility context, i.e. the ability to move in and out of strategic groups, these results can be seen in a different light.

Group specific barriers such as mobility barriers do not only protect from outside threats of entry, but also from firms within the industry belonging to other groups. This provides an explanation for why firms that earn higher profits than others are not immediately imitated. Mobility barriers are created by firms that discover how to exploit differences in initial assets, i.e. entrepreneurial activities, accepting the risk that comes with such moves.

In traditional theory, industries have queues of potential entrants and they are all assumed to enter the industry at a zero starting point. Strategic groups face similar queues of potential entrants but they also face firms at different levels of existing output with related initial assets. Thus for example, if we consider Coca-Cola and Pepsi as a strategic group, we see that the group not only faces entry threats from firms that have never bottled anything, but also from firms in other strategic groups, such as beer bottlers behavioural.

Mobility Barriers as Exit Barriers

Mobility barriers are not just barriers for entering groups, but also for leaving them. Exit barriers can be critical, especially in the case of declining industries. Harrigan (1980) and Rafferty (1987) have argued that it may be easier to enter an industry than it is to exit. Harrigan (1980) identified a number of different barriers to exit. She argued that strategic exit barriers would deter a firm from closing plants or entire businesses which were not achieving performance goals. She found that strategic considerations did influence firms' behaviours with respect to declining businesses.

Specifically, Harrigan identified four strategic exit barriers, namely: corporate image barriers, customer linkage barrierscustomers, short-term reporting goal barriers, and vertical integration barriers (Harrigan, 1980:382). Addressing the same subject, Rafferty (1987), suggested that strategic groups analysis using discrete variable mapping could assist in planning strategic turnaround. It was pointed out in the study of the TV rental industry that "the plotting of strategic positions of major competitors in end-game environments can enable exit strategies to be chosen on the basis of strengths and weaknesses." (Rafferty, 1987:86).

Hatten and Hatten (1987) point out that mobility barriers can become transformed to exit barriers, trapping firms within strategic groups who are unable to extract themselves from an industry in an orderly fashion. Strategic moves to enter other groups are jeopardised by the burden of maintaining a hold on the industry one wishes to exit (usually in decline). Large fixed costs in the form of non-depreciated initial assets act to inhibit the transition from one industry to another.

Sources of Mobility Barriers

Mobility barriers are not symmetrical. Just as each strategic group may have a distinctive strategy, it will also build up unique barriers. McGee and Thomas (1986) have pointed out that mobility barriers are not always created by firms. For example, some firms may enjoy high mobility barriers around their group due to cheap labour and/or government intervention. McGee and Thomas have identified three sources of mobility barriers: market related strategies, general supply characteristics of the industry; and features specific to the management and ownership of the firm. The asymmetry of mobility barriers is an important consideration in this study, since the barriers formed may reflect managerial perceptions of strategic dimensions.

Cool and Schendel (1987), on the other hand, sum up mobility barriers as the structural forces impeding firms from freely changing their competitive position, and as substantially independent of the individual firm's actions.

The Limitations of Studies on Entry and Mobility Barriers

The limitation of the concepts of entry barriers and mobility barriers in essence stems from the narrow focus of strategy itself within the "positioning school" of Porter et al. The problem with entry barriers and mobility barriers from this perspective is that they are seen as a generic position or condition of an industry. They are not seen from a unique perspective. At one level, they reduce the process of strategy to a formulation of a position, which is arrived at from a restricted list of conditions.

For example, the fast-food hamburger outlets within the restaurant industry are such that clusters of strategic groups can be matched from industry conditions. These conditions may be so broad that strategic groups can be rendered on the basis of such things as "fragmentation" or "maturity" within the industry. At another level, because a firm cannot gain the benefits of national advertising due to its regional location, it becomes positioned into a particular strategic group which might be labelled "regional competitors". In other words, firms are perceived as belonging to one club or another, which in itself dictates the generic portfolio of strategies to be pursued.

The Positioning Approach

The implications of this approach are that the use of entry barriers and mobility barriers as a means of "boxing" particular strategies (in Porters case, the so-called generic strategies), focuses the research in strategic groups on particular conditions or categories. This approach ignores the nuances of managerial cognitions and the differences in their perceptions which inform their actions. Mintzberg, Ahlstrand and Lampel (1998) have referred to this as the cluster static research of the positioning school.

What they challenge is the view that firms within an industry pursue similar strategic dimensions which identify them as strategic groupings, simply because factors such as entry barriers and mobility barriers exist in their industry. They argue that, since these "boxes" are based on past (and even existing) behaviours, researchers are tempted to become codifiers of the past and hence have a bias towards categorising firms as "staying there" rather than "getting there" (Mintzberg, Ahlstrand and Lampel, 1998:117).

While entry barriers and mobility barriers may well describe conditions and categories, they do not inform us of the richness of strategic learning and emergent strategy which takes place in the management process and the inventiveness of firms. For strategy to be meaningful, it must surely be seen as perspective rather than (or perhaps as well as) position. Porter has argued in response to criticism about his "generic" formation that, "if strategy is stretched to include employees and organisational arrangements, it becomes virtually everything a company does or consists of. Not only does this complicate matters, but it obscures the chain of causality that runs from competitive environment to position to activities to employee skills and organisation." (Porter 1997: 162)

Positioning as a Chain of Causality

However, this seems a rather narrow and deterministic view of the strategy process. Surely strategy does concern itself with everything a company does or consists of? Porter's chain of causality argument also suggests that strategy runs in a linear direction. This model and its methodological implications for research have much in common with Porters analysis of internationally successful industries, which he clusters on the basis of demand conditions and vertical relationships. His theory of national competitive advantage assigns important roles to demand conditions and vertical relationships in order to group industries into "upstream sectors", "industrial or supporting functions" and "final consumption goods industries." (Porter, 1990; 287). He suggests that his cluster chart based on these relationships has "…. some similarities to Leontief's input-output tables because it seeks to represent vertical flows among industries." (Porter, 1990; 797).

Porter's writings on the Competitive Advantage of Nations are not coincidental to his earlier "positioning" work on generic strategic groups. Both stem from the same basic model of the chain of causality. But this obscures the ongoing process of strategy. Porter's model is based on what military strategist refer to as the "come as you are" approach to strategy. In other words, once the strategic battle begins, you are stuck with what you have. You can change only before or after (Mintzberg et al, 1998: 120). However, in the dynamics of business competition, the necessity to make discrete strategic moves as part of an on-going strategy process becomes an imperative. As Sun Tzu writes of the strategist in battle, "All men can see the tactics by which I conquer, but what no man can see is the strategy out of which great victory is achieved".

By implication, Porter's "chain of causality" argument about strategy and those of others in the positional school suggests that strategic groups also conform to a chain of causality, in that the groups mirror the strategic dimensions pursued by incumbent firms. In the same way that there is a chain of causality in industry sectors, there is a chain of causality in strategic groups and the formation of mobility barriers. The 'chain of causality' perspective has particular relevance for specific firms in certain industries, although it may not hold true in other industry contexts. In this study, the UK Brewing industry features as the source of the exploration of strategic groups. It is an industry with a long history and one where the structure of the industry reflects a strategic pathway that has exhibited considerable consistency towards consolidation. From the 19th century as a consequence of the integration of mass production with mass distribution, the industry continued to evolve the process of the internalisation of firm transactions that had previously been carried out by the market. This evolution was characterised by adaptation and co-ordination that coalesced the structure of the industry and developed a strong identity with the strategy of concentration and consolidation as a marked feature of the industry. At the level of the industry, there is a historical 'chain of causality' that gives firm's a positional dynamic. However, it does not follow that at the level of the firm there exists cognitive groups who develop a strategic group identity in the sense that they mutually share the same perceptions about strategic dimensions, and that strategic groups consist of firms with managers who strongly identify with each other through their cognitions about strategy.

Strategic Group Implications

Hunt (1972), who first conceived the concept of strategic groups, observed conduct differences between firms in product diversification, quality and distribution methods, and suggested that these differences were asymmetries preventing oligopolistic consensus. Newman (1978), conducted his study of 34 U.S. producer goods chemical industries, assuming that homogeneity only needed to be measured for the leading firms.

Defined by size, Newman (1978) identified groups on the basis of their relationships with these leading businesses, calculating the concentration of identified groups with the Herfindahl measure. He concluded that heterogeneity of strategic groups increases rivalry within industries and makes consensus between groups difficult. This means, according to Newman, that the traditional goal congruence of oligopoly theory does not hold, as the presence of strategic groups results in companies pursuing different strategies and aiming for different goals. This situation may be compared with the prisoner's dilemma as described in game theory.

Newman's (1978) conclusions provide the basis for an understanding of why firms in industry sectors do not pursue a common strategy. As in the prisoner's dilemma, the interests of the groups and their degree of opposition and utility, will determine the extent of strategic group rivalry within industries. Such firms as may be found within strategic groups may possess distinctive competencies dynamic which distinguish them from other members but may also be inter-related by their degree of unity and opposition, thus giving the strategic groupings specific forms of interfirm association. The implication here is that a strategic group is a social organisation in which the parts may not be affected by the whole.

Newman (1978) further argued that different base industries and patterns of vertical integration suffice to stratify groups, and that attention to the factors that determine market conduct improves the understanding of the basis of market power and allocative distortions within an industry. Hatten and Schendel (1977), in their survey of the U.S. brewing industry, showed that the relationship between profitability, conduct and structural environment is not always constant within firms. Their study, which identified groups by their marketing and manufacturing allocations of resources, was unique in that it was the first to focus on individual firms rather than industries.

Game Theory

By definition, strategic groups mirror situations where the decision-makers within firms (players) interact strategically; and in this sense they not only interact with each other within the same firms, but with decision-makers in other firms within the same industry. This "strategic" interaction differs from, say, decision-making within an industry where there is only one firm, i.e., when there is a monopoly. In a monopoly situation, decisions can be made without regard for competitors since, in theory at least, none exist. However, when there are competitors in an industry, what these decision-makers do in a strategic sense may potentially affect the revenues and returns of other firms in the same market (following similar strategic dimensions). Thus, players' strategic decisions result in the formation of group clusters or strategic groups within an industry based on the need to take account of their actions on the other firms in the market and importantly, how these other firms may react to their decisions. This interaction therefore becomes important in the decision-making process within incumbent firms. The importance lies in anticipating the reactions of other firms to any particular firms' strategic decisions within the group. In this sense, any firm's decision-making will need to reflect anticipating how others will react to its decisions. Such interactions can be characterised in the models of cooperation and conflict utilised in the sphere of game theory.

Game theory has developed from oligopolistic theory, and is concerned with independent decisions involving conflicts of interest. The basic idea is to step away from the notion that competitive games have to result in zero outcomes. A zero outcome means that the utilities of the players always sum to zero, i.e. one's gain must be someone else's loss. Non-zero sum games, which is the issue here, recognise that the outcome does not have to be zero, as long as the player's interests are not directly opposed, and hence it may be possible for the players to gain from co-operation. The classic example is the so called "prisoner's dilemma".

The prisoner's dilemma involves two prisoners under interrogation. Each prisoner has two options, either to "grass" or to remain silent. If one prisoner talks and the other does not the squealer will get a pardon, whilst his comrade will hang. If both confess, they will both hang, but if neither confesses they will get a reduced sentence due to insufficient evidence. Hence a prisoner's utility will be the greatest if he squeals and his friend does not, and the lowest if he hangs. There is the third option of both remaining silent, where the combined utility of the prisoners will be greater than if one squealed and the other did not, or if both squeal. Now, the prisoner's dilemma is whether he can trust his fellow prisoner or not.

For example, in non-colluding oligopolistic industry structures, strategic decision-makers may perceive that they face a Kinked Demand Curve. In essence what this suggests is that decision-makers need to take account of how their competitors will react to decisions made by them. As a consequence of decision-makers anticipating the reactions of others (rivals), price is often a stable dimension in oligopolistic industries and firms' compete on clear strategies of differentiation.

The Kinked Demand Curve

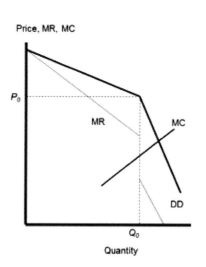

Price, MR, MC

- An oligopolist who increases price will not be matched by competitors
- An oligopolist who reduces price will be matched by competitors
- the 'kink' means that MC can change without affecting price

Figure 5. The Kinked Demand Curve

Consider how a firm may perceive its demand curve under oligopoly (figure 5). Decision-makers can observe the current price and output (market share), but must try to anticipate rivals reactions to any price change. The firm may expect rivals to respond if it reduces its price, as this will be seen as an aggressive move. Therefore, demand in response to a price reduction by any particular firm is likely to be relatively inelastic, since rivals are likely to respond immediately. Consequently, the demand curve will be steep below p_0 and overall industry revenues will fall with a price reduction strategy. For a price increase we can anticipate that a firm's rivals are less likely to react since, everything else being equal (ceteris paribus), a price increase will stimulate substitution effects as customers switch to the now lower-priced rivals. Demand will therefore be relatively elastic above p_0 and decision-makers will perceive that they face a kinked demand curve. Given this perception, strategic decision-makers in oligopolistic industries will see that revenues will fall whether price is increased or decreased and that the best strategy is to maintain the price level at p_0. Prices will tend to be stable, even in the face of increasing marginal costs. Facing a kinked demand curve, the perspective of oligopolistic competition means that competing on price is not a feasible strategic option for the firm. Instead it becomes clearer that a strategy of differentiation is the rational choice for the oligopolist.

Differentiation

The term differentiation implies that markets do not perceive products and services as indistinguishable. Indeed when used to signify a strategic intent, while many products and services may be perceived as similar, there are properties that can be identified as corresponding with specific consumer tastes and preferences that in turn, correspond with individual demand curves. Since market demand curves are simply the sum of all individuals' demand curves, they correspondingly reflect consumers' preferences for differentiated goods and services and importantly, their marginal utility curves. Moreover, heterogeneity in preferences and tastes reflects both variety and variable quantities in consumers' demand curves. In a strategic sense, the product/service differentiation approach implies that decisions are driven by the need to position supplier offerings to match particular, discrete (finite values) demand curves; while defending that position from competitors who may attack with other discrete offerings. This strategic position is often preserved through branding and consumers' perceptions of quality.

Discrete demand curves reflect the utility (satisfaction) that consumers gain from goods and services. However, in this context, it is useful to make the distinction between *total utility* and *marginal utility*. Total utility (*TU*) reflects the satisfaction that a consumer gains from all of the consumption of a particular good or service within a given time frame. So that the consumption of five cups of coffee a day would reflect a person's daily total utility from coffee and the satisfaction derived from those five cups.

Marginal utility (*MU*), on the other hand, is the additional satisfaction gained from consuming one more unit (an extra unit) within a given time frame. Thus, we might ponder the marginal utility we gain from our third cup of coffee of the day over our second cup of the day. In doing so we may conclude that we experience *diminishing marginal utility* as we consume more cups of coffee. As we increase our consumption by an extra unit we may experience less additional utility than we did with the previous unit and our marginal utility will continue to diminish the more extra units we consume.

It is clear that the more of a commodity we consume, the greater will be the total utility. However, this utility is also discrete in the sense that our consumption within a given time frame will be finite when our total utility is at its maximum. Within a given period of time no additional satisfaction can be gained by consuming extra units of the product or service. Therefore, when we reach our maximum total utility, our marginal utility will be equal to zero. Consuming an additional sixth cup of coffee will yield no marginal utility and may even result in dissatisfaction and negative marginal utility.

In an analysis of differentiation strategy and discrete demand curves we must address the link between total utility and consumers' incomes. In doing so we address the issue of how to measure utility. As we have alluded to above, while consumers may have similar experiences, they may derive different preferences and outcomes that provides them with unique utility; 'your experience may not be my experience'.

Two peoples satisfaction from the same product (cups of coffee) confronts us with the problem that utility is inherently subjective. A solution to this problem is to link utility with a measure of monetary value. Thus, a consumer's total utility may also be reflected in the monetary value they place on their consumption. In terms of a consumers' marginal utility, this can then be viewed as the value (the amount of money) they place on obtaining one more unit. It follows that what value is placed on one extra unit may differ from person to person. Notwithstanding that the price of a product may be the same for two consumers, one consumer may place a value on an extra unit of the product, which is higher than the value placed by the other. Thus, if my marginal utility is greater than the price I am expected to pay then I will consume an extra unit of the product, assuming my income allows for this. The difference between my marginal utility and the price, is a measure of the value of my marginal utility; $MU>P$ equals the worth of my utility.

This worth represents the difference between what I am actually prepared to pay and what I am expected to pay and is my *Marginal Consumer Surplus*.

$$MCS = MU - P$$

It follows that the *Total Consumer Surplus* for a product, service or market is the summation of the marginal consumer surpluses obtained from all the units consumed and represents the difference between the Total Utility (*TU*) from all the units, and consumers' actual Total Expenditure (*TE*) on them. If the total consumer surplus is greater than the amount they actually spend, then we can refer to this as the *Reservation Price* (RP) of the consumer; the price the consumer would have been prepared to pay to match their utility with a monetary value.

$$TCS = TU - TE$$

and $TCS = RP$

Since Total Expenditure (*TE*) and Total Revenue (*TR*) are synonymous (price x quantity), with the exception that Q is the quantity purchased by the consumer as expenditure and Q is the quantity sold by the supplier as sales, then we can summarise the above as:

$$TCS = TU - (P \times Q) = RP$$

Differentiation strategy, therefore, reflects consumers' preferences, heterogeneity and the characteristics of products and services that coincide with these preferences. The discrete nature of consumers' choice is also reflected in the distinguishing characteristics that new products, services and innovations bring to the competitive arena. These new products and innovations, when successful, are identified by markets as possessing discrete characteristics that make them readily distinguishable from similar market offerings (Belleflamme and Peitz, 2015; Lancaster, 1966).

Thus, preferences are not merely defined in a broad product-market sense, but by discrete choices where particular characteristics provide utility and lend themselves to brand creation and reinforcement. Typically, examples of these discrete choices are reflected in consumer products such as beers, watches, clothing, automobiles, holiday destinations and even health care, where consumers differ in their brand preferences and in their demand curves (exhibiting varied amounts of quantity)(Belleflamme and Peitz, 2015). In market terms, brand loyalty is the return for the successful implementation of a discrete choice differentiating strategy.

In terms of a simplified mathematical description or process, the discrete choice approach allows for the assumption that consumers will purchase one product or service over another and therefore, will display a purchasing pattern that reflects either a zero purchase or a definite purchase, which we can regard as one complete entity (finite value). The alternative to this assumption is to postulate that all consumers are the same, but exhibit a variable demand for all entities; what Belleflamme and Peitz (2015:112) refer to as the 'representative customer approach'.

Taking products and services as entities with discrete characteristics is the fundamental assumption underpinning the concept of branding. The discrete characteristics are bundled and packaged as products, where the premium reflects the marginal utility of the package. The logic of branding and that of premium pricing, in many respects mirrors the dichotomy of variety and quality in individual demand curves. This view emphasises the demand-side of discrete characteristics. However, there is a supply-side influence in that the costs of discrete characteristics affect the firms' competitive performance. Thus, we could say that premium branding occurs when consumers prefer one product over another and when the *Reservation Price* exceeds the premium price. When prices are set at marginal costs, the *Reservation Price* reflects the optimum utility to the consumer. This proposition enables us to analyse market structures where oligopoly depends on the ability of suppliers to bundle characteristics that create brand differentiation according to consumers' perceptions of discrete market offerings.

Since in theory, as we have observed above, oligopolies would be advised not to compete on price, but compete in markets through differentiated products and services; product specification and design configurations, combined with marketing branding creates a discrete choice approach to markets that is central to the differentiation strategy. We can model this strategy under certain assumptions. For example, we can consider non-price decision factors based on a differentiated strategy in oligopolistic market structures through dimensions such as location decisions of the firm, or its strategic business units, for competitive advantage. By assuming price to be constant in oligopolistic structures, we can model how variables such as location, as a strategic dimension, influences the extent of the specifics of product differentiation in markets.

The location model serves as a simple illustration of a differentiation strategy where price competition is avoided, and consumers' discrete choices drives strategy implementation based on market preferences and individual demand curves. The maintenance of a premium price differentiated strategy depends on fulfilling consumers' needs of these discrete preferences, so that the consumer faces a market price p_m that reflects perceived differences. Based on this approach the firm may make rational assumptions, for example, about strategic dimensions that corresponds with consumers' ideal choice of location in the product-market space interface.

Differentiation and the location dimension

To begin with, we must make a distinction between vertical and horizontal differentiation. In a vertically differentiated product-market space, commodities differ in quality and all consumers agree on the preference ordering of the commodities. In a horizontally differentiated product-market space, the consumers do not agree on the preference ordering; thus if all commodities are sold at the same price the optimal choice depends on the particular consumer preferences.

Location models (sometimes known as address models) are models in which consumers view each firm's product as having a particular location in product-market space and where consumers also differ in their location; in this sense, the location of a consumer may define their most preferred product. In this respect it is useful to regard location as a metaphor for a one dimensional characteristic rather than a specific position; for example, assuming we wish to set up a cold drinks stand on a hot day in a park that is representative of our market space with no competitors. Whereas the demand curve for a competitive firm would be horizontal and the firm would be a *price taker*, such a firm (our cold drinks stand) would have monopoly power and face a downward sloping demand curve, where to maximise profits it is simply required to search the price-quantity choices on its demand curve. In this situation of monopoly power the firm is a *price searcher* because it controls the price in the absence of competition. The monopoly's market power over the price reflects its control over its output and, therefore, its control over the market supply. However, the closer two firms' products are in market space, the closer substitutes they become.

Thus, in our simple model we can include the availability of a close substitute. Assigning a substitutability coefficient (τ) to substitutes enables us to assume that the smaller the value of τ, the closer the substitutability of a product; that is, consumers are willing to purchase certain 'non-ideal' products. The substitutability coefficient allows us to specify how willing consumers are to trade-off characteristics for location and how much utility a consumer loses from purchasing a product that does not match their 'ideal'.

The location of a preferred product is a significant factor in representing consumers' 'ideal', when products are priced equally. It seems reasonable to assume, *ceteris paribus*, that consumers close to a preferred product supplier/producer would be unlikely or unwilling to buy from a different producer and therefore in location models, competition may well tend towards *localisation* and firms' may exhibit some degree of monopoly power (in oligopolistic market structures an increase in the price of one product may not impact on the demand for products that are far away).

The most widely known location model of horizontal product differentiation is Hotelling's (1929) linear city model. The basic features of the model assumes two firms at different locations in a product-market space. Consumers also have locations and incur utility loss (often referred to as transportation costs) from consuming a product that is not their ideal.

Location models require us to specify how consumers are distributed in the product-market space and we can assume that consumers are distributed in the market on an interval range of [0,1], with the market having a total mass of 1. We can also assume that the location of an individual consumer would reflect, as near as possible, their preferred geographical position in market space (i.e., city, town, etc). In a city representation of market space, product/service offerings would ideally be situated on a continuum of, say, a High Street or Shopping Centre. It is rational to assume that consumers' preferences are for locations that are accessible.

The two firms are denoted as $i = 1, 2$; y is used to denote the location of the firms. The location of firm 1 is $y_1 = a$, where a is the measure of the distance from the left city boundary, 0 (the left limit of the linear product market space). The location of firm 2 is $y_2 = 1 - b$, where b is the measure of the distance from the right city boundary, 1 (the right limit of the product market space). In this notation, since firm 1 is the nearest to the left city boundary it can also be denoted as $y_1 = a \leq 1 - b$. In this model x denotes the location of consumers in the product market space.

The reservation value of the consumer is denoted as r for a product location under two constraints; the price p and the cost of not consuming the ideal, where there is a diminished consumer surplus arising from the consumer preference and the product purchase. As alluded to above, the parameter $\tau > 0$ measures the strength of preferences; the larger τ is, the less consumers are willing to consume non-ideal products (an opportunity cost).

Thus we can specify the utility υ of the preferences in the quadratic[1] expression:

$$v_i = r - p - t(x - y)^2$$

Since the consumer will choose the product that maximises their utility, consumers located at x will purchase from firm y1 when,

$$v_i = r - p_1 - t(x - a)^2 \geq r - p_2 - t\left(x - (1 - b)\right)^2$$

or alternatively if,

$$v_i = p_2 - p_1 \geq \tau(x - a)^2 - \tau\left(x - (1 - b)\right)^2$$

Otherwise, consumers will purchase from firm y_2.

Since the linear location model is representative of the linear function depicting the equation of a straight line, expressing the form of the function of the second degree as a quadratic function eliminates the negative values.

The Nash equilibrium outcome of the location model occurs when each firm chooses its location to maximise its demand given the location of the other firm.

Thus, $a = b = 1/2$ $or, l_1 = l_2 = 1/2$

In linear location models, the Nash equilibrium leads to clustering in the centre. When prices are effectively inert, firms will attempt to position themselves to attract the largest number of customers by meeting consumer tastes. The resultant outcome, known as 'the principle of minimum differentiation', is a cloning effect in market space.

In the simultaneous location game, no firm has an incentive to deviate, since any firm that deviates will serve less than half of the market. For any different location, $l_1 \neq \frac{1}{2}$ and $l_2 \neq \frac{1}{2}$, at least one firm has an incentive to deviate because if firm i is located, for example, to the left of ½, then firm j has an incentive to move slightly to the right of firm i . Thus, the location Nash equilibrium implies that the firms locate strategically at the centre.

In the Nash Equilibrium solution here, neither player (firm) can improve his or her payoff given the other players strategy. That is, given the location strategy of firm i_1, firm i_2 can do no better, and given firm i_2's strategy, firm i_1 can do no better. Each location strategy is a best response against the other player's location strategy.

The clustering reflects a strategic grouping in market space and the location model provides an illustration of a strategic dimension that influences the grouping. The insight of this equilibrium is that while oligopolies will compete on differentiation (of the horizontal variety); where substitutability is high, their strategic decision-making may be more influenced by market share considerations that are determined by specific strategic dimensions such as branding and location as a means of best meeting consumer tastes and preferences. In general we can observe this phenomenon in the distribution networks and location functions of firms, and in the branding investment of oligopolistic market structures.

In the cluster analysis factor solution discussed in chapter 6, there is particularly strong evidence indicating support for a horizontal differentiation strategy in the brewing industry. In Figure 14, the communality of the location variables (strategic dimensions) V1 and V2 account for 32.7 per cent of the variance explained by the factor solution. This indicates a significant correlation between the location dimension and the strategic group clustering in market space of firms in the brewing industry pursuing a horizontal differentiation strategy.

Under oligopolistic market conditions, a horizontal differentiation strategy drives market share competitiveness and highlights the complementarity that exists between cost leadership and differentiation. The mutuality between cost leadership and differentiation features strongly in the Three Factor Solution discussed later in chapter 6, and provides an opportunity to explore the 'generic strategy' proposition from a more critical empirical standpoint based on the orientation of the strategic groups in the industry.

Identifying Strategic Groups

Porter argues that strategic groups and mobility barriers provide an explanation as to why within industries there are subtle differences between firms in their competitive strategies, and why there are persistent intra-industry differences in profits. Porter's (1974) study of 38 consumer goods industries in the U.S. indicates that barriers within industries are asymmetrical and that the degree of rivalry within industries increases with the number of strategic groups. In his study he identified groups by dividing firms into "leaders" and "followers", on the basis of their shares of the industry's total sales revenue.

Oster (1982) has focused on the movements between groups within industries and barrier and group existence over time. She assigned firms from 19 consumer goods industries to strategic groups by analysing their advertising to sales ratio. Oster (1982) concluded that differences in strategies persist over time between strategic groups, although profit rates were not the same, and that mobility between groups is low. The conclusion of mobility barriers protecting groups was combined with the finding that it is the durability of barrier investments that maintains group structures. Oster also found that small and large firms can belong to the same group, contrary to Porter's study. Large size would then be an indication of efficiency.

McGee and Thomas (1986 b) did not conduct an empirical survey, but instead analysed the works and methods of other researchers. Their paper highlights the main features of strategic group research and points to several problems with how surveys have been conducted. Furthermore they note the arbitrary way that variables, from which strategic groups have been defined, have been chosen. They also suggest that theoretical concepts such as mobility barriers, isolating mechanisms and controllable variables would be of better use in forming a classification system. In other words, they are best used as codifiers of conditions, rather than as a means of describing the strategy process of strategic groups.

Mascarenhas and Aaker (1989) identify strategic groups through mobility barriers, following some of McGee and Thomas' arguments. Their survey of the oil-well drilling industry argues that mobility barriers are industry specific, and hence an in-depth knowledge of competitive conditions is essential. Their most important findings were that highly protected groups, contrary to traditional belief, did not always display higher profitability than less protected groups, and that as Hatten and Hatten (1987) had argued, mobility barriers can be asymmetrical.

Cool and Schendel (1988) saw, as noted above, scope and resource commitments as the key strategic actions of interest in determining strategic groups. They also hypothesised that if one assumes that group members have different risk profiles, and if risk and return are related, performance would be expected to vary between firms within groups.

In this context, McNamee and McHugh (1989) conducted a study, where they utilised the Porter model for identifying strategic groups in the Irish clothing industry. However, they attempted to advance Porter's model by capturing the competitive pressures that strategic groups face. This competitive pressure is measured by the variation from the standard deviation of the net profit before tax of firms in strategic groups. The result of this measure is to portray group competitive intensity by means of an ellipse on a group intensity competitive map. The mapping of groups in this way suggests different risk profiles associated with the strategy and structure of groups and consequently differing performance profiles Schendel.

Problems with Group Identification

There are two main problems with identifying strategic groups: first, the problem of correctly defining the industry, separating close and not-so-close substitutes. Second, identifying what data is necessary for the analysis and what is available. When these problems can be overcome, as Cool and Schendel suggested, "strategic group analysis provides an instructive diagnostic framework for evaluating the need to adjust or change competencies, if possible, or to change current strategy" (Cool and Schendel, 1988:221). Accordingly, it is suggested that strategic group analysis can be a valuable tool for the analysis of industries and competitors, and an aid in strategic investment decisions and strategic planning. The concept can help analyse rivalry within the industry and the consequences of strategic movements between strategic groups by individual firms.

A strategic move does not necessarily mean that firms move directly from their present group to the desired group. If the mobility barriers protecting the desired group are too high to be overcome, a firm can move via a third group in order to build up enough of the assets and skills required to move into the preferred group. In this respect, several Japanese companies would appear to have done just this, by moving from low cost to standard quality to high quality groupings. Each successive strategic move has been from a position of strength on the basis of the mobility barrier erected along some key strategic dimension, such as market share.

Strategic Groups as a Predictive Tool

It has been argued that strategic group analysis can also predict the impact of industry rivalry through three key variables (Porter, 1979). First, the number and distribution of groups and secondly, the strategic distance between groups. The strategic distance refers to the degree to which strategies in different groups differ in terms of key strategic variables, such as advertising, quality, pricing and so on. If there is a significant distance, this means that the market is heterogeneous and oligopolistic co-ordination is replaced with intense rivalry. The third variable is the market interdependence among strategic groups. This is the degree to which different groupings compete for the same customers.

The more diverse strategies are, the more enhanced will rivalry be amongst groups with high interdependence. All three of these factors interact, which means that rivalry will not be symmetric across the industry. It should also be added that if there is only one large and a few small groups, rivalry will tend to be insignificant if the small groups create no threat to the large.

Profitability, as one measure of competitive performance, is not only affected by industry rivalry, but also by the degree of rivalry within groups. Groups with high mobility barriers protecting them are likely to be more profitable than those with small. Nevertheless, if there is intense rivalry amongst the group members, profits are more easily eroded, as there are no barriers protecting the individual firm. Moreover, warfare within the group, especially a dominant one, is likely to affect not only the profitability of member firms but also firms in groups, in relation to the barriers, ranking below the fighting group. However, this need not be the case. For example, if the warfare is not connected to price, a price umbrella may be created protecting lower groups.

Mapping Strategic Groups Dimensions

Strategic groups can be visually analysed through mapping. The strength of this is that it allows the strategist to communicate complex relations amongst strategic dimensions simultaneously. Mapping can be done either in the simple way shown in Figure 4, with the limitation of looking at only two dimensions at a time, or in the complex way of Day et al (1987), where several variables are plotted on the same graph. However, while illustrating more variables than the Porter mapping, the Day et al analysis suffers from the same shortcomings in that clustering based on measures of profitability, advertising expenditure, price, cash flow, market segments, reflect outcomes of strategic action rather than informing us of the dynamics of competitive behaviour and strategy.

The positional school suggests that, when firms are prospecting for new opportunities to exploit, they would do well to compare their topographic maps of market segments with those of strategic groups. An overlay of these may suggest opportunities that can be developed if they are poorly covered by current suppliers. Hatten and Hatten (1987) concluded that strategic groups provide a tool for analysing companies that pursue the same strategy but are not in competition with each other. This way it may be possible to exploit other experiences in the search for an emergent competitive strategy. In this study, it is partly intended to research this view and to see if it is supported by the cognitive perceptions of strategic dimensions shared within the brewing industry analysis.

Imitative Dimensions

Strategic dimensions are imitative and this accounts for the fluidity of perceptions amongst small and large competitors alike. McGee and Thomas (1986) have summarised their argument on strategic groups into three basic hypotheses. The first is that size is not the only key variable in assessing strategic groupings. Secondly, mobility barriers are an extension of the conventional barriers to entry argument and a counterpart of strategic group formation. Thirdly, isolating mechanisms indicate the individual firm's abilities to exploit and imitate a strategy together with the skills and resources that those firms possess.

Finally, they put a question mark to how strategic groups form and whether there is a relationship between groupings and industry evolution, or whether it is between groupings and individual actions. However, what they do not investigate is whether actions are determined by perceptions of strategic dimensions, and if these coincide with groups formed as a result of industry evolution and asset commitments.

Taxonomy and Strategic Groups

Porter (1980) recognises that his theory of strategic groups is richer in the conceptual sense than the crude leader/follower dichotomy and the simple measures of industry structure used in his study. Newman's (1978) empirical work, as Oster (1982) points out, is somewhat closer to the spirit of a concept of strategic groups. However, in spite of the emergence of the above studies, and in particular, the popularisation of the notion of strategic groups by Porter (1980), industry performance rather than strategic groupings remains the major seam of strategic management research (Cool and Schendel, 1987 and Cosier and Rechner, 1985). This, it can be argued, is due to the dynamics of competitive behaviour, which makes the robust construction of a classification system problematic.

Few studies have attempted to plot the development of strategic groups over time on the basis of multivariate research rather than concentrating on one or two variables, such as size. Perhaps a reason for this lies in the use of different measures and weightings in studies on strategic groups. The diversity of classification measures is a feature which does not facilitate useful comparisons of results (McGee and Thomas, 1986 b). Chrisman et al, (1988) have developed this criticism, calling for a standardised classification system. The theory and practice of taxonomy offers four objectives for classification systems: differentiation, generalisation, identification, and information retrieval.

Differentiation facilitates generalisation, which makes studies comparable, and identification ensures consistency, whilst information retrieval makes it possible to use and apply generalisations made in comparative studies (Chrisman et al, 1988). In addition, all categorised levels in a classification system have to be mutually exclusive, internally homogeneous, collectively exhaustive, stable and based on a relevant language.

However, while classification has played a major part in the development and understanding of phenomena, it is questionable whether the application of taxonomy to the notion of strategic groups is valid. By their very nature, firms exist in an ever-changing competitive environment. While research into strategic groups may be based on the choice of convenient industries, which assists the process of classification, the reality of firms' operational characteristics within industries may be based on multiple business activities. If research on strategic groups is to reflect the complexity of strategic conduct, then it seems unlikely that a classification process, as manifested through the theory and practice of taxonomy, is of sufficient sophistication to allow this to be done.

As yet, researchers on strategic groups have not ventured into the realms of forecasting based on a conventional classification system in an attempt to predict the long-run evolution of industry structure. Placing firms in strategic groupings on the basis of conventional classification systems (i.e. the theory of taxonomy) may be a fruitless exercise and, consequently, the robustness of industry forecasts will prove questionable.

It could be argued that the concept of strategic groups may be in the process of being shaped into a potentially powerful analytical tool. However, from the above analysis, the identification of groups shows that, in some industries, these have been ignored from one very important perspective, namely, that of the managers within firms. Robinson (1956), writing over forty years ago, suggested that a precise and meaningful definition of an industry is a vain objective, and perhaps the lack of a classification of strategic groups on the basis of economic constructs in more recent times, supports this view.

With a few exceptions, the strategic management literature on strategic groups has perhaps vainly failed to thoroughly examine and identify strategic groups from a "managerial perceptions" perspective. As insiders and strategic decision-makers, managers' perceptions of strategic groups within their industry, and their identification of strategic dimensions, can but only enrich the understanding of strategic group structures.

Strategists' Perceptions of Strategic Groups

Reger and Huff (1993) examined the problem of strategic groups from the point of view of strategists. They argued that, "logically, strategists would think in terms of clusters of competitors to cognitively simplify a complex environment" (1993:105). They contended that commonalities among firms could be expected independent of individual precepts due to the pressures of isomorphism and inertia inhibiting strategic change. Their research was a counter to the attack by Barney and Hoskisson (1990) who argued that the idiosyncratic positions achieved by some firms associated with competitive advantage, rendered strategic group theory fundamentally flawed. For Barney and Hoskisson (1990), the empirical evidence suggested that it was possible for firms to be idiosyncratic in strategically relevant ways. The empirical evidence of this research appears to support this view.

Reger and Huff (1993) focused on determining if strategists could perceive differentiating commonalities among firms and, if this was the case, on examining the nature of those perceptions. They advanced the proposition that if groups of firms were "real" for strategists, the research at the strategic group level could establish the significant importance of groups and hence overcome the criticisms that they were merely the result of researchers' analytical exercises. This research moved the investigation of strategic groups from simple assumptions based on structure/conduct observations. Their inquiry into how strategists perceive similarities among sub-groups of firms in an industry really only advanced the level of investigation to group participants in the industry. Strategists in the industry may group firm participants in that industry in similar ways and indicate a shared sense of group structure in the industry.

However, while strategists may group firm participants in their industry, this does not provide sufficient evidence to support the proposition that competitive strategies can be observed from strategic groupings based on managerial perceptions of competitive dimensions. To this end, Reger and Huff's proposition that their data reveals "a range of agreement on the similarity of firm strategies" (1993:105), is tested in this study through a cognitive lens perspective of strategists' perceptions. Reger and Huff conclude that strategic groups may well be amplified by cognitive studies using strategists as data sources. In many ways, their research can be seen as exploring the views of Barney and Hoskisson (1990), in that they bolster our understanding of why firms achieve the kind of idiosyncratic positions Barney and Hoskisson indicate.

Managerial Perceptions and Cognition

In the literature on strategy, many writers concur with Hofer & Schendel (1978) who, for example, list goal formulation, environmental analysis, strategy formulation, strategy evaluation, strategy implementation and strategy control as the six complicated responsibilities that managers are expected to address in strategic management. Clearly, managerial perception and cognition plays a central role in all of these. However, many writers who define strategic groupings simply on the basis of these responsibilities or even on the basis of size or performance, have overlooked the significant ecological aspects of managerial cognition, which is the source of a font of evidence about decision-making.

Following on from the work of Reger and Huff (1993), Peteraf and Shanley (1997) have argued that research emanating from organisational ecological studies provides compelling evidence of the existence of strategic groups on the basis of managerial cognition. They develop the concept of 'strategic group identity' as, "a set of mutual understandings, among members of a cognitive intra-industry group, regarding the central, enduring and distinctive characteristics of the group" (Peteraf and Shanley, 1997:166). They contend that strategic group identity emanates from "a set of *mutual understandings…*rather than from the *shared understandings* that underlie organisational identity" (*op cit*: 166). They also contend that a cognitive group, "requires a common understanding among its members that a group of some sort exists" (*op cit*).

Peteraf and Shanley (1997) do much to explore the efficacy of strategic groups and cite common institutional histories, firm size, product quality, overlapping social networks and experience of the industry setting as central characteristics of the mutual understanding of cognitive strategic groups (*op cit*: 167). Importantly, they argue that a 'dominant managerial logic' may inform the collective of a cognitive perspective, "that can be thought of as a kind of knowledge structure that evolves over time out of the cumulative effect of the firms' strategic decisions" (*op cit*: 168). The explicit existence of cognitive strategic groups is marked by a strong identity that enables the group perspective to have an influence on firm level behaviours and outcomes (*op cit*: 174). On the other hand, Peteraf and Shanley argue that a 'weak' cognitive identity will be insufficient to effect firm level behaviours.

By exploring this aspect of competitive behaviour, we are able to distinguish strategic groups, which help us to explain more precisely why it is possible for firms to be idiosyncratic in strategically relevant ways, as we realistically observe them to be in competitive environments. Stubbart (1989) also holds that cognitive organisation precedes and shapes competitive strategic behaviour and suggests that this aspect of strategic management is essential, if not dominant, in the strategic management process.

The Conventional Paradigm and the Dynamics of Strategy

Previously, the strategic management prescriptions which underlie the conventional wisdom on strategic groups have been outlined. The fundamental natures of these prescriptions are derived from a conventional paradigm. The perspective from which we view a situation is termed a paradigm, the general way that we use to make sense of the world around us. The paradigm is the lens through which we look at the world and it underlies what we perceive. Thus, a paradigm is a set of beliefs and assumptions we make about the world. These beliefs and assumptions normally exist beneath our level of consciousness and are rarely challenged or at best questioned.

The particular set of beliefs about strategic groups which underpins the unquestioned assumption of the prescriptive studies, is that the dynamics of industry structures are those of stability and a certain reliability leading to predictive behaviour. The validity of such studies which purports to identify strategic groups on the basis of key dimensions, either by the researcher or by clustering by managers, depends on what has been referred to as the stable equilibrium organisational paradigm (Stacey, 1993).

This paradigm assumes patterns of behaviour and performance that are consistent with each other. Change, per se, is accepted as a consequence of change in the environment and the organisation is driven by the need to achieve a predetermined goal that requires adaptation to the environment. In this paradigm, the factors which affect goal achievement must match and balance, with interactions between people in the organisation being consistent with goals and plans.

The Illusion of Stability

On the face of it, this perspective seems reasonable. It presupposes that firms build on their strengths. However, Miller (1990), on the basis of empirical studies, suggests that companies who build on their strengths actually move along trajectories whereby they either reach a state of explosive instability, or they reach a state of stable equilibrium. The outcome, for both situations, is that the company will fail. It is argued that this "no win" scenario develops because "companies do not innovate and transform themselves and they become out of touch with the changing world and the competitive environment" (Stacey, 1993:209).

Earlier in chapter 2 it was pointed out that one of the enduring problems of prescriptive perspectives in the area of strategic groups is the absence of a theoretical framework or tool which enables the prediction of a firm's behaviour within an industry. This criticism could also be levelled at the entire field of strategic management. This is related to the fundamental problem of competitive dynamics and the evolution of industries as complex non-linear structures. Perhaps the clearest analogy of this dynamic can be seen with reference to chaos theory.

Chaos Theory

Chaos theory, which is the study of non-linear dynamic systems, provides a useful conceptual framework that reconciles the essential unpredictability of industries and strategic groups with the emergence of distinctive patterns (Levy, 1994). Lorenz (1963), while studying the dynamics of turbulent flow in fluids, pioneered chaos theory. The problems explored in chaos theory can be illustrated with reference to the observation of a metal ball suspended over two or more magnets. The ball will trace a series of patterns that never exactly repeat themselves, and yet are not totally random.

The paradox is that the motion of the ball is driven by the same Newtonian mathematics which enables us to predict the orbits of planets around the sun with a high degree of accuracy. Since we know the original location, speed and direction of the ball, we ought to be able to predict its path with a reasonable degree of accuracy. The problem is that we cannot, and this gives rise to the question, which relates to industry dynamics, in that how is it that deterministic systems can give rise to unpredictability? The explanation for the ball is that timing variations in the motion of the ball are magnified every time it swings past one of the magnets. The combination of the divergence with the repeated interactions with the magnets gives rise to "chaotic behaviour".

Strategic Groups and Chaos Theory

To appreciate the relevance of chaos theory to our understanding of strategic groups, we need to conceptualise industries as complex, dynamic, nonlinear systems. Firms interact with each other and with other actors in their environment. Small exogenous disturbances to chaotic systems can cause unexpectedly large changes. The implication for strategic groups and for business strategy in general, is that the entry of one new competitor or the development of a seemingly minor technology can have a substantial impact on competition in an industry. Examples of this from the brewing industry can be found in the introduction of the Beer Orders and the invention of the widget.

Utilising the analogy of chaos theory, the path followed by a particular firm may have an underlying pattern (or even a hidden pattern), but the specific nature of the firm's behaviour may be completely random and hence unpredictable in the long-term.

In this sense, Pascale (1990) has argued that the firms that succeed are the ones who sustain contradictions. These contradictions generate tensions; tensions create energy; with energy firms innovate and transform themselves and survive. Similarly, Stacey (1993), following Pascale (1990), has suggested that successful firms are the ones that operate in a "state of non-equilibrium, following circular, dialectical processes of rearranging paradoxical forces" (Stacey, 1993:209).

There is thus a constant fractal dimension in strategy, where firm behaviour mirroring chaos reflects order (a pattern) within disorder (random behaviour).

This process may apply equally to groups of firms who, on the face of it, appear to follow a specific path due to the fact that they share particular resource configurations. At one level, there may be distinguishing characteristics which manifest themselves in a particular pattern. However, at another level, these firms may exhibit different strategies, which reflect behaviour intent on managing the dynamic paradoxical forces of competition. The results discussed in chapter 6, elaborating the cost leader differentiation strategy, provide just such an example. In contrast to the traditional prescriptive paradigm based upon linear relationships and equilibrium, the simultaneous pursuit of cost leadership differentiation suggests that more complex strategies and organisational forms, reflecting the chaotic dynamics of competition, will depict the interactions between firms who might otherwise be seen as dissimilar. Likewise, the apparent dissimilarity between strategic groups in an industry may disguise managerial perceptions of key dimensions within these groups, which in reality reflect more complex interactions than group structures suggest. On this basis, it follows that attention must now turn to the twin subjects of perception and cognition.

Summary

In developing his definition of strategic groups, Porter (1980), suggests that an industry could have one strategic group if all the firms followed essentially the same strategy. However, he adds that usually there are a small number of strategic groups that capture the essential strategic differences among firms in the industry. Porter suggests that there is homogeneity within strategic groups and that firms within strategic groups will resemble one another closely, respond in the same way to disturbances and anticipate each other's reactions accurately. This view conforms with the orthodox economic position of rational choice and utility maximising managers and reflects the influence of classical notions of equilibrium, in the way that a firm's actions and organisation are determined by the "laws" of supply and demand.

This view poses the question of why all firms in an industry do not follow the most successful strategy that can be identified in the industry. The literature on the subject addresses this question by pointing to the fact that firms are likely to have different goals, different histories, different technologies and subtle, but important, differences in products. Firms will also be subject to competitive barriers to entry and mobility barriers due to access to different sources of materials, brand differences, the timing of investments and the availability of capital.

In the literature on strategic groups, particular emphasis is placed on the importance of mobility barriers. The idea of group barriers is made more specific and underpins the homogeneity aspect of strategic groups, by reference to particular mobility barriers around groups which not only protects them from outside threats of entry, but also from firms within the industry who belong to other groups. This notion also underscores the pre-occupation with order and equilibrium in strategic behaviour and alludes to a taxonomy of strategic groups.

The problem with the concept of entry and mobility barriers is that they are seen as a generic position or condition of an industry. They discourage the view that strategic behaviour can be seen from a unique perspective. They reduce the actual process of strategy to a formulation of a position, arrived at from a restricted set of conditions. This approach ignores the nuances of managerial cognitions and the differences in managers' perceptions, which inform their actions.

The prescriptive view of strategic groups further limits our understanding of competition to solely that of an adversarial pursuit. It does not countenance the co-creative co-operation inherent in the learning and knowledge process portrayed through the nuances of managerial cognition. Even within the so-called rational decisions of game theory, we can see that the equilibrium outcomes are indeed a process of cognitive co-operation, based on knowledge and co-creative perception. In the prisoner's dilemma, the prisoners as "insiders" reflect a process of strategy making which has to remain flexible but rely on co-operation in a hostile environment. In the same way in which the prisoner's dilemma is seen only as a rational decision from a prescriptive point of view, the main research on strategy and strategic groups has failed to examine the managerial perceptions perspective and the process of knowledge creation in strategy.

A major shortcoming of prescriptive studies in the strategy field, which is characterised in particular by strategic group's theory, is the illusion of stability. However, while it is recognised that a degree of temporal stability and continuity is a central feature of competitive markets, prescriptive studies fail to investigate how the swirling events of complex non-linear competitive dynamics are dealt with in the reality of strategic decision-making. The constant fractal dimension in strategy, in reality, produces a vision of firm behaviour as mirroring order within disorder. Managing chaos over time reflects a strategic pattern, within which managerial behaviour may at times be completely random. This paradox requires a more elaborate explanation of the process of strategic management than that provided by prescriptive paradigms, and which can only begin to be addressed through an understanding of the complex interactions of managerial perceptions.

Chapter 3 Cognition, Perception and Construct Theory

Cognitive Groupings

Research on managerial cognition and competitive positioning (Reger, 1990) and strategic groups, as the result of perception and cognition (Reger and Huff, 1993), (Peteraf and Shanley, 1997), has attempted to advance the empirical evidence of the similarities and differences among competitors. To date, the basic premise of this research has been that it is logical to presume that strategists will think in terms of clusters of competitors to cognitively simplify what is otherwise a complex environment.

It is argued that the broad pressures impinging on firms create similar isomorphous organisations and, consequently, commonalities among firms should be expected (Reger and Huff, 1993; Di Maggio and Powell, 1983). In their endeavours to identify strategic groups on the basis of cognition, researchers have examined the proposition that strategists will perceive similarities among subgroups of firms in an industry and that strategists in the same industry will group participants in that industry in similar ways.

A starting point in cognitive research is the recognition that the environmental stimuli impinging on strategists' makes their situation one of information overload. The way this overload is dealt with is by managers simplifying the cognitive complexity of their environment by organising competitors into groups in order to facilitate the process of analysis. Grouping competitors, it is argued, develops cognitive frameworks to facilitate strategic decision processes and helps to reveal a range of agreement on the similarity of firms' strategies.

Cognitive Groupings and Managerial Groupings

The above approach, emanating from the descriptive school, suffers from the same preconceptions as the economic organisation studies. While the cognitive studies utilise the perceptions of managers, rather than the convenient selection of economic data by the researcher, the real difference between them may only lie in the practical experience of the practitioner over the academic.

In a comparative sense this may be significant, but the way experienced managers group competitors will be influenced by the same, similar broad characteristics as those to which, say, journalists, analysts and academics are exposed. It is likely that the cognitive groupings of competitors by strategists will be influenced by perceptions of firm size, sales levels, financial data, assets and so on. Methodologically, groupings on the basis of perceptions about these variables, even by experienced managers, still do not inform us of shared similarity or commonality among managers in different firms about strategic dimensions. Moreover, there is still an underlying assumption that grouping a large number of competitors in this way reveals a range of agreement about firms' strategies.

The method does not explore the differences and similarities among strategists about key competitive strategic dimensions. We could make an analogy with this simplification process by reference to a situation where we might ask certain individuals in a large room filled with people, to group the occupants. The groupings may be done on the basis of some agreement related to certain visible characteristics. These might be height, weight, hair colour, dress sense and so on. Grouping on the basis of visible characteristics would simplify the problem of analysing the large number of people in the room.

However, it would not inform us of the similarities between people in different groups on the basis of their personalities, likes and dislikes and cognitive rationalities about how they viewed the world. In short, while serving the purpose of simplification, our groupings would be superficial. In this sense, it can be argued that asking strategists to simplify the complex competitive environment by grouping competitors in an industry is also a somewhat superficial exercise.

The groupings may have widely shared characteristics, but this does not provide us with evidence of the group members' mental models of competition, which may well be highly asymmetrical and idiosyncratic.

The Contribution of this Research

The originality of this research, in contrast to the earlier studies referred to above, is that this research is investigating the empirical evidence of shared cognitions of strategic dimensions among managers. Earlier studies on strategic groups have, *a fortiori* (transitive related inferences), determined groups with reference to key strategic dimensions. Some studies have utilised Porter's identification of strategic dimensions (Cool and Schendel, 1987; McGee and Thomas, 1986) and elaborated on these.

Others have elicited key strategic dimensions, which have incorporated some of Porters dimensions, but have also included industry specific aspects (Reger and Huff, 1993). However, the clustering of commonalities of key dimensions among managers has not been examined.

Moreover, while the commonality of strategists' key dimensions among firms within clusters has been assumed, this commonality has not been tested. This research attempts to bridge the gap in strategic group studies by examining strategic group clusters identified on the basis of managers'/strategists' perceptions of key strategic dimensions. The hypothesis that these clusters should match strategic groups as formulated by the prescriptive method is put to the test.

Perception

A basic issue, which has confronted man and confounded philosophers, is the perception of reality. How is it we see and experience the world as we do? It is clear any perceptions of the world and our environment must have some relationship to the "real" world, otherwise we would long ago have been devoured by predators. The problem is fundamental. Physics suggests that the world is made up of collections of atomic particles and waves of energy, but it most certainly does not look like that.

Our sensory systems - touch, hearing and vision - are the bridge between the real world and our experience of it. Sensory receptions transform the energy of physical stimuli into nerve impulses, which travel to the brain to produce sensations and perceptions. Our experience of the world and our environment corresponds much more closely to the patterns of activity of neurones in the brain than it does to the patterns of impinging stimulus energy (Békésy, 1957 and Michael, 1972).

This raises the question: do two people's perceptions of the same reality differ? In examining the area of managerial perceptions and strategic groups, we confront the very same question.

Perception and Shared Experience

Suppose, for example, that two people are looking at the same green leaf at the same time. How do we know that they are having the same experience? There seems no possible way of answering this question; for what one person observes in other people are only the signs which they show to him or her, so how can we be sure that other people use words to stand for the same experiences? It seems possible that although two people call the leaf green, that they have different colour experiences on looking at it. For example, one might see it the colour, which the other calls "blue". Therefore, it might be said that we can never know whether two people are having the same experiences.

This question appears to be one which is eternally unanswerable, but yet one whose meaning is perfectly clear and comprehensible. It appears that this is so because we understand the sense of the question. We think we know exactly what is meant by every word contained in the question, for example, what an 'experience' is, and what the word 'same' means. This enables us to make sense of the apparently illusory question. Even if we consider that the words may have more than one meaning, they are used according to different conventions in different contexts.

Take the word "same" for example; it could mean that one object is the same in terms of its function as another object. In this sense, we understand the concept of a chair because it possesses the characteristics of "chairedness" consistent with the function for which a chair is used, although, clearly, not all chairs are the same. This raises the issue as to what it means to say that two people have the same experiences when they look at a coloured leaf. If we say, "this leaf is the same green as that", then we give the experience a precise sense.

Personal Construct Theory

George Kelly's (1955) theory of personal construct psychology provides a very useful explanation of precisely how we make that sense. Personal construct theory examines a person's psychological processes by looking at the way in which he or she anticipates events, how events are anticipated in terms of the person construing the replications of those events and how this enables the person to construe similarities and contrasts.

According to Kelly, in construing similarities and contrasts, a person forms bi-polar constructs, so that both similarity and contrast are features of every construct. An example of a construct can be illustrated as follows: suppose one person regarded another person as entirely trustworthy. An occasion arises when the trusted person asks the other person to lend them money. This request has not been made before but the lender has no difficulty in complying with the borrower's request because the person's trustworthiness has been formed.

However, the borrower, having obtained the loan never mentions or repays the money to the lender and continues on with their past relationship as if they had never borrowed the money in the first place. The lender's construing of similarity and contrast on which their bi-polar construct of previous events was formed, has now been significantly disturbed. The borrowing incident does not equate with previous replications of trustworthy dealings with the borrower and, consequently, the lender's anticipation of trustworthiness of subsequent dealings with the lender will mean that both similarity and contrast will be anticipated differently.

The Postulate and Corollaries of Construct Theory

Kelly's construct system can be conveniently viewed as hierarchically linked sets of bi-polar constructs and these can be systematically assembled using a simple grid method (Fransella and Bannister, 1977). The use of the grid technique obviates the need to explore these linkages without experimental bias being generated by the researcher. The central tenets of personal construct theory are stated in the form of a fundamental postulate supported by elaborative corollaries (Fransella and Bannister, 1977). Kelly's fundamental postulate argues: "A person's processes are psychologically channelised by the ways in which he anticipates events". His corollaries are as follows:-

- people differ from each other in their construction of events.
- each person evolves, for the convenience of anticipating events, a construction system which embraces ordinal relationships between constructs. This implies a hierarchical system, in which some constructs are more important than others and in which some constructs are subordinated to, and embraced by, other more super-ordinate constructs.

Charniak and McDermott (1985) reinforce the notion of a hierarchical system as being the most efficient way to represent information about an object or concept in memory. A hierarchical system is more efficient because it enables information to be represented only once, reducing the amount of redundant information.

The hierarchical information is based on a semantic network where nodes representing concepts, ideas and objectives, are linked with arcs which form the association between the nodes (Collins and Quillian, 1969; Stubbart, 1989). Abstract information is held at higher levels in the network, while more specific information is held at lower levels.

For example, abstract information about strategy in an industry would be held at a higher level, while information about specific companies would be held at a lower level.

- there are a finite number of dichotomous constructs composing a person's construction system.
- a person will choose the alternative within a dichotomised construct through which he or she anticipates the greater possibility for the elaboration of their system.
- in our example of the lender and the borrower, the former has no difficulty choosing to lend the money because this presents an opportunity to elaborate on their perception that the borrower is trustworthy.
- similarly, the anticipation of a persons construct of local versus regional brewers will be based on specific reference to firms which he or she categorises on the basis of the similarity associated with the elaboration of that construct.
- a construct is convenient (applicable) for a finite range of events only.
- a person's construct system varies as he or she successively construes events.
- this variation is limited by the openness (permeability) or closedness (impermeability), to new events, of the construct within whose range of convenience the variants lie.

Kelly argues that a person's worldviews are open and ambiguous. Closure is only temporary, while the people commit themselves to a decision about choice. This includes cutting themselves off from ambiguity and uncertainty while a decision is made related to the range of convenience of construct alternatives.

- a person may employ a variety of construction subsystems which are inferentially incompatible with each other, and which may imply inconsistency to the outside observer.
- to the extent that one person employs a construction of experience which is similar to that employed by another, his/her psychological processes are similar to those employed by the other person.
- to the extent to which a person construes the construction processes of another person, he or she may play a role in a social process involving the other.

The bi-polar constructs in the theory of personal construct psychology make the communication of perceptions possible. Together they give us a structure of the experience. They overcome the idea that the contents of different people's minds are shut off from each other by insurmountable barriers, so that what is experienced is externally private and inexpressible. The idea that we are, so to speak, imprisoned behind bars through which only words can escape (as though it were a defect in language that it consists wholly of words), is removed. In sum, they enable the identification of cognitive structures which could not otherwise be articulated.

Repertory Grid Techniques

Kelly developed several methods of construct elicitation which appear useful for exploring a person's construction of their world. These methods were used in his application of Role Construct Repertory Test and have been modified in subsequent grid designs dealing with construct elicitation in general (Fransella & Bannister, 1977). The appeal of Repertory Grid technique to the exploration of managerial perceptions of strategic groups is considerable. The essential feature or elements, which represent their world in the competitive/industry structure sense, can be easily presented and are representations with which managers will be familiar.

The first stage of the techniques involves identifying the elements in the domain of interest of the managers. For example, identifying firms in a given industry which are representative of the activities of firms in that industry. The second stage involves eliciting constructs. Constructs are the qualities which people use to think about the elements. In other words, the constructs are the descriptors of the elements. To elicit the constructs the method of triading is most commonly used. Triading involves drawing three cards at random. Each card represents an element (i.e. in this case a company). The respondent is asked to identify the two elements that are most similar and is then asked to state how these two are different from the third element.

The elements and constructs are arranged on a repertory grid and the construct elicitations are then arranged onto a second grid to enable a ranking of the construct descriptors.

The use of the triad of elements method in elicitation enables constructions to be drawn out of the manager/person without causing the person to create artificial constructions. The repertory grid technique also enables a mathematical formulation to be developed from the relationship of elements to elicited constructs.

The representation in mathematical terms of the relationship between the respondents and constructs in the grid is an important aspect of the analysis of the elicitations. The subtle relationships between respondents and constructs can be ascertained using statistical packages which, among other things, calculate the distances between respondents, thus enabling the hierarchical clustering of elicitations to be compared and mapped out diagrammatically.

A visual representation of a person's mental model can be produced by subjecting the ranked order grid to principal components analysis and/or cluster analysis. Cluster analysis shows how the rated elements are grouped with the respondents. Principal components analysis provides a map that shows the underlying dimensions or factors that are responsible for differentiating between the elements.

The Robustness of Repertory Grid Techniques

The repertory grid is flexible and can elicit reasons for the structure of persons' mental maps. However, as stated above, the maps are derived from complex statistical operations on raw data and, therefore, a certain amount of researcher interpretation is required in the process.

Daniels, de Chernatony and Johnson (1992) have investigated an alternative to repertory grid in order to assess the degree of subjective interpretation on the part of the researcher. They contrasted the repertory grid techniques with a hierarchical taxonomic sorting technique. In this the respondent is asked to name the elements (companies) that represent competitors in his/her industry in a step analogous to the repertory grid techniques described above. The respondent then sorts the cards on which the element is written and is asked to place these together on the basis of closeness/similarity. This provides physical clusters arranged by the respondent.

However, the mental models are constrained by the two dimensional arrangement (since they are arranged on a flat surface) and subsequently there is the possibility that the technique lacks sufficient complexity, and context similarity, in producing mental maps. This may be overcome by eliciting multiple mental maps. However, the first map elicited is regarded as the dominant map.

It is argued that visual card sort mapping is a valid method for mapping managers' mental models of competitive industry structures. It was found that there was significant convergence between the maps elicited by visual card sort mapping and those elicited by the grid technique. In a study of 29 respondents on visual card sorting, as well as triading (the method used in repertory grid techniques), the means and standard deviations of average rated importance for elicited constructs were significantly convergent (3.91, 3.75 and 0.565, 0.715) (Daniels, de Chernatony and Johnson, 1992). However, it was also concluded that the issue of access and time constraints in relation to the managers presents additional problems for this method of research.

The foregoing rationale for this research into strategic groups and managerial perceptions is facilitated by the standards and criteria provided by Repertory Grid as a formal and systematic method of inquiry. This method has formed the basis on which the pilot and extended study undertaken in this research has been conducted and the data analysed.

Knowledge and Judgement

The literature suggests that researchers understand competition in industry sectors through the use of strategic groups and that firms within groups follow similar strategies. It seems a reasonable hypothesis, as outlined above, that managers (insiders) will cognitively organise competitive factors in the process of formulating strategies and in so doing perceptually determine the existence of strategic groups within their industry sector. In other words, strategic groups, reflecting homogenous perceptions of strategic dimensions, are a real phenomenon in the competitive environment.

The cognitive construction of important competitive factors involves knowledge building, in the sense that the manager's personal constructs will be tested continually against their experience of existing in the competitive environment. Knowledge in the form of the relevant substantive facts will be intertwined with judgements, dealing with the way uncertainties are resolved. Knowledge and judgement will combine in the reconciliation between abstraction and practical reality. In this way knowledge and judgement inform managers' learning and memory, which are intimately bound up with their particular contexts of activity and experience.

Managerial judgements will be influenced by long-term memory. Information in long-term memory is processed by grouping concepts and events together in terms of contiguity (Schank, 1982; Schacker, 1989). Short-term memory processes information for storage and retrieval in long-term memory and has a limited capacity (Miller 1956). The contiguity of long-term memory associates concepts by time, function or shared dimensions.

These concepts are organised for efficiency in memory through a hierarchy (Charniak and McDermott, 1985). The relationship between judgements, encompassing knowledge, memory and experiences, precedes our actions in a particular context. We can postulate, therefore, that managers' cognitive organisation of competitive dimensions informs their actions in the process of formulating competitive strategies.

A cognitive framework of managerial perceptions

In managerial cognition, the interpretative processes of the key strategic dimensions through which managers enact responses to environmental/organisational changes, are strongly emphasised. These cognitions are linked to managerial actions and strategic change is inferred from these actions. The writer's model, incorporating the cognitive lens perspective strategy, is contained in Figure 4.

The cognitive lens perspective model shown in Figure 4 reflects a sequential, planned search by rational managers for a fit between the firm and its environment, through the creation and implementation of a competitive strategy. Competitive strategy is a concept which incorporates discrete changes in a firm's business level strategies. Business level strategies are meant to improve the competitiveness of the firm. In the model, the competitive environment is objectively determined and manifests a source of opportunities and threats. The competitive environment directly influences the perceptions of managers and their cognition of strategic dimensions. In turn, the strategic decisions, which they predicate, change the organisational conditions and the content of strategy.

The Cognitive Lens Model

In the prescriptive studies, it is explicitly implied that strategic group formations should manifest the commonality of key dimensions among firms in the industry. Moreover, the business level strategies which firms implement do not necessarily need to reflect the diversity of assets under particular corporate umbrellas within an industry. In this sense, the traditional Structure-Conduct-Performance paradigm which models a direct *one-way* causal link running from industry structure to managerial conduct and then on to corporate performance, is considerably flawed. The one-way causal link of the SCP model will be subject to a variety of feedback effects that create difficulties for the identification of cause and effect.

Competitive advantage is not a unitary concept in the sense that the magnitude of corporate asset commitments is linked to various levels of response and variations in performance. Competitive strategies leading to competitive advantages may be viewed as an iterative process, whereby managers effect changes designed to adjust the organisation to the competitive environment.

Central to this iterative process is the cognitive lens perspective of key strategic dimensions, which inform managerial decisions and actions about the combination of changes in competitive strategy.

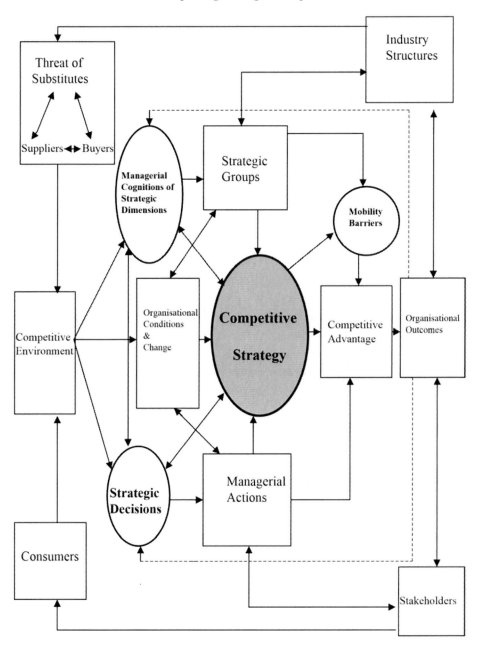

Figure 6. A Cognitive Lens Perspective

The Environment, Organisational Conditions and Change

Several studies have indicated that deregulation or specific regulatory changes are positively related to changes in firms' strategies (Smith and Grimm, 1987; Zajac and Shortell, 1989). In response to deregulation, it was found that firms pursuing defender – like, efficiency – orientated, or less focussed strategies, tended to change to more prospector-like, more innovative and more focussed strategies (Rajagopalan and Spreitzer, 1996). Defender type strategies refer to actions that provide for continuity and security. Prospector type strategies refer to actions that reflect product and market development and are supported by a flexible and creative approach to change (Miles and Snow, 1978).

In the past twenty-five years the Beer and Brewing industry in the UK has been characterised by an environmental/organisational context which has been uncertain and dynamic. Undoubtedly this has been a source of information uncertainty and cause – effect ambiguity for managers. The contention here is that managers in the UK brewing industry would attempt to understand their ambiguous environment through a series of iterative actions informed by their cognition of strategic dimensions.

Such actions would involve information gathering, not only aimed at probing their perceptions of the external context, but also aimed at influencing their cognitions in a proactive sense. Managers, through the iterative process of strategic change and competitive strategy, can shape the opportunities and constraints posed by the competitive environment and organisational conditions.

These actions are aimed at reducing uncertainty stemming from the environment and may lead to a better understanding and more focussed development of mobility barriers. In this sense, managers learn from the ongoing iterative process of strategy formulation and use this knowledge to reinforce actions which enhance mobility barriers.

What is being suggested here is that strategic change, leading on from managerial cognitions of key dimensions, seldom emerges in a linear fashion. Similarly, groups at the competitive strategy level will not emerge solely from asset configurations that imply that the content of strategies is unidirectional.

Industry structures may imply unidirectional approaches to industry competition, as in the concentration ratio of the UK brewing industry. However, this belies the reality of adjustments to firms' strategies and the grouping of firms on the basis of their strategic responses to dynamic environmental conditions. These groupings may in fact be viewed as idiosyncratic when the asset configuration of group members reflects a contrast rather than homogeneity. However, they may also reflect valid relationships that mirror the historical continuity in firms' strategic responses.

Such relationships may not have been previously supported by empirical data, because such data relied on the same operational antecedents. That is, although researchers may have claimed to approach the problem of strategic groups from different perspectives, namely, the economic organisation and managerial perception perspective, they have in fact relied on the same basic methods for grouping competitors.

Shortcomings of Strategic Group Research

In the area of economic organisation, strategic group research has been used to describe the symmetry of operations observed between firms in an industry. The identification of systematic differences observed through accounting and financial data has also been used to explore the concept of strategic groups. However, dissatisfactions have arisen with these approaches due to the different, perhaps even haphazard, selection of strategic dimensions. Moreover, the lack of sufficient theory and or model construction has left this field of research on strategic groups essentially inconclusive. Indeed, the most critical writers on this prescriptive area of strategic group research have questioned whether strategic groups actually exist and consequently whether a firm's performance depends upon strategic group membership (Barney and Hoskinson, 1990:187).

A Cognitive Lens Perspective of Strategic Change

In general, the literature on strategy manifests two schools of thought. As suggested in Chapter I, the "prescriptive" school focuses on the rationality and structure content of competitiveness on the basis of an input/output relationship, while the "descriptive" or "process" school focuses on the role of managers in the strategic change process, utilising behavioural in-depth studies based on grounded theory.

However, while these approaches often reflect findings which highlight the schisms between the schools, they may not be mutually exclusive. It is possible that a cognitive perspective aimed at synthesising economic organisation with the management of change, may provide guidance for future research concerned with the integration of these schools of thought (Rafferty, 1997).

The managerial cognition's perspective in the strategic change process explicitly focuses on the cognitive interpretations of managers. Reger has argued this perspective is "more useful" than the economic and structural positioning view because the "objective reality" of the researcher, from this perspective, may not be meaningful to strategists and may not guide their decision-making (Reger, 1990:71).

The cognitive lens perspective views managerial actions in the environmental/organisational context against a backcloth whereby knowledge, beliefs, cultures and structure cannot be objectively de-coupled from managerial actions concerned with the context of strategy. As J. C. Spender has put it, "organisational behaviour ..... is managed through the ideas adopted by the people in the organisation" (Spender, 1989:185). These ideas reflect what managers think about their own companies and "as different firms develop different strategies and experience different results, messages are broadcast back to others in the industry about what works and what fails" (Spender, 1989:193).

In cognitive lens studies, cognitions are linked to managerial actions and strategic change is inferred from managerial actions (Rajagopalan and Spreiter, 1996). Through its recognition of organisational ideologies, the cognitive lens approach also makes tacit distinctions between evolutionary and transformational strategic changes (Webb and Dawson, 1991). Incremental shifts in the knowledge structures which essentially do not disturb the dialectic of managerial cognition's are associated with evolutionary strategic change, whereas strategic change of a transformational nature is a manifestation of a profound shift in knowledge structure and ideologies (Johnson, 1987; Rafferty, 1988).

Cognition and Shared Perceptions

Managerial cognitions can have little effect on strategic change unless they are turned into actions or lead to inaction. However, managerial cognitions can be altered through actions that seek to inculcate a different and shared perspective about the need for change based on a new or adjusted cognitive lens perspective. This view is summed up in Richard Pascale's argument that it is easier to act ourselves into a better way of thinking than it is to think ourselves into a better way of acting (Pascale, 1990).

On the one hand, it can be argued, in the cognitive lens perspective that the environment cannot be objectively determined, but instead is enacted by managers through cognitions (Johnson, 1992). It can also be argued that the competitive environment may impinge on managerial cognitions in a way that creates a shared perception amongst some managers in different organisations within the same industry.

The fact that the organisational context and the organisational structure form part of a much broader organisational ideology, in which "inseparability" and "embeddedness" (Hofstede, 1980) may mitigate against strategic change, does not preclude the interpretative processes, through which managers enact, being shared on a strategic group basis across different organisations. This view is related to what Spender (1989) refers to as an industry recipe, a shared set of ideas. The shared set of ideas may point to the reasons or the apparent homogeneity of strategic groups when these have been formulated by managers' perceptions of groups in their industry.

Several researchers (e.g. Barr et al, 1992; Child & Smith, 1987; Pettigrew, 1987; Webb and Dawson, 1991; Whipp et al, 1989) have indicated that strategic change occurs when changes in the environmental conditions are accompanied by major changes in top management's cognitions. Moreover, research has indicated that there can be significant variations in managerial cognitions of similar environmental events (Ginsberg & Abrahamson, 1991; Grinyer & McKiernan, 1990; Meyer, (1982).

Managerial Perceptions and Organisational Conditions

The above studies highlight the shortcomings of the rational perspective. They point to an explanation for the failure of some strategic changes, but not others, in response to the same environmental changes, when the intervening effects of managerial cognitions differ significantly within the same industry, and indeed within the same firm.

Managerial interpretations of internal factors which were linked to declining performance have been shown to initiate strategic change (Barr et al, 1992; and Lant et al, 1992). Transformational strategic changes, as opposed to evolutionary incremental strategic changes, have been accompanied by changes in top management's belief structures (Child and Smith, 1987; Pettigrew, 1987; Webb and Dawson, 1991). What these findings may demonstrate is that managerial perceptions of altered organisational conditions influence the need for strategic change more readily than the rational perspectives more commonly associated with prescriptive approaches.

Managerial Cognitions across Firms

A methodological issue confronting cognitive lens studies has concerned the measure of dimensions at individual manager level and the aggregation of these to the level of the firm. However, this approach has limitations in that researchers who exclusively use the cognitive perspective at the level of the individual manager rarely distinguish cognitions across firms in an industry. The weakness here is that researchers using a cognitive perspective may draw conclusions from case studies without reference to a well-defined construct which make explicit, linkages between managers in firms across an industry.

Using a strategic group approach (rather than an individual firm) as the basis of analysis could provide a common ground across which managerial perceptions of strategic dimensions bridge the gap between the cognitive and rational lens perspectives. In this way, it may be possible to make more valid comparisons of managerial cognitions across an industry sector, thus avoiding the results of biases drawn from individual case studies. Moreover, the critical assertions of strategic group theory that strategic groups exist, can be tested and greater light shed on the assumption that firms are idiosyncratic in strategically relevant ways (Barney & Hoskisson, 1990).

Reger and Huff have suggested that, "strategic groups can be defined in a way that allows some strategically important variance among firms within each group" (1993:104). In this sense, the emphasis is not on a modified version of group structures aimed at the understanding of profitable strategic choices. Nor is the emphasis on the different cognitive perspectives and actions linked with economically successful strategic change. As Reger and Huff argue "predicting firm profitability … is not the key contribution of a cognitive approach to strategic groups" (1993:104).

Identifying the variances in managerial cognitions within an industry may be the key contribution to the theory of strategic groups, which explains not only the differences in group formations, but also illuminates the idiosyncrasies of strategically relevant actions. The empirical question is not whether strategists and managers share perceptions of strategic dimensions with each other (and how), but rather with whom they share. In this sense, this research attempts to focus on the patterns of shared perceptions across an industry at the strategic groups level.

Structure, Strategy and Managerial Perceptions

There is a certain imitative dimension to shared perceptions, as suggested earlier (Spender, 1989), regarding the communication across an industry about what works and what fails in terms of strategies. As Spender has commented "it is probably a mistake to make a computer look like a washing machine" (1989:184). However, managers are not precluded from implementing similar strategies at the competitive level. The fact that some brewing firms may imitate a hotel company in the way that some building societies may imitate a bank does not mean that we can presume that corporate performance is a direct function of industry structure. What is suggested here is that the process of developing a structure is different from the process of creating a strategy. As Lessem has suggested, "the main emphasis is on the interplay – the fluidity among particular perspectives …. The particular product or process is always in the process of being reworked in the process of change" (Lessem, 1997:56).

Industry Structure

The notion of an industry and its members has posed particular problems for economists and other researchers for some time. We speak of the steel industry or the automobile industry, but it could be reasonably argued that the steel industry, through its constituent supplies, is part of the consuming automobile industry.

While it may be possible to argue that industries have no identity other than that created by firms, sharing a common interest with other firms, it is a mistake to identify strategic groups as providing a characteristic remedy to this problem by clustering firms, on the basis of measures, which ignore the inner workings and thoughts of managers. For example, Hunt (1972), in his initial study of strategic groups in the "white goods industry", clustered his groups on the basis of three dimensions: the extent of vertical integration, the degree of diversification, and the degree of differentiation. These measures were validated with reference to corporate performance and not concerned with managerial behaviour or thought.

The industrial economics view, popularised by Porter et al, of strategic groups is principally concerned with overcoming the problems of industry definition by classifying an industry as consisting of different homogeneous groups. This view of industry presents a model, where firms' performance is a function of the group performance and the firms' resources. However, there is little empirical evidence to support the view that performance variations within these homogeneous groups are significantly any different from the performance variations between them. Thus, predicting profitability from homogeneous group structures does not seem particularly sound.

Notwithstanding the efficacy of proposing a predictive model from the categorisation of homogeneous strategic groups, the issue of change is also marginalised by the categories from industrial economics. Managerial perceptions reflect what managers think about their companies in the competitive environment. Change takes place because of what happens to companies in that environment. The changes, which occur in companies, influence the perceptions of managers in other companies and their actions will also change. Thus, the shared perceptions may change and ideas and actions previously representative of a particular group of managers may be reflected among a new group representing different firms.

From an outside observer's point of view, the considerable simplification of clustering firms on measures related to physical homogeneity (Hunt, 1972), obscures the experiences and events which rearrange the perceptions of managers and their manoeuvrings for competitive advantage. Successful competitors do not rely on competitive advantage as a closed formula. There are numerous and legendary failures which testify to that fact. Strategy is a rationality which remains open and is often ambiguous due to the different interpretations, nuances and circumstances that managers understand and experience. In practice, analysts may view particular groups as homogeneous, when in reality there is considerable heterogeneity across, and even within, firms in an industry.

The hypothesis to be tested in this study is directly concerned with this reality and examines the issue of whether managerial perceptions of competitive dimensions are homogeneous within and across strategic groups.

Summary

Cognitive studies in relation to strategic groups have focussed on how managers perceive similarities among subgroups in an industry. However, cognitive groupings of competitors by strategists have been influenced by the same perceptions of firm size, sales, financial data, asset configurations etc, as those of outsiders such as academics or journalists. Moreover, a grouping of sub groups of firms in an industry relies on the underlying assumption that there is a range of agreement within the groups about firms' strategies.

This research departs from the above method by investigating the empirical evidence of shared cognitions of strategic dimensions among managers. Utilising Kelly's (1955) theory of personal construct psychology, managers' perceptions of key competitive dimensions will be elicited and explored as a means of testing the range of agreement in relation to strategic groups. Utilising the repertory grid technique in conjunction with principal component analysis and cluster analysis, a visual representation of strategists' cognitions of key strategic dimensions will be produced.

The cognitive construction of important competitive dimensions, as perceived by managers, is a knowledge-building process. The interactive process, whereby managers effect changes and inculcate new knowledge, can be illustrated in a cognitive lens model which links the competitive environment with managerial cognition and competitive strategy.

The cognitive perspective provides a synthesis of economic organisation and the management of strategic change. The hypothesis tested in this research is directly connected with the reality of this synthesis and, as such, it is to the realities of the Brewing industry which we must now turn in Chapter 4.

PART II INDUSTRY CONTEXT

Chapter 4 The UK Brewing Industry

Introduction

The UK brewing industry dates back to the Middle-Ages and can be regarded as somewhat unique among industry sectors. As alcoholic drinks manufactures, brewers, historically, have been regulated by the British Government. Consequently, fiscal pressures on brewing has enabled reliable data to be gathered on the industry and on the number of firms involved in it. The effects of direct government taxation on brewing products has also meant that accurate information on the structure of the industry, market shares, distribution and pricing have been reliably gathered through HM Customs and Excise and the Brewers and Licensed Retailers Association (BLRA).

The modern history of the brewing industry really begins around 1830 with the passing of the Beer Act into legislation. The Beer Act of 1830 can perhaps be regarded as one of the most significant statutes of legislation of the nineteenth century. The objective of the Beer Act was to achieve 'free licensing' in the trade and sale of beer (Gourvish and Wilson, 2008)[1]. However, the main significance of the Beer Act was as an indicator of the reassessment that had occurred of the political, economic and social situation after 1815 in the 'Age of Reform', and the necessity to bring about change of the magnitude being promulgated by political economists such as Adam Smith.

Prior to the Beer Act of 1830, licences of all retail beer outlets were entirely under the control of magistrates and increasingly the influence of brewers in gaining possession of licences and consequently outlets, sharpened the antagonisms of economic theorists and liberal thinkers. Regulation gave authoritarian powers to magistrates and local and regional monopolies to brewers.

The Beer Act created a fourth type of public house (following Taverns, Inns and Alehouses); the beer house. In effect, the Act allowed any householder who paid rates to apply for an excise license (at a cost of two guinea's) to sell beer and importantly, to brew it on their premises.

By 1838, 46,000 beer houses had been added to the 51,000 premises in operation before 1830. For the advocates of free trade, the Beer Act was a milestone (Gourvish and Wilson, 2008). Industries like brewing depended on agricultural products and agricultural areas welcomed the urban demand for their outputs. For Adam Smith, the gains of both town and country for these relationships was reciprocal; "and the division of labour is in this, as in all other

---

[1] For an excellent history of the industry see, Gourvish, T. R. and Wilson, R. G. (2008), The British Brewing Industry 1830-1980, Cambridge University Press.

cases, advantageous to all the different persons employed" (Briggs, 1974:37).

However, the phenomenon that the 1830 Act was in large measure designed to address, the 'tie', was not definitively curtailed. The historical distribution, involving the networks of brewery owned tied public houses, resulted in the industry evolving a monopoly structure at local and regional levels. This structure proved a consistent focus of criticism from both consumer and government sources beginning in the 1960's, which, over the next 30 years, led to competition policy investigations culminating in the Monopolies and Mergers Commission Report in 1989. This report was the harbinger of the introduction of regulations known as the "Beer Orders" that were aimed at altering the monopoly structure of the tied house distribution network and which, between 1991 and 2005, brought about significant competitive changes in the industry. The following analysis tracks the impact of these changes and highlights the strategic reorientation of the industry through the period of the late 1990's to the early years of 2000.

Since the 1930's there has been a long term, steady reduction in the number of large, well-established breweries. In 1900 there were approximately 6,000 breweries operating in the UK. By 1930 there were in excess of 500 brewery companies in the UK. By the end of the 1960's there were less than 100. The BLRA differentiates between the long established breweries founded before 1971 and those established since then. The group founded before 1971 includes all the national and major regional brewers and consists of 62 companies who between them controlled 85 active breweries. The number of breweries established before 1971 and still in existence between 1980 and 1998 is summarised in Table 1.

Table 1: Number of Breweries Established before 1971, 1980 – 1998

	1980	1985	1990	1995	1998
Companies owning breweries established before 1971	81	73	65	64	62
Operating breweries established before 1971	142	121	99	93	85

The striking trend in the brewing industry over the period 1980 – 1998 is the degree of concentration. A feature of this concentration has been the polarisation between the national groups such as Scottish Courage and Bass and the regional and local brewers. However, as can be seen from Table 1, despite concentration as a marked historical feature of this industry, by the late 1990's the core of the industry still consisted of 62 long established companies.

Industry concentration in the UK was a national phenomenon in the 1960's and 1970's. In the merger mania of that period in British economic history, the Brewing industry was just one of a number of sectors that experienced the disappearance of firms through mergers and acquisitions. Overall during that period, British companies vanished at a rate of 856 per annum. This compared with rates of 291 and 460 in 1954-58 and 1974-80 respectively. In 1968 the 100 largest companies controlled 41 per cent of total net output of the economy, compared with 22 per cent 19 years earlier. The majority of mergers and acquisitions were of the horizontal variety resulting in increased concentration levels across industries (Gourvish and Wilson, 2008).

Among the most virile in the 'merger mania' era were firms in the brewing industry. Whereas in the mid-1950's the top five brewers owned 11 per cent of the country's licensed retail outlets, by the mid -1970's this had risen to 38 per cent. Over the period 1954-1973 production facilities fell from 479 to 162, with the number of companies dropping from 305 to 88. The level of concentration resulting from the merger mania period produced a cluster of firms who, by the early 1970's, accounted for 80 per cent of total UK beer output. The so called "Big Seven" consisted of Allied Breweries, Bass Charrington, Courage, Scottish and Newcastle, Watney, Whitbread and Guinness. Between 1958 and 1970 the "Big Six" (excluding Guinness) brewers closed 44 per cent of their 122 breweries while achieving four-fold increases in output (Gourvish and Wilson, 2008).

Mergers and Acquisitions Rationale

Notwithstanding the level of mergers and acquisitions in the UK economy in the 1960's and 1970's, this activity took place against a backcloth of international developments that witnessed an initial flurry of moves that grew into an international phenomenon. In that sense the events in the UK were not comparatively abnormal. Generally, across international frontiers, stock markets were beginning to flourish following the post-war adjustment. This economic environment facilitated deals. Capital was available and seeking opportunities and many deals took advantage of share issues to raise funds, which they combined with share exchanges to complete the transactions. The pursuit of economies of scale was an important dimension in the growth strategies of firms. Increasing and consolidating market share to discourage new entrants and exercise a degree of market power in the anticipation of growing multinational competition also became an important strategic consideration.

Throughout this period UK political economic influences also played its part as British Governments oscillated between discouraging and encouraging industry concentration. On the one hand, while politicians moved to strengthen the powers of the Monopolies Commission to intervene in mergers and acquisitions in the public interest; on the other hand, Government actions through Industrial Policy initiatives were eager to encourage mergers in sectors such as the automotive industry based on concerns about scale economies from overseas competitors. The general industrial sentiment this created was that certain industries would benefit from increased concentration as a competitive strategy in the face of growing international competition.

Consumer demand also played an important part in the merger and acquisitions activity in the brewing industry. Between the late 1950's and the late

1970's beer consumption increased by over 70 per cent. Almost all of this was met by domestic production. Figure 5 illustrates the growth in output and consumption of beer between 1955 and 1990.

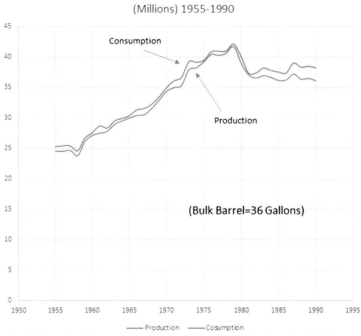

UK Beer Production and Consumption in Bulk Barrels (Millions) 1955-1990

Figure 7. UK Beer Statistics (adapted from UK Statistical Handbook, 1990. Source cited in Gourvish and Wilson (2008), p.630).

In addressing an analysis of the brewing industry in the context of the concept of strategic groups and indeed, cognitive strategic groups, the historiography of the industry is of particular importance. Taking a longitudinal perspective, two recurring themes have run through the British Brewing industry for almost two hundred years; namely, regulation and concentration strategies. Indeed, in the post WWII era it could be argued that the rate of concentration has been characterised by greater velocity as a consequence of regulatory intervention that has witnessed the disappearance of firms, beers, public houses and tied corporates.

Perhaps the most striking feature of the changes in the industry over this period can be seen in the demise of the public house, the 'pub'. There were approximately 100,000 pubs in the UK at the turn of the century. By 1980, this figure had declined to approximately 69,000. Figures from the British Beer and Pub Association record that this number had fallen to 51,900 by 2014. In the intervening period fluctuations have occurred with the number of closures between 1980 and 1994 increasing by 12 per cent, whereas in the period between

1994 and 1999, the number of pubs actually rose by 1 per cent. However, between 1999 and 2014 the number declined by 16 per cent.

A number of causes can be identified to explain the decline. Prominent among these are the Beer Orders themselves combined with changing lifestyles towards healthier diets and changing social attitudes towards the consumption of alcohol (for example, the Institute of Alcohol Studies argue that duty should not be cut but raised by 4 per cent above inflation for societal reasons). Since the sixteenth century, brewing has almost continually attracted government intervention because it produces a product that, while popular, is a potentially dangerous drink and has been a major source of government revenue. The excise duty on beer has consistently outstripped inflation with the 'duty escalator' between 2008 and 2013 providing an example of excise duty increasing by 2 per cent above the rate of inflation. While there has been a duty cut of 1 pence between 2013 and 2016, there is evidence that duty cuts actually damage the pub trade by reducing the relative price of alcohol in supermarkets, which have seen their share of the market increase at the expense of the on-trade. Falling real incomes since the 2008 financial crisis and the recession that followed has mirrored the declining popularity of beer and drinking in pubs, as has the apparent effects of the UK smoking ban in public places. There has also been a more heightened attitude towards pubs with low turnover that has been reflected in divestments as property values have risen considerably.

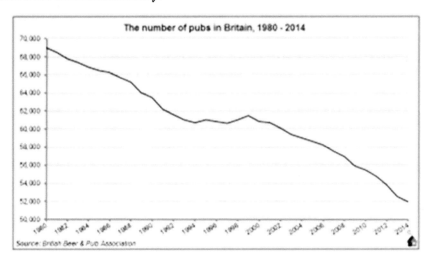

Figure 8. The UK Pub Decline

However, these changes have been met with diversity; the growth in the popularity of lager; the emergence of new product segments based on average gravity, premium gravity and specialist beers; reinvigorated competition through the creation and promotion of new brands and new independent micropub brewers established over the last ten years; all as a means of best meeting consumer tastes and preferences. In fact if we were to summarise and encapsulate the longitudinal strategy of the brewing industry it would be as an industry consistently pursuing a horizontal differentiation strategy.

The New Brewers

The period since 1971 has been generally regarded as the period of the development of the modern breweries. Between 1971 and 1997, over 200 new breweries became operational, with over 100 of these opening since 1987 (BLRA, 1997). In addition to these breweries, the industry has seen the development of the "brewpubs", where small-scale brewing takes place and which historically mirror the origins of the brewing industry in the 12th century. In 1987, there were approximately 70 of these and by 1998 this number had grown to 215 (see Table 2). Similarly, the growth of the microbrewers has reinvigorated the industry somewhat, so that by 2014 the number of UK breweries had risen to 1,424 (see Fig. 6). While the development of the brewpubs were initially the creations of the new free-house owners, recent developments in this area have come from investments by the national brewers in establishing chains of brewpubs. For example, Carlsberg – Tetley created the Firkin chain of 21 public houses, which brew their own beer on site. The 'craft' ales are demanding premium prices for premium products, with the new microbrewers now becoming targets as niche businesses for their profitability in the food and drinks market.

Although operationally small, the number of microbrewers established in recent years has had an influence on the development of specific segments of the industry. For example, Archers Ales, which was established in Swindon in 1979, while only operating three of its own tied houses, supplies 180 other free trade houses. It is estimated that the vast majority of microbrewers produce speciality beers, which they supply as guest beers to an average of 50 or fewer local free houses (BLRA, 1998). However, while the increase in the granting of brewing licenses since 1980 had altered the trend in the number of operators by the late 1990's and 2000's, the effects of concentration are more evident by examining the beer market.

Table 2: Total Number of Breweries in the UK, 1998

Breweries founded before 1971	85
Stand-alone Breweries founded since 1971	200
Brewery public houses (Brew Pubs)	215
Total	500

Source: BLRA, Key Note, 1998

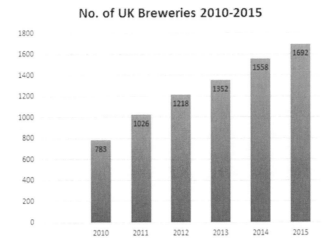

Figure 9. Growth in the number of UK Breweries 2010-2015

The Market

UK consumers are estimated to have spent £30.513 billion on alcoholic drinks in 1998, representing just under 6 per cent of total expenditure on all goods and services. By 2014 expenditure on alcoholic drinks was estimated at approximately £50 billion.

In relation to the total volume of consumption, the market for beer can be characterised as mature. Throughout the period 1991 – 1998, consumption of beer remained virtually unchanged at approximately 6,200 million litres per annum. Over the period this volume has fluctuated by an average of 0.3 per cent with the maximum downward variation of 3.3 per cent occurring between 1991 and 1993. In value terms, by 1998, the market was estimated at £16.75 billion, equivalent to 54.8 per cent of the alcoholic drinks market. This was divided into the on-trade (public houses) worth £13.28 billion and the off-trade (supermarkets, grocery multiples, off licences), valued at £3.47 billion.

Notwithstanding the continuous decline in the consumption of beer over the past 20 years or so since 1995, beer consumption actually rose by 1 per cent in 2014. This small rise is attributed to the cuts in excise duty that were implemented in the 2012 and 2013 budgets. Overall, beer took approximately 36 per cent of the UK drinks market in 2014, with wine in second place at 33 per cent. Spirits

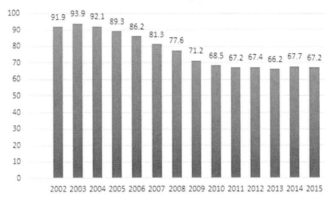

Average number of litres per head consumed annually in the UK

Figure 10. Average consumption per head in the UK

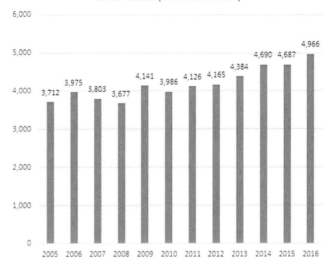

Consumer spending on Beer in the UK from 2005-2016 (in Millions GBP)

Figure 11. Consumer spending on Beer, 2005-2016

accounted for approximately 21 per cent of the market and cider and 'alcopops' took up 8 per cent and 2 per cent respectively.

In 2015, alcohol was almost 60 per cent more affordable in the UK than it was in 1980, highlighting the overall trend of increasing affordability over the period. 'Affordability' is the price of alcohol related to adult's disposable income (base year: 1980). It has been estimated that in 2014 in the UK the average weekly household spend on alcohol consumed in the home was £7.90. This compares with £7.20 spent on alcohol consumed outside the home (Health and Social Care Information Centre, 2016, Statistics on Alcohol). The split in household spend crystallises the key dichotomy in the alcohol market and emphasises the rather precarious road ahead for the beer sector in particular.

Prices

Levels of beer consumption in the UK are at a 16 year low, notwithstanding the 1 per cent rise in 2014, the total national consumption stands at 4.375 billion litres annually. This equates with a per capita consumption of 67.7 litres. While volumes have remained relatively stable around this level since 2014, prices have outstripped the Retail Price Index by over 100 per cent in certain periods. For example, between 1990 and 1995 the retail price index rose by 18.5 per cent, whereas beer prices rose by 46.3 per cent in the same period (Office for National Statistics, 1998). Between 2002 and 2014 average beer prices rose by approximately 60 per cent while inflation increased by approximately 50 per cent.

Prices have risen much faster in the on-trade (brewery owned public houses and free houses) than in the off-trade (supermarket sales, grocery multiples and off-licences). While prices in the on-trade rose on average by 36 per cent throughout the 1990's, the off-trade increase has been in the region of 21 per cent. Indeed, in the period between 1993 and 1994 prices actually fell by 1.6 per cent in the off-trade, reflecting a deflationary lag resulting from the volume decline between 1991 and 1993.

The draught beer market accounts for approximately 65 per cent of sales by volume, with the remaining 35 per cent being accounted for by packaged and bottled beers. In 1998, Lager accounted for approximately 57 per cent of total sales of draught, with dark draught beers accounting for 39 per cent and dark packaged beers, the remaining 4 per cent. By 2016, lagers' share of the market had fallen to just over 50 per cent as the craft beers and a modest increase in traditional beers made in-roads into the market. In terms of pricing, lager products on average are between 13 and 15 per cent higher than dark beers, with some lager brands retailing at a premium of 33 per cent over the average dark beer price (Keynote Report and Office of National Statistics).

Excise Duty and Taxation

The Government's predilection for scrutinising the brewing sector has as much to do with fiscal policy, as competition policy. The sales value of the market is partly governed by levels of taxation in the form of excise duty and value-added-tax. Customs and excise revenues from beer sales amounted to £4.92 billion in 1998, of which £2.57 billion came from excise duty and £2.35 billion from VAT. In the late 1990's excise duty on beer products represented about 32.3 pence per pint, or some 17 per cent of the weighted average retail price in the on-trade. By contrast, excise duties in 2015 amounted to approximately £15.5 billion or around 100 pence per pint.

Table 3: Average Price and Tax per pint, 2002-2014

Year	Pre-tax price	VAT per pint	Duty per pint	Price per pint
2002	1.44	0.3	0.28	2.02
2003	1.57	0.32	0.29	2.18
2004	1.62	0.33	0.3	2.25
2005	1.68	0.35	0.31	2.34
2006	1.75	0.36	0.32	2.43
2007	1.83	0.38	0.33	2.54
2008	1.91	0.4	0.36	2.67
2009	1.97	0.36	0.39	2.72
2010	2.02	0.42	0.41	2.85
2011	2.04	0.5	0.44	2.98
2012	2.10	0.52	0.47	3.09
2013	2.18	0.53	0.46	3.17
2014	2.24	0.54	0.45	3.23

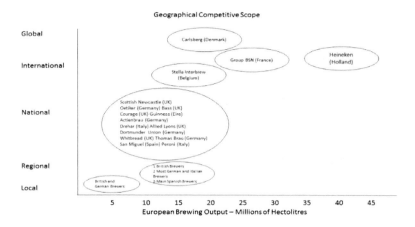

Figure 12 European Brewing Industry

In the post-Brexit environment of the UK, it would be somewhat unrealistic to speculate on what the British market may look like in isolation. However, Figure 12 illustrates European Brewing output in relation to the geographical competitive scope of the European industry and it can be seen that there are no serious International or global players among the UK suppliers; who in the main compete at national, regional and local level. UK personal imports from Europe account for more than 20 per cent of the official off-trade in beer, equivalent to some £1.55 billion.

Table 4: Major European Union and other sources of Imports by country of origin

	%	%
European Union		
Republic of Ireland	39	
Germany	27	
Netherlands, France	11	
Belgium	10	
Italy	2	
Spain	11	
		91
Others		
US	3	
Czechoslovakia	1	
Mexico	1	
Australia	3	
Others		9
Total		100

The excise duty differentials between the UK and the other European Union producers, provides the rationale for the growing trend of personal imports from France, Germany, Spain and Belgium. Table 5, provides a comparison of the excise duties in Continental Europe compared with the UK.

Table 5: Comparative Excise Data on Beer across Europe

	Pence per pint	Value Added Tax (at 5% Alcohol by % Volume)
United Kingdom	45	20
Ireland	48.5	21.0
France	4.6	20.6
Belgium	8.5	20.5
Netherlands	10.8	17.5
Spain	3.9	16.0
Germany	4.4	15.0
Denmark	22.6	25.0
Sweden	57.2	25
Finland	75.0	22.0

Source: Brewers and Licensed Retailers Association (BLRA)

The cross channel trade in personal imports is regarded as "bootlegging" by licensed retailers and producers in the UK, and post-Brexit it remains to be seen what the future holds for both consumers and suppliers.

The UK consumes 12 per cent of all beer sales in the EU, but pays nearly 40 per cent of all beer duty in the EU. Over the last ten years, beer taxes in the UK have risen by 43 per cent. The UK's beer taxes are estimated to be three times the EU average and ten times higher than those of the largest producer, Germany.

In March 2017 the Chancellor of the Exchequer raised duty on beer by 3.9 per cent (based on the OBR forecast of RPI inflation at September 2017). The March increase of just under two pence per pint was heralded by the BLRA as a return to the much resented Beer Duty Escalator that, it has been argued, contributed to 75,000 job losses, 3,700 pub closures and a 24 per cent fall in beer sales in pubs.

The new tax increase will inevitably lead to higher prices in pubs and place more pressure on pub closures. As Brexit looms it will be interesting to see if the tax burden on beer will be eased to support an industry that employs in the region of 900,000 UK jobs.

Market Segmentation

Over the last decade segmentation has become on increasing feature of the market. This segmentation has become more complex as basic market segments have overlapped each other to produce a complex pattern of branding. For example, the on-trade has different ratios of sales between lager and dark beers, with lager accounting for 46.6 per cent of sales and dark beer (including packaged) 53.4 per cent. Packaged lager's share of the off-trade is approximately 81 per cent of sales.

Table 6: Basic Market Segmentation by percentage of volume

	%
On-Trade	70
Off-Trade (Take home)	30
Total	100
Draught	65
Packaged/Bottled	35
Total	100
Lager	55
Dark Beers	45
Total	100

Source: Keynote Report

Packaged beer is mainly sold in the off-trade, but on-trade consumers are increasingly opting for bottled products. This in turn is altering the packaging dimension. The basic divisions of the market are listed below in Table 5.

A further development in the last two decades has seen the increasing trend of consumers choosing the same brands to drink in the public houses as they drink at home. This marks a significant change in the industry since initially many brands were developed for either the public house or the off-license. Thus, there is a convergence in the market of particular products, while at the same time the number of brands has increased.

Traditional Beers versus Lager

The basic axis of the market is the split between lager and traditional dark beers. Lagers share of the market has grown from 31 per cent in 1981 to its current position of approximately 50 per cent market share by volume. However, since the early 1990's and 2000's, dark beers have been fighting back through new product development, more sophisticated marketing and the introduction of in-can draught systems (the widget) in the take home trade. Brands such as Boddingtons (Whitbread Plc), John Smiths and Gillespie's (Scottish Courage) and Caffrey's Irish Ale (Bass), have been at the forefront of the recovery. The innovations by the larger producers in the dark beer segment have benefited many of the regional brewers who were unable or unwilling to compete in the multinationally-based lager sector. In addition, the in-roads of the 'craft' beers have been mainly responsible for the erosion of lagers share in the last five years or so.

However, the progress of lager's share of the market appears only to have been slowed rather than halted. It is estimated that lager has been losing share by about 1 per cent a year over the past five years or so, compared with the 2 per cent per annum increases in the 1980's and 1990's.

The innovations in the dark beer segment have been matched by the introduction of dry beer and ice beer in the lager segment. Similarly, lager producers have responded by developing the "full flavour" characteristics of their brands. Premium lager brands have also been developed in response to the innovations in dark beers and these have proved highly competitive in segmenting the 18 to 25 year old market, with 51 per cent of draught premium products being consumed by this segment.

Brands

Traditionally brand awareness was low in the draught beer sector. Public house drinkers would tend to order generically (i.e. pint of bitter, pint of lager) rather than by brand. Product allegiance was as much a function of public house preference as subconscious brand awareness. This situation clearly benefited the brewers who owned large numbers of public houses (tied houses) through which their beer was distributed. Two developments encouraged brand competition. Firstly, the growth of the off-trade through supermarkets and multiple grocery chains, whose branding (either by manufacturers' or retailers' own label) is of crucial importance, heralded the beer drinker into the world of fast-moving consumer goods. Secondly, the government's concern over the impact of the traditional tied-house on free competition in the late 1980's eventually led, in 1991, to a set of industry regulations entitled the beer orders which forced the big six brewing groups (Bass ,Whitbread, Courage, Allied Breweries, Guinness and Scottish and Newcastle) to greatly reduce the number of public houses they owned.

The Impact of the Beer Orders

Government concern in the late 1960's, over the impact of the traditional brewery tied house on free competition, led, in 1991 (following the Monopolies and Mergers Commission investigation in 1989), to a set of industry regulations entitled the Beer Orders. These regulations forced the "Big Six" brewing groups, at that time, to either sell off a substantial proportion of their public houses or withdraw from brewing. Consequently the pattern of public house ownership changed dramatically after 1991.

The Beer Orders forced the largest brewers to reduce the size of their tied public house estates to no more than 2,000 public houses. Only one national competitor, Grand Metropolitan chose the alternative of quitting brewing completely and it sold its breweries to Courage (then owned by Foster's Brewing in Australia). As well as Grand Metropolitan, several important regional brewers took the same step. The largest of these are now known as Greenall's Group and Boddington Group, specialising in drink's distribution and leisure. In 1994 the two ex-brewers came together when the Greenall Group acquired Boddingtons Group. There are now approximately 58,000 public houses in the U.K., of which some 26 per cent or 15,000, are owned by the top 5 national brewers.

The Grand Metropolitan Courage agreement was quickly followed by an important merger in 1993 involving Allied Lyons (Allied Breweries) and the UK subsidiary of Carlsberg of Denmark. Carlsberg – Tetley was the result of the merger, taking each company's leading lager and bitter brands as the new name. Since then Allied Lyons has become Allied Domecq by taking over the Pedro Domecq drinks empire in Spain.

Whitbread and Bass, two of the big six in the early 1990's, reduced their large pub estates in line with the ceilings stipulated in the Beer Orders. Whitbread also took the step of selling off many of the minority shares it held in a dozen independent regional brewers.

Historically, the UK Government has often intervened to prevent the brewing industry from becoming too concentrated in an effort to safeguard the independence of the regional brewers. The Beer Orders in 1991 were introduced to further reduce concentration and vertical integration by the big six. The market shares of the leading six companies in 1991 are shown in Table 6.

Table 7: The "Big Six" Brewers Market Shares in 1991

	%
Bass	22
Courage	21
Whitbread	12
Scottish Newcastle	11
Allied Breweries	9
Guinness	6
Total	81

The most distinctive feature of vertical integration in the UK brewing industry is the traditional tied system involving breweries and pubs. The Beer Orders undoubtedly triggered the scaling down of the vertically integrated empires of the largest brewers. The government's measures were designed to destabilise the historical structure of vertical integration in order to protect the regional brewers and increase competition.

However, it is doubtful whether the changes envisaged could have anticipated the resulting far reaching strategic reorientation of the industry. Polarisation, rather than concentration, has ensued throughout the mid to late 1990's, with product branding, innovation and product development becoming among the key factors in competition. At the same time the brewing majors have pursued extensive diversification in leisure related sectors.

The Strategic Orientation following the Beer Orders

The Beer Orders forced the major nationals and the large regional brewers to either pursue a retailing strategy or concentrate on brewing. Both options required competitors to strengthen and develop their brand positions. Consequently, building brand image and brand position became the strategy that dominated the activities of the industry throughout the 1990's.

Innovation

Since the mid 1980's, premium beers and lagers had been introduced into the market. In addition, market segmentation by age and social class had taken place. Innovation with fashionable brands had also led some to be positioned as icons among younger consumers (e.g. Sol & Beck's). Guinness developed the widget for canned beers, followed closely by the same development with premium products. Widgets were subsequently developed for bottled products, which gave a new impetus to darker ales and stout. The development of the widget enabled producers to follow premier pricing through brand differentiation, with premium widget cans retailing for up to 33 per cent more than non-widget products.

The widget improvement, while not adding to the alcoholic strength of the products, nevertheless improved the texture and taste of traditional products. The improvement in canned beers led to the introduction of better draught products. Subsequently there was a resurgence of interest in stouts and ales, both in public houses and in the off trade. For those brewers who misjudged the premium lager boom, but with specialisation in dark cask-conditioned beers, the drive to compete with premium lagers placed an emphasis on developing stronger ties with the free trade sector. Similarly, there was a greater emphasis on discounts and brewing loans in an attempt to regain their market position.

Diversification, Mergers and Acquisitions

The growth in demand for foreign lagers linked with the development of "free trade houses", placed emphasis on the negotiation of licenses, to produce foreign brands domestically and create new distribution arrangements in the free trade sector. The Beer Orders heralded major horizontal diversification's among the major groups with moves into wines and spirits (Guinness, Allied Domecq), hotels (Bass, Whitbread), food manufacturing (Grand Metropolitan, Allied Domecq) and even holiday camps (Scottish and Newcastle).

Free trade ownership dramatically altered the market trends, resulting in a considerable contraction in the number of major holding companies involved in brewing, further concentrations of market share, and a rise in shares for major national brands at the expense of minor or regional brands. Moreover, the acquisition of Courage by Scottish and Newcastle (Scottish Courage) in 1995 signalled a shift from the British Governments historical view, that beer production and distribution should be regulated to a greater extent than occurs in other industries.

The Beer Orders were the harbingers of the most important changes in an industry whose origins date back to the Middle Ages. These changes are still progressing and indeed it can be said that the last 5 years have witnessed the most far-reaching developments.

In 1900 there were 6,000 breweries operating in the United Kingdom. According to the Brewers and Licensed Retailers Association (BLRA), there are now only 64 brewing companies operating breweries that were established before 1971. While these companies continue to operate 90 breweries, the number of licenses issued by HM Customs and Excise to the so-called "minibrewers" has increased from 1 in 1979 to 350 by 1997.

While the number of long-standing brewery companies has declined, the contraction has resulted in 85 per cent of the beer consumed by volume in the UK being controlled by four companies. As the so-called "big four" reduced the over-capacity in the industry, they also diversified heavily, leaving room at the local level for small specialised mini-brewers who could supply free houses with limited quantities of beers which the large nationals could not justify producing. Thus, while the entry barriers at local level have been lowered, the mobility barriers have increased both on the brewing side and in the area of related horizontal diversification.

Scottish Courage's major diversifications have been in the leisure industry, where they own and operate the Centre Parc chain of all-year holiday villages as well as the Pontin's holiday centres. Bass have also diversified into leisure activities, essentially comprising of gambling, with ownership of Coral Racing, bingo and fruit machines, and entertainment through the Hollywood Bowl Tenpin bowling. Bass also controls British soft drinks and internationally it has diversified into hotels through its acquisition of Holiday Inn International.

Allied Domecq have diversified into spirit drinks with the acquisition of Teachers whiskey, Beefeater Gin, Lambs Navy Rum, Tia Maria Liqueur and Cockburn's Port. In addition, Allied has acquired Victoria Wine off-licenses, Baskins Robbins and the fast food catering business, Dunkin Donuts.

Whitbread have developed as an important restaurateur with the ownership of Beefeater, TGI Friday and Pizza Hut. In the hotel industry, Whitbread has acquired Travel Inns and Marriot Hotels and in the leisure sector they have acquired a chain of private sports clubs, the David Lloyd Leisure group. In addition, Whitbread is also the leading specialist off-license operator through its acquisition of Peter Dominic. Thus, product differentiation both at local and national level through segmentation, combined with retail consolidation and diversification, has been the major strategic thrust of the industry, particularly in the last five to six years. The 3 factor strategy emerging from this study, identified from the principal components analysis in chapter 6, clearly corresponds with the evidence from the above industry developments.

Polarisation between the National and Regional Brewers

The polarisation following the Beer Orders centred on the majors widening the gap between the national and independent regional brewers. This was achieved by the largest brewers concentrating on volume capacity on a national geographical basis, linked to the acquisition of regional brands

One particular acquisition serves to illustrate this development. In 1995, Scottish and Newcastle paid £600 million for the acquisition of Courage Breweries, owned by Fosters of Australia. This acquisition created the biggest brewing group in the United Kingdom and catapulted Scottish and Newcastle (now Scottish Courage) to the top of the brewing giants. The acquisition of

Courage by Scottish and Newcastle completed a remarkable transformation for the Scottish firm. In 1989, Scottish and Newcastle was itself under siege from Elders IXL, then owner of Fosters.

Elders £1.6 billion bid in 1989 was referred to the Monopolies and Mergers Commission and following a very robust political campaign when the "tartan card" was undoubtedly played to great effect, Scottish and Newcastle fought off the Elders bid. Following this, Elders went into rapid decline. The decline eventually highlighted Elders debt problems and by 1994 Fosters appeared to be close to drowning under the burden of balance sheet debts of £1.9 billion.

At the time of Scottish and Newcastle's bid for Courage it seemed inconceivable that the move would escape the attentions of the Office for Fair Trading. However, following the Beer Orders in 1991, it was clear that there was a major threat to sales of traditional ales as European lager brands literally poured into the market. Between 1990 and 1994, lagers share of the draught market, both standard and premium, rose by 2 per cent per annum. The acquisition of Courage would mean that Scottish and Newcastle would enjoy an extraordinary geographical fit. Based in Edinburgh, Scottish and Newcastle were strong in Scotland and the North of England. Courage's operations were concentrated south of Birmingham. The acquisition would create a portfolio of top brands, including Fosters famous "Amber Nectar" lager brand, which was part of the deal. Consequently, the acquisition avoided the serious scrutiny often associated with government departments in this industry and the outcome was the creation of Scottish Courage.

Market Shares

The Scottish Courage deal undoubtedly influenced strategist's perceptions of competitive factors. The message to the majors was clear. The door appeared open to pursue concentration on volume output of outstanding national brands. This view seemed valid until the autumn of 1997, when the President of the Board of Trade blocked Bass's attempt to acquire the whole of the share capital of its smaller rival, Carlsberg-Tetley. Indeed, the decision by the Department of Trade and Industry to order Bass, the second largest brewer, to sell its 50 per cent interest in the company seemed once more to herald a turning point in the intervention and regulatory history of the sector. Table 7 illustrates the effect of the polarisation in the industry of the major's and regional brewers share of the market.

As can be seen from Table 7 below, the "big four" majors at this time controlled 88 per cent of the market by volume (Beer market shares are expressed in volume since the value shares are normally identical). Notwithstanding the failure of the Bass/Carlsberg-Tetley merger, the industry became as concentrated in terms of market shares than it had ever been.

Table 8: Brewers Market Shares (% volume), 1998

	%
Scottish Courage	33
Bass	24
Whitbread	16
Carlsberg-Tetley	15
Guinness	5
Regional and local brewers and imports	
Total	100

Source: Keynote Report, 1998

As can be seen from Table 7 above, the "big four" majors at this time controlled 88 per cent of the market by volume (Beer market shares are expressed in volume since the value shares are normally identical). Notwithstanding the failure of the Bass/Carlsberg-Tetley merger, the industry became as concentrated in terms of market shares than it had ever been.

Two companies, Scottish Courage and Bass, share over half the UK beer market and the top five competitors have 93 per cent of the market between them. However, when we consider the position of the regional and local brewers, the sheer scale of brewing must be taken into account. With a total turnover of £16.75 billion in 1998, the 7 per cent share of the market represents sales of £1.17 billion. Deducting imports share of this UK residual sales value, leaves sales of £1.03 billion for UK regional and local brewers.

Concentration and Market Structure

Using the 3-firm concentration ratio, the market share of the top three firms, we can see that the industry has a concentration ratio of 0.73 (Table 7), with a market value of £12.23 Billion. Economic theory of market structure suggests that with such a large concentration ratio, the three leading firms have very large economies of scale relative to the market size. In this sense the evidence from the industry would tend to support the theory of market structure. However, a corollary to the high concentration ratio, in theory, is that the number of plants should be very low. Conversely, where the number of plants is very high, economies of scale of the larger firms would be less important and they would control a much smaller market share.

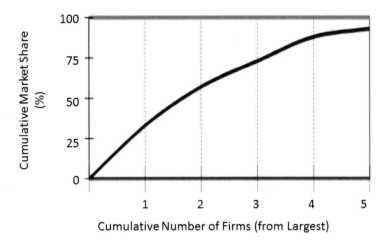

Figure 13. Cumulative Concentration Curve

However, as has been discussed, the number of firms in the industry has actually been increasing over the last two decades to reach its current level of 500 brewers (Table 2). Indeed, given the concentration ratio of 0.73, even the pre-1971 core of established brewers appears relatively high at 62 (Table 1).

The concentration ratio only indicates seller concentration at a particular point on what is otherwise a cumulative concentration curve, as Figure 6 indicates.

The concentration ratio tells us little about the number of firms that we might expect to be sustained in a situation where the 3-firm ratio was very high, as in this case. As previously discussed in chapter two, researchers have concluded that mobility barriers, in relation to strategic groups, are a function of efficiency, with levels of efficiency being correlated with size (Oster, 1982). In this sense strategic groups have been identified on an efficiency basis by reference to their market shares (acting as mobility barriers) and these have been used to determine the concentration of an industry.

Using a three firm strategic group concentration ratio (or even a five firm ratio) may lead us to conclude that this indeed may be a mobility barrier. However, it does not, per se, lead us to conclude that the rest of the industry is inefficient and unable to compete. As mentioned earlier (page 34) the problem with concentration ratios is that the result is not always clear and unambiguous. In our analysis of the brewing industry it seems clear that notwithstanding a five firm concentration ratio of 93 per cent, the trend of new entrants in the form of "microbrewers" is evidence of competitive behaviour, which is not constrained by the limitations of scope and scale.

Clearly other competitive dimensions must be overriding the influences of efficiency accruing to the leading incumbents. We can partly account for new entrants as a result of the turbulence brought about by the Beer Orders in 1991. These forced a strategic reorientation on the majors and provided fresh opportunities for the regional and local brewers. However, much of the strategic reorientation has concerned itself with combining differentiation dimensions with market segments, which has enabled the micro-competitors to exist in the same markets as the industry giants. With 500 competitors in an industry dominated by four firms, the competitive dimensions are clearly more common across the industry than the efficiency and scale dimensions.

The Herfindahl Index and Industry Rivalry

The brewing concentration ratio also obscures measures of the number of sustainable firms in the industry. Utilising the normally preferred Herfindahl Index found in the literature on strategic groups, provides a similarly unsatisfactory outcome in relation to gauging the number of groups that could exist within the industry. Using the Herfindahl Index we can calculate a theoretical measure of the number of firms, which we could expect this industry to support, based on the known market shares. It will be recalled (page 34) that the Herfindahl Index notation is,

$$H = \sum_{i=1}^{n} Si^2$$

where n = number of firms and Si = % market share.

Taking the five largest firms with a cumulative market share of 93 per cent produces an index where $H=0.2171$, which equates with an industry structure where the minimum efficient scale is 4.6 firms.

Table 9: Herfindahl Index

Firm	S	S²
Scottish Courage	0.33	0.1089
Bass	0.24	0.0576
Whitbread	0.16	0.0256
Carlsberg-Tetley	0.15	0.0225
Guinness	0.05	0.0025
	0.93	0.2171
Where $n = \frac{1}{H} = 4.6$		

On the basis of the Herfindahl Index (Table 9) and the corresponding number of firms, the conclusion would be that the output at minimum efficient scale relative to the size of the market, should support 4 firms. Theoretically, the suggestion is that there is over-capacity with five firms and that expansion of output with increasing economics of scale by the top four firms would produce a more efficient market structure.

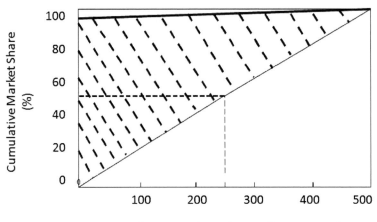

Cumulative Number of Firms (from Largest)

Figure 14. Lorenz Curve of Relative Concentration

From Table 2, it can be seen that there are in fact 500 breweries in the UK. As an absolute concentration measure the Herfindahl Index obscures the inequalities in the shares of the total number of firms actually producing for the market. A selective concentration measure accommodating these irregularities can be constructed in the form of a Lorenz Curve as shown in Figure 7.

The diagonal straight line in Figure 7 shows what a distribution of complete equality in firm shares would look like. The extent to which the Lorenz Curve deviates from this line gives an indication of relative seller concentration. For example, the diagonal line shows how we might expect 50 per cent of market sales to be accounted for by 50 per cent of the total firms. In fact, 57 per cent of the total sales are accounted for by the largest 0.4 of one per cent of total firms, as the curve indicates.

The Lorenz Curve coefficient (the Gini coefficient), which is calculated by dividing the shaded area below the curve by the area below the line of equality gives a measure of the extent to which the Lorenz Curve for a particular market deviates from the linear diagonal. The greater the equality, the closer the Gini coefficient will be to zero. When there is complete inequality the coefficient will be equal to one. From Figure 7, it can be seen that the Gini coefficient for the UK brewing industry is only marginally less than one (this can be seen without the need to calculate the measure).

Strategic Groups in the Industry

The relative inequality from the Lorenz Curve has a significant bearing on the question of strategic groups in the UK brewing industry. From an industrial economics viewpoint it could be argued that the identification of strategic groups is a fairly straightforward matter. Given the seller concentration as indicated by the Gini coefficient and the minimum efficient scale suggested by the Herfhindhal Index, it would seem reasonable to conclude that the industry reflects an oligopolistic structure. However, it also seems that the industry conforms to monopolistic competition where approximately 7 per cent of the market share is competed for by a large number of firms exhibiting downward sloping demand curves. Monopolistic competition among these firms takes the form of differentiation based on locality, product specialisation, loyalty and personalisation.

While the categories of firms in the industry-multinationals, national brewers, regional and local brewers and importers-remained a feature following the Beer Orders, the balance of competition shifted between these sectors. While multinational firms such as Heineken, Carlsberg and Anheuser-Busch had been present for many years in the UK market-the two latter companies operating their own breweries-the balance of market power shifted in the late 1990's. This shift favoured the multinationals. Prior to the late 1990's, foreign multinationals had less than 25 per cent of the UK market. The changes heralded by the Beer Orders enabled the globalisation influences in world brewing to be felt in the UK in the early 2000's. By 2002-2003 an estimated 60 per cent of the beer sold in the UK was produced by companies with foreign headquarters. Table 9 illustrates the shift in market penetration in 2005 by foreign multinationals and the market share impact on the formerly integrated British brewers.

Table 10. Market Shares in UK Brewing by value, 2005.

Company	Ownership origin	Market share
Scottish Courage	Scottish & Newcastle (UK)	27%
Coors Brewers	Molson Coors (Canada/US)	21%
InBev UK	InBev (Belgium)	18%
Carlsberg UK	Carlsberg (Denmark)	13%
Diageo	Diageo (UK)	6%
Others		15%
TOTAL		100%

Source: Keynote

On the basis of size and scope, the top four firms would be clustered as one group, with the regional and local brewers being grouped accordingly. Guinness, who in this approach seems somewhat awkwardly positioned, would be on its own. The asset configuration of the big four would, not unreasonably, reinforce the differences between the groups. We could also conclude that the big four, with more economies of scale than a monopolistically competitive industry but less than a natural monopoly, represent an oligopoly. We can also observe that, in a mature market, attempts to expand the outputs of any of the top four firms would quickly encounter decreasing returns to scale and prevent the incumbents from expanding to drive competitors out of business.

This confirms the weakness of analyses, which overlook the underlying competitive strategies of the complete range of firms in the industry. Analyses wherein competition is viewed as somehow independent of intrafirm organisation, where managers are capable of responding as strategic agents who may implement actions which relax the constraints of their position, even in markets of almost unitary inequality.

Thus it could be argued that the UK brewing industry provides the benchmark case for a rebuttal of the positioning approach of strategic group analysis – 495 firms may be testament to that. An industry with an oligopolistic structure, yet with 500 competitors, exists in this form because of the strategic dimensions, which firms pursue at the competitive level. To ignore the possibility that this strategic competition based on key dimensions does not cut across all firms in the sector and accounts for the fact that many firms survive, is to ignore the realities of the industry.

The inequality of the Lorenz Curve is not the end of the analysis, but the picture, which throws into focus the question of how the vast majority of the "unequals" compete strategically. This question is explored in Chapter 6 and in doing so shifts the emphasis once more onto the role of managerial perceptions and strategic groups.

Summary

As has been shown in Chapter four the UK brewing industry, which provides the industry context of this exploration, has undergone a significant strategic reorientation in the past eight years. During this period the industry has become more concentrated yet more competitive, in a market that has experienced little or no growth in terms of its overall size.

Historically, brewers have invested in barriers to entry through vertical integration in order to avoid retail competition, achieve economies of scale and pursue absolute cost advantages. However, since 1991 these barriers have not protected the traditional brewers from new entrants. Some 200 brewers have entered the industry since 1971 with 100 of these entering within the last ten years. In addition, the growth of brewpubs has boosted the total number of licensed brewers to 500. This growth is in stark contrast to the position thirty years ago when there were approximately 85 operating breweries in the industry.

In the last eight years the spark, which undoubtedly fired the motor of change in the industry, has been the impact of the Beer Orders.

The Beer Orders represent a classical example of regulatory change imposed on an oligopolistic industry structure that provided local and regional monopolies through the tied house system. The Beer Orders were intended to go straight to the heart of competition policy in the industry. The competitive protection afforded the major brewers through the tied house system was the cornerstone of their vertically integrated structure. To the extent that the Beer Orders forcibly reduced the degree of this vertical integration, they provided scope for much smaller competitors to effectively build mobility barriers through focussed brand differentiation, which gave smaller firms' advantages relative to the incumbent majors.

The turbulence and fluidity of the industry environment after 1991 produced a time period of more acute strategic instability than had previously been experienced. From a research perspective this period presents the opportunity to examine the concept of strategic groups and to test the inherent assumptions underpinning these groups, against managerial perceptions of strategic dimensions in order to investigate the asymmetry of groups. The nature of this research will also enable such asymmetries as may exist within firms, to be explored.

PART III CLUSTERING GROUPS

Chapter 5 Research Methodology

Introduction

In the field of strategy research it is well recognised that strategic change often occurs in response to external influences such as technological change, deregulation or new entrants (Cool, 1985; Figenbaum, 1987). Consequently it is important to distinguish between what may be regarded as relatively stable periods from those that manifest significant, important external change. Contrasting these periods of significant change with periods of relative stability enables the dynamics of strategic reorientation to be observed.

This research investigates the concept of strategic groups during a postregulatory period in which it is reasonable to expect strategic reorientation to take place and thus, for analytical purposes, provide a richer background against which the findings can be interpreted (Tushman and Romanelli, 1985).

By evaluating strategic groups in a post-regulation industry, the focus is on a time period of more acute strategic instability. Previous research into strategic groups has in the main ignored regulatory turbulence and focussed entirely on stable strategic time periods. For example, Mascarenhas (1989) identified strategic groups within three periods of stability. Cool and Schendel (1987) and Figenbaum and Thomas (1990) identified four and nine stable strategic time periods respectively in their studies.

While the choice of time period for this research is not to engage in the debate over stability versus turbulence , but merely to examine the findings against a more dynamic industry background, it is worth pointing out that some researchers have taken serious issue with those studies which have ignored instability in strategic group research.

For example, Bresser, Dunbar and Jithendranathan (1994) have taken issue with the prescription that meaningful strategic group research "must … be focussed upon identifying periods of homogeneity and similarity in competitive strategic behaviour…." (Figenbaum and Thomas, 1990:198).

They argue that such views prematurely close-off periods that should be the focus of heightened research into strategic groups and provide the most informative studies from the point of view of practical interest.

The writer concurs with this view, since the prescription of environmental stability is more likely to result in groupings, which reflect custodial decisions about asset and resource commitments, rather than inform about rivalry and competitive behaviour.

By examining strategic groups through managerial perceptions of strategic dimensions during periods of heightened environmental change, it may be possible to identify different types of group responses as well as different strategic groups from those anticipated on the basis of asset configurations. For example, it may be possible to identify firms that hold on to strategies which were effective prior to regulation, and others whose strategies are emergent from the new strategic options.

This chapter addresses the following topics:

* The Hypothesis
* The Sample
* Questionnaire Design
* Pilot Study
* The Survey
* Strategic Group Clusters
* Hypothesis Testing

The Hypothesis

The data was gathered from the Breweries and Beer Industry via a sample of companies drawn from a Standard Industrial Classification four-digit activity group (SIC 4270). The first step in the decision-making procedure of the research was to state the null hypothesis (H_0). As the hypothesis of no differences, the null hypothesis is usually formulated for the express purpose of being rejected. If it is rejected, the alternative hypothesis (H_1) may be accepted. Thus, the alternative hypothesis of this research is the operational statement of the research hypothesis. The *research hypothesis* represents the prediction derived from the theory under examination.

In making a decision about differences, we are testing H_0 against H_1. Therefore, H_1 constitutes the hypothesis (the assertion) that is accepted if H_0 is rejected. The theory of strategic groups that is being tested would lead us to predict that managerial perceptions of competitive dimensions are homogenous within and across strategic groups. This prediction is our research hypothesis. Confirmation of that prediction would lend support to the theory from which it was derived.

From the arguments propounded in the previous chapters the following hypothesis was addressed:

H_0, Managers' perceptions of key strategic dimensions are homogenous within strategic groups.

The null hypothesis

H_1, Managers' perceptions of key strategic dimensions indicate heterogeneity within strategic groups.

The alternative hypothesis

Sample Survey

Using the ICC (Inter Company Comparisons) database in the form of the Lotus One Source by the Lotus Development Corporation (1992), a list of 101 companies operating in the Breweries and Beer Industry (SIC 4270) was compiled. The ICC database itself is compiled from the Companies Registrations Office for England and Wales, and Scotland and Northern Ireland, and covers over 130,000 companies from 250 industries and 330 four digit SIC codes, including financial data held in accordance with UK accountancy standard practice.

From the list of 101 companies, three brewing companies were selected from which to draw the initial sample of managers for the pilot study. Each company was asked to identify strategic decision-makers within the firm that were familiar with competition in the industry prior to the 1991 Beer Orders. 15 managers from these three firms agreed to participate in the initial pilot study.

Following the pilot study and the creation of the key dimensions questionnaire, all of the 101 companies generated from the ICC database where invited to participate in completing the questionnaire on the basis of strategic decision-makers familiar with the industry prior to regulation. In all, 53 "strategists" from 36 companies participated in the full study (see Appendix XVII, page 173), providing usable data for a 35.6 per cent firm participation rate.

Confining the study to one industry rather than using a multi-industry sample, is strongly supported by the argument that empirical research, which aims to investigate links between competitive dimensions of Strategic Business Units (SBU's), is best served by moderating the effects of the industry environment. The impact of the industry structure and the greater likelihood of consensus on the competitive methods employed is best served by a single industry approach. While it has been argued that the power of some industry research is made more substantial by the attempt to identify predicted relationships across a widely divergent industrial sample (Snow and Hambrick, 1980). The different industry environments in which managers are located may obscure the results when the consensus of competitive behaviour is being studied (Dess, 1987).

Moderating the links between perceptions and strategic groups are the effects of management experience and values, in their particular industry, together with the cognitive bases that these provide in the consensus approach. In previous studies into strategic groups, single industry SBU samples were used. Moreover, while the samples of other studies on strategic groups have been similar to and indeed, in some cases of a smaller size, they have conformed with the normative assumptions implicit in Porters (1980) work.

For example, Hunt (1972) based his findings on 4 case studies; Hatten and Schendel (1977) on 13 businesses; Dess and Davies (1984) on 19 non-diversified firms; Lewis and Thomas (1990) researched 16 grocery multiples; Porac et al (1989) and Reger and Huff (1993) studied 17 and 18 firms, respectively. Other studies have used somewhat larger samples. Harrigan (1985) surveyed 92 retailers; Fombrun and Zajac (1987) used a 113 firm sample; Kim and Lim (1988) used a 54 company sample; Figenbaum and Thomas (1990) investigated 33 insurance companies: Boeker (1991) used 49 firms and Bresser, Dunbar and Jithendranathan (1994) investigated 218 savings and loans institutions. Thus, the sample used in this study can be viewed as comparable with other studies.

Cross-industry studies undoubtedly have significance for the investigation of strategic groups based on managerial perceptions of competitive dimensions. The implications for firm performance when examined from a cross-industry perspective may strengthen the hypothesis that managers' perceptions of competitive dimensions are homogeneous (thus supporting the Hypothesis H_1). However, such studies would by necessity require multiple single industry research, which is outside the bounds and scope of this study. It is hoped that this study will provide a benchmark for further research based on the cognition of managers, in a cross industry enquiry in the spirit suggested by Porac et al (1989).

The Pilot Study

In the literature on strategic groups, many research methodologies have employed data sources not available to managers (e.g. Newman, 1978; Uster, 1982). Others have had limited interpretative value for specific industries, for example the use of the Pims database (Galbraith and Schendel, 1983; Caves and Ghemawat, 1992) and the use of financial data (Bresser, Dunbar and Jithendranathan, 1994). Financial data from a specified time period does not provide a conceptual understanding of what determines strategy, nor does it reflect managers' cognitive maps in periods of instability and reorientation.

Moreover, the use of normative measures (Porter, 1980) implied that strategy could be inferred on the basis of the importance or emphasis of particular asset configurations available to the firm, and has remained oblivious to the connections between perceptions and realised strategy. The descriptive approach, found from investigating managerial cognition of competition (Reger and Huff, 1993), acts as an informed enquiry of strategic group formation based on manager's grouping of companies according to corporate strategy variables. This, it is argued, provides a more reliable method of clustering strategic groups.

The main research instrument used in this study is a questionnaire containing 26-key dimensions, which were identified by senior managers (strategists) as being important to competitiveness in the brewing industry (see Appendix II, page 152). Each manager was required to rate his/her views on the importance of the dimensions to competitiveness on a scale of strongly agree to strongly disagree. The key dimensions questionnaire was initially generated from a 15 respondent pilot study using the Repertory Grid methodology. The purpose of the pilot study was threefold. Firstly, the sample of 15 respondents from 3 brewing firms was chosen to test the efficacy of the Repertory Grid methodology. Secondly, the pilot data enabled the clustering technique to be assessed using SPSS/PC+ and Miniplan version II statistical procedures. Thirdly, the pilot was used as a basis for a guide to a wider sample of the industry population. An additional advantage of the pilot study was that it enabled a comparison to be made with Porter's list of competitive dimensions, which he identified as "strategic dimensions" (Porter, 1980: 127).

As outlined in Chapter 3, the data gathering approach utilised the Repertory Grid technique and this was initially tested in the Pilot Study consisting of 15 respondents. Each respondent in the pilot study was interviewed separately. Following the standard procedures for the minimum context card format, the 15 respondents were presented with different elements (firms) three at a time. The sequence of presentations of triads was random and the same for each respondent. Each respondent identified key dimensions until their boredom level rose substantially.

The methodology conformed to the assumptions of personal construct theory (Kelly, 1955,) in that the elements chosen (the firms in the industry) were within the range of convenience of construct elicitation (i.e. the formation of the bipolar constructs manifesting both similarity and contrast) (see Appendix III, page 155). The elements (firms) were representative of the industry from which they were drawn to enable the respondents to relate their elicited constructs to that industry. This ensures that each respondent is able to apply the constructs elicited to elements (firms) other than those from which the constructs have been elicited (Fransella & Bannister, 1971).

Seven representative elements (firms) were chosen from the SIC four digit group within the Breweries and Beer Industry, namely Scottish and Newcastle, Watneys, Courage, Greene King, Ruddles, Whitbread and Aylesbury Brewing. These were given a random number from 1 to 7, to facilitate the randomisation of triads of elements (firms) (Appendix IV, page 156 and V, page 157).

The Repertory Grid Technique

Using the Minimum Context Card Form (Kelly, 1955), a randomly selected triad of elements (firms) was presented to each subject who was then asked to specify **"in what ways are two of the three companies similar and in what way is the third dissimilar from the other two"**. (Appendix VI, page 158). The use of the triad of elements and the task set by the question ensures that the constructs elicited are explicitly bi-polar and the answers to the question provide a "contrast pole" (Appendix III, page 155).

In eliciting the bi-polar constructs, the contrast pole provides elicitation's of the interaction of elements and consequently is related to the subjects role construct system. For example, a respondent may describe Aylesbury Brewing

Company as different from Scottish and Newcastle and Whitbread on the basis that the latter two are national competitors.

Thus the order of showing the triads of elements was generated by:

(i)   Matching a randomly selected element with a random number (Appendix IV).
(ii) Matching randomly selected triads of elements with randomly selected letter codes (Appendix V).
(iii) Randomly selecting the triad element letter codes (Appendix VII) to give the order of showing the triads to the subjects.

Table 10, lists steps followed in the Pilot Study Procedure.

The triads of elements (i.e. the three firms) were presented on separate cards spread out in front of the subject. For example, the first order of showing the triads of elements from the randomly selected letter codes was code L (Appendix VII, page 159).

This equated with the randomly selected triad of, Whitbread's, Scottish and Newcastle, and Courage. When the two firms are selected by the subject on the basis of similarity between them and dissimilarity with the third, the subjects are asked to elaborate in what ways the first two were alike and in what way the third was dissimilar from the other two. This latter procedure, described as laddering (Hinkle, 1965), allows for increasingly super-ordinate constructs to be elicited. Super-ordinate constructs are constructs of a higher order of abstraction than those elicited from the triads of elements.

For example, subjects may cite branding or pricing as a similarity/dissimilarity between elements. Thus the procedure involves eliciting constructs using the minimum context card form and then asking the subject the question "why" about the contrast pole.

The question of why elements are similar/dissimilar is asked until the subject is unable (or unwilling) to produce more contrast dimensions of a higher order of abstraction than the initial bi-polar constructs. The following table summarises the procedure adopted to elicit the key dimensions.

Having elicited the contrast dimensions through the laddering procedure, the pilot sample enabled a list of dimensions to be selected on the basis of the repetition of these across the sample by every respondent. For example, in eliciting similarities/dissimilarities between elements (firms), different respondents might mention quality or price as a differentiating dimension. The consistent dimensions were identified and re-presented to the respondent sample, to confirm the validity or otherwise of the dimensions as being important to competitiveness in their industry.

This list was then compared with Porter's (1980) list of strategic dimensions against which strategic groups could be identified. Table 11 lists the repeated dimensions elicited, and contrasts these with those proposed by Porter (1980). It is interesting to note that not all of Porter's dimensions were listed by the subjects in the pilot study, but included several others.

Table 11: The Pilot Study Procedure

Step 1 Lis t compiled of 101 firms in the brewing industry (SIC 4270)

Step 2 3 representative firms chosen from which to select respondents. 15 respondents provided

Step 3 7 representative elements (firms) chosen for pilot triads and allocated a random number as shown in Appendix IV, page 156

Step 4 Triads of elements (firms) randomly selected and matched with a letter code as shown in Appendix V, page 157

Step 5 Letter codes randomly selected to provide the order of showing the triads. Appendix VII, page 159

Step 6 Respondents shown randomly selected triads and presented with a card containing the question as illustrated in Appendix VI, page 158

Step 7 Laddering procedure adopted to elicit dimensions until respondent is unable or unwilling to produce contrast dimensions

This would suggest that certain competitive dimensions are industry specific and the "generic" nature of Porters dimensions disguises the importance of industry specific perspectives of competitive dimensions. For example horizontal integration, discounts and loans, reflects the importance of "public house" competition, a key factor in formulating a coherent strategy in the industry, which will be examined in greater detail in Chapter 6.

From the sample, an initial number of 19 dimensions were listed (six more than Porter). These were then used to produce a contrast pole/dimension matrix rated across a "strongly agree – strongly disagree" scale (Appendix VIII, page 160) which eventually formed the basis of the final questionnaire (Appendix II page 3, page 154). The scale "strongly agree - strongly disagree" was given a numerical value from 5 to 1 respectively (unknown to the respondents) enabling a quantitative analysis using descriptive statistical techniques to be applied to the data.

In the initial pilot study a sample of 15 managers (respondent subjects) were chosen from three brewing companies. This enabled three important areas to be addressed, namely:

1. An epistemology of the repertory grid methodology.
2. The generation of a list of dimensions that would provide the basis for a survey of a wider sample of the industry population.
3. To enable the descriptive statistics of cluster analysis and principle

components analysis utilising both SPSS PC + and Miniplan, to be compared in testing the proposition developed in the thesis.

Table 12: Pilot Study Respondent Scores

Key Dimensions		A	B	C	D	E	F	G	H	I	J	K	L	M	N	O	Ave. Scores
		15 Respondents															
*1	Location	3	5	5	4	5	3	2	5	2	4	3	5	4	3	4	3.8
*2	Prices	2	4	5	4	5	2	4	4	5	4	4	5	4	5	5	4.1
* 3	Quality	3	3	5	4	5	3	4	3	4	5	3	5	4	5	5	4
4	Advertising	5	2	4	3	4	5	1	2	2	4	4	5	5	3	4	3.5
5	Image	4	3	3	2	4	4	4	3	2	4	4	5	4	4	5	3.7
*6	Prod Range	4	3	5	2	3	4	2	3	1	3	2	3	3	2	3	2.8
*7	Econ of Scale	4	5	3	2	4	5	2	5	4	2	2	3	4	2	4	3.4
*8	Prod Brand	5	4	4	4	3	4	2	4	2	4	2	4	3	4	4	3.5
9	Horiz Integ	4	3	3	2	2	3	3	3	3	2	2	2	3	3	2	2.7
*10	Service	3	3	4	3	3	3	3	3	3	2	2	2	3	3	2	2.7
11	Pay	3	4	3	2	1	1	3	4	4	2	3	2	2	3	2	2.6
12	Packaging	1	4	3	4	4	4	4	4	3	4	3	5	3	4	4	3.8
13	Org Eff	4	5	4	4	3	3	3	5	3	4	3	5	4	4	3	3.8
*14	Vet Integ	3	3	3	1	3	2	1	3	1	1	2	3	2	3	1	2.1
*15	Outlet Mix	4	1	3	2	3	2	4	1	4	2	3	3	3	3	2	2.7
16	Market Share	2	4	3	3	3	4	4	4	2	2	3	4	4	3	3	3.2
17	Process Tech	4	5	3	4	2	4	3	5	3	3	3	4	4	4	2	3.5
18	Discounts	1	3	5	3	3	1	3	3	3	2	2	4	3	4	3	2.9
19	Loans	2	3	4	2	3	4	3	3	3	2	2	4	3	4	3	3

Note: Each lettered column represents a different respondent case
* Denotes dimensions of competitive strategy identified by Porter (1980:128)

The Statistical Analysis

Strategic groups have been identified using bivariate and multivariate analysis. Hunt (1972), Porter (1979) and Newman (1978) argued that groups could be identified from a few key factors essential to success. These "key factors" were identified from secondary sources, based on asset commitments, rather than on factors emanating from managers' perceptions of dimensions important to competitive behaviour. For example, Porter (1980) plotted groups on two axes for different variables, illustrating their group position by their aggregate sales (Appendix I, page 151). Harrigan (1980) and McNamee and McHugh (1989) also employed this methodology. McNamee and McHugh charted their "Strategic Group Maps ... based on company structure, geographical market specialization, company size and pricing ... taken two at a time" (1989:89). Harrigan suggested in her study of the Receiving – Tubes Industry, that "there were two strategic groups: (1) the producers and (2) the merchandisers" (1980:75).

However, when investigating competitive strategies and the dynamics of competitive behaviour, the fewer the number of variables considered, the less meaningful and accurate the analysis will be. Harrigan (1985), employing Porter's (1979) selection of key factors, found that utilising cluster analysis provided a more thorough result. She suggested that, "techniques such as factor analysis scales and cluster analysis inter-differences matrices can be better used [than *a priori* groupings] to gauge the diversity of firms placed into different groups (Harrigan, 1985:55). Hatten and Hatten (1987) have also argued that multivariate analysis is a significant enhancement to previous methods as it can creatively use all available data to a greater extent, avoiding the limitations of preconceived ideas about what factors are important. Consequently, cluster analysis, combined with Factor Analysis and Principal Component analysis models, have been used in the study of strategic groups.

Table 11 represents the scores on the 5 - 1 scale generated from the rated order grid used in the pilot study (Appendix VIII, page 160). It includes 19 elicited dimensions from the 15-person survey, producing a 19x15case/variable matrix. Appendix IX, page 161 gives a short summary of the variables in the pilot survey based on the SPSS/PC+ configuration. This shows from left to right the variable code (e.g. Lo for location), the mean value of the responses to specific variables, the minimum and maximum value given by respondents and the dimension variable label and how many responses there were to each.

The Clustering Technique

Two statistical packages were used to produce the cluster analysis in the pilot study, SPSS PC + and Miniplan. This was done as a precursor to the main study to ascertain both the efficiency of the process of data analysis and its interpretative value.

In the trial clustering of the pilot data it was assumed that managers, in evaluating the rated order grid (Appendix VIII, page 160), would rate highly the contrast dimensions that were most important to the strategic conduct of their firms.

In the clustering procedure, firms are assumed not to be homogeneous, and the dissimilarity in responses is measured by the Euclidean distance between each possible pair of firms and translated into a data matrix. The standard Euclidean distance measure is as follows:

$$Distance\ (X, Y) = \sqrt{\sum_i (X_i - Y_i)^2}$$

The lower the dissimilarity coefficient between two subjects, the more homogeneous they are in their attitudes. By taking two subjects with the smallest coefficient and pairing them together we find our first cluster, and by agglomeration (the cases being combined at each stage) we build clusters until all firms belong to the same and only cluster. Taking the average distance between clusters enables the selection, in order to maximise the distance between the formed groups. Using SPSS PC + we estimate, and at what level, it seems reasonable to form clusters.

The pilot study was initially clustered using SPSS PC+ (Appendix X, page 162). The clustering and dendogram (Appendix X page 3) produced what appeared to be four groups, namely; B,H(2,8), [1] G,I(7,9), A,F(1,6) and C,D,E,J,K,L,M,N,O(3,4,5,10,11,12,13,14,15). This result highlighted the problem of the level of homogeneity that we could regard as acceptable for the formation of groups. The clusters were formed for subjects that have responded to the question of what key factors of success are important and which are unimportant.

If we look at the data in Table 11 (in conjunction with the cluster analysis in Appendix X) for the four groups above, we find that respondents in group one (B,H) give the same score to every dimension (with a coefficient of 0.000). Group two (G,I) scored the same eleven times out of the nineteen possible. Group three (A,F) scored the same nine times (there are also many similar scores), and with group four no scores are the same for any member of this group. The question then arising is what level of scores, in terms of homogeneity, indicates a group?

Similarity Levels

Within SPSS PC+ we can determine which scores are relevant for group formation by imposing a cut-off value. For example, all scores with a value less than 4 could be entered as 0 (zero) in order to skew the clusters to reflect a level of similarity in group formations, which minimised the distance within the clusters. However, as mentioned in relation to Porters (1980) key factors, utilising a larger sample of dimensions and scores enables between group average clustering to maximise the distance between clusters and provide a more meaningful exploration of the differences between groups.

Clustering using the Euclidean distance measure, via SPSS PC+, did not distinguish a similarity cut-off level in relation to the scores. The researcher through a visual analysis of the corresponding dendogram determined this. On the other hand, Miniplan Version II, enabled this subjective choice to be minimised by allowing the level of similarity to be determined as a parameter within the computation of clusters. For example, similarity levels could be set at 50, 60 and 65 per cent similarity. The discussion on similarity levels illustrates the effect of

---

[1] The letter codes and numbers (shown in brackets) correspond with Table 11, for example, B,H (2,8) relates to respondent No:2 denoted by the letter B in Table 11.

setting different similarity levels, on group formations. The resulting Miniplan dendogram (Appendix XII, page 168) reflects a consistency of approach, which caters for the range of scores across dimensions that are relevant for the formation of strategic groups. Clearly the lower the parameter for the similarity level, the smaller the number of clusters formed. On the other hand, the higher the similarity, the more stringent the test of clusters becomes and consequently we will find a larger number of clusters.

Hierarchical Clusters

A hierarchical cluster technique can be either agglomerative or divisive. One of the primary features distinguishing hierarchical techniques from other clustering algorithms is that the allocation of an object to a cluster may be irrevocable. That is, once an object joins a cluster it is never removed and fused with other objects belonging to some other cluster (Dillon and Goldstein, 1984). Agglomerative methods proceed by forming a series of fusions of the n objects into groups (see Appendix XI, page 165). Divisive methods partition the set of n objects into finer and finer subdivisions.

Thus agglomerative methods eventually result in all objects falling into one cluster, whereas divisive techniques will finally split the data so that each object forms its own cluster. In either case, the issue is where to stop. The assignment criteria or assignment rule as it is often referred to is concerned with this issue and what is the optimal (i.e. correct) number of clusters to form.

Determining the Clusters

Ward (1963) proposed a method of forming clusters where the assignment rule rests on the increase in the error sum of squares induced by combining every possible pair of clusters. This value, which is denoted by E.S.S., is used as an objective function. Ward's method is based on the loss of information resulting from the grouping of responses of individuals (respondents) into clusters, and is measured by the total sum of squared deviations of every observation from the mean of the cluster to which it belongs. The number of clusters is determined by ending the agglomeration when the initial cluster variance is less than X percent of the error sum induced by combining individuals to form a new cluster.

The objective of Ward's method is to minimise the error sum of squares and this results in small close clusters. A non-optimal solution will occur only in those circumstances where the "natural" clustering of the respondents' profiles is quite weak (Dillon and Goldstein, 1974).

In the research on strategic groups using managers as the respondents, where clustering analysis has been used to identify groups, Ward's method has been most commonly utilised (Reger & Huff, 1993).

The E.S.S. is computed as:

$$E.S.S. = \sum_{j=l}^{k} \left(\sum_{i=l}^{nj} X_{ij}^2 - \frac{1}{n_j} \left(\sum_{i=j}^{nj} X_{ij} \right)^2 \right)$$

Where X_{ij} denotes the dimension value for the ith individual in the jth cluster, k is the total number of clusters at each stage, and nj is the number of individuals in the jth cluster.

Since in Ward's method we were able to predefine the cluster criteria or assignment rule in advance of optimising the agglomeration, we can express the notation of the distance between the ith individual and the lth cluster as follows:

$$D(i, l) = \left(\sum_{j=1}^{p} [X(i,j) - \bar{X}(l,j)]^2 \right)^{1/2}$$

Where p represents the partition that results in each of the i individuals being allocated to one of clusters 1, 2 ..... l, and D(i,l) is the Euclidean distance between individual i and the cluster mean of the cluster containing the individual. It will be noted that this method in actuality effects a partition of the data and that the allocation of an individual to a cluster is not irrevocable. The above notation can be defined (Dillon and Goldstein, 1974) as:

$$E[P(n,k)] = \sum_{i=l}^{n} D[i, l(i)]^2$$

where, P(n,k) is the partition that results and E the error component by moving individuals from one cluster to another until no transfer of an individual results in a reduction in E.

Figenbaum and Thomas (1990); Galbraith and Schendel (1983); Cool and Schendel (1987); Fairburn and Zajac (1987); Figenbaum and Thomas (1990); all determined the number of clusters using Ward's method. While Ward's method has been widely used, the assignment rule determining the agglomeration cut-off or similarity level (E), is nevertheless a parameter set by the user.

In this respect care should be used in setting parameter values and in keeping with the above researchers, the similarity level for the data analysis in this inquiry was set at 65 per cent throughout the pilot and the main study.

In computing the pilot study data using both SPSS PC+ and Miniplan Version II, it was found that Miniplan facilitated setting the similarity level as a parameter value. SPSS PC+ did not allow the same efficiency of approach, relying on the more subjective selection of the number of clusters formed on the basis of a visual identification of clusters from the dendogram. Thus, on the strengths of Miniplan over SPSS PC+, the former was adopted as the most effective descriptive statistical package with which to process both the pilot data and the data from the extended population study.

The Pilot Clusters

The cluster groups formed from the 19x15 pilot matrix with a 65 per cent similarity level are illustrated in Appendix XI, page 165. The hierarchical cluster analysis produced 14 clusters, which contrasts with the 4 clusters produced using SPSS PC+. As discussed above, Ward's method, combined with the similarity assignment parameter, produces a more stringent analysis, which results in small close clusters. This provides a more relevant formation of groups on the basis of those contrast perceptions that inform us of the importance of respondents' strategic dimensions.

It can be seen that from the 15 respondents, cases 2 and 8 (B,H) have complete homogeneity, forming one cluster. At the 65 per cent level, the remaining 13 respondents do not cluster and display complete heterogeneity. Hence we have 14 clusters, one with two members and thirteen with a single member. However, below 60 per cent similarity we can see that the number of clusters, reduces to 12, and below the 50 per cent level we have 9 clusters (see Appendix XI page 1, page 165). This compares with the 4 clusters produced using SPSS PC+ and illustrates the potential discrepancies in terms of the robustness of the clusters between the two statistical approaches. In this sense the pilot study examined the efficiency of the statistical packages as a means of ensuring the most significant analysis of the extended population study.

14 clusters were formed when a similarity level of 65 per cent was assigned to the partition of the data. This compared with 4 clusters when the pilot data was analysed using SPSS PC+. In cases 2 and 8 (B,H) (Scottish and Newcastle and Courage) there is complete homogeneity with a coefficient of 0.000. The differences in the number of clusters formed demonstrate the level of stringency between the two processes. The interchange involving the assignment parameter in Miniplan, compared with the subjective reduction of the number of scores analysed in SPSS PC+, mitigates against the limitations of multivariate data.

The step reduction in the number of clusters reflects the fusion of respondents into groups. As the similarity level is lowered, the Euclidean distance is relaxed in relation to the computation of the reduction in the total error sum of squares as this represents the information lost by merging a fusion (Everitt, 1974). In sum, subsequent levels of aggregation result in the analysis suggesting that there are non-significant differences between cluster means. Harrigan (1985) has argued that the squared Euclidean distance between groups may represent the height of mobility barriers and that the average distance between observations within a group is an indication of the degree of homogeneity. Consequently, from the standpoint of an inquiry into managerial perceptions of competitive dimensions, it seems important to ensure that differences are identified and hence the level of the criteria value should be set at least above 60 per cent. The level set for this research was 65 per cent.

Principal Components Analysis

To supplement the multivariate analysis of variance, a principal component analysis was performed on the data using Miniplan Version II. Principle component analysis entails identifying factors (i.e. principal components) which explain "as much of the total variation in the data as possible, with as few of these factors as possible" (Dillon and Goldstein, 1974:24). The factors are extracted so that the first principal component accounts for the largest amount of the total variations in the data. Principle components analysis is, thus, the linear combination of the original set of variables into a smaller set of linear combinations that account for most of the variance of the original set. The linear combination of the observed set can be written as follows:

$$PC_{(n)1} = \ddot{W}_{(n)1}X_1 + \ddot{W}_{(n)2}X_2 + \cdots \ddot{W}_{(n)p}X_p$$

where the weights $\ddot{w}_{(n)1}$, $\ddot{w}_{(n)2}$ .. $\ddot{w}_{.(n)p}$ represent the weightings which minimise the ratio of the variance of $PC_{(1)}$ to the total variation.

PC is the principal component n which is a linear combination of the original variables X_1 to X_p whose sample variance is the greatest (where n = 1) for all the coefficients $\ddot{w}_{n1}$ to $\ddot{w}_{np}$ (Everitt and Dunn, 1991).

Interpreting the Principal Components Analysis

Appendix XIII, page 169, displays the principal component analysis matrix in relation to the dimensions. There are 3 principle components (Factors), which account for 60.4 per cent of the total variation in the data. The matrix measures, in terms of the spatial distance, the strength of the correlation's between these 3 factors and each of the remaining dimensions. The higher the absolute value displayed for each principle component in relation to the dimensions, then the stronger the correlation between that principle component and the dimension. The more negative the values, the less the dimensions are correlated with the principal components.

For example, from Appendix XIII it can be seen that variable (dimension) C38 (Trade discounts) has the strongest correlation with Factor 2 (PC2) with a positive correlation of 0.349. Variable C38 has its weakest correlation with Factor 3 (PC3) with a negative correlation of − 0.305. Finally, variable C38 can be said to be almost neutral with Factor 1 (PC1) with a slight negative correlation of -0.008.

Appendix XIII lists the Eigan values for each variable. Appendix XIII illustrates a Scree Plot of the Pilot data showing the total variance associated with each factor. The conventional criteria suggests that only factors that account for a variance greater than I (eigan value >I) should be taken into account. The scree plot enables the researcher to pinpoint the distinct break between the steep slope of the large factors and the gradual trailing off of the remaining factors. Experimental evidence indicates that the scree begins at the kth factor (i.e. where the eigan value <I), where k is the true number factors. From the scree plot, it appears that a six factor model is sufficient for the community example provided by the pilot data.

The principal component analysis (Appendix XIII) displays the coefficients that relate the variables (dimensions) to the factors. For example the figures show that the Quality index can be expressed as:

$$C35 = 0.234F_1 + (-0.163F_2) + 0.029F_3 \ldots + XF_n$$

Each row contains the coefficients used to express a variable (dimension) in terms of the factors. These coefficients are the factor loadings, since they indicate how much weight is assigned to each factor. Factors with large coefficients (in absolute value) for a variable (dimension) are closely related to that variable (dimension). For example, Factor 3 is the factor with the largest weighting for the advertising index (C24) (Appendix XIII), with a loading of 0.505.

The Rotated Factor Diagram

As can be seen from the Principal Components analysis in Appendix XIII, Factor 1 accounts for 23.8 per cent of the total variance (with an eigan value = 4.5126). Factor 2 accounts for 20.8 per cent and Factor 3 for 15.8 per cent, giving a cumulative proportion of 60.4 per cent of the total variance between the scores of the dimensions accounted for by the three factors. Thus, we would expect the subjects in each cluster to be spatially represented in terms of their proximity to each other when measured in relation to their correlation with the principal components. Plotting each subjects score against the principal components provides a vector co-ordinate, which is displayed on the Rotated Factor diagram (Appendices XV, page 171 and XVI, page 172).

Interpreting the Rotated Factor Diagram

Appendices XV and XVI display the rotated factor analyses based on the 3-factor model. From Appendix XIII, page 169, it can be seen that Factors 1 and 2 account for 44.6 per cent of the total variance between the scores of the dimensions. The key symbols to the right of the Rotated factor diagram (Appendix XV) represent the clusters and since respondents 2 and 8 had identical scores, there are fourteen clusters. The respondents corresponding to the clusters are spatially represented in terms of their proximity to each other when measured in relation to their correlation with the principal components. The rotated factor diagram represents each respondents score plotted against the principal components to provide a vector co-ordinate. The diagram provides an additional form of confirmation of the correlation between the scores of the subjects and the principal components. For example, taking cluster 1 (represented by a circle in the diagram) (Appendix XV) the two members B and H have identical correlation's with the principal components and are spatially positioned in terms of their absolute values (i.e. PC_1 = - 2 and PC_2 = - 4.5).

Clusters 7 and 10 are positioned in close proximity with Cluster 8 (respondent N) in relation to their correlation with the principal components. However, the main benefit of the rotated factor analysis diagram is that it highlights the differences in the data analysed, and so provides greater clarity about possible groupings than would be provided by reference to the dendogram alone. Combining both the cluster analysis and the principal component analysis provides a more robust method of identifying groups which avoids the potential for significant error caused by relying solely on the cluster solution. The principal component analysis adds additional quantifiable significance to the raw data in terms of the confidence level that one might attach to the cluster groupings.

Summary

The pilot study enabled various aspects to be explored in relation to the proposed methodology utilising the Repertory grid technique. The pilot facilitated the epistemology of the repertory grid methodology to be enhanced in the context of the selected industry sector. It provided a list of dimensions for comparison with the normative dimensions selected by Porter (1980); and it allowed the efficiency of the descriptive statistical techniques to be tested.

The pilot study also confirmed the view that a larger number of variables (dimensions) provide a more realistic means of testing for cluster groupings. This is due to the fact that information is not "lost" by assuming a few "key dimensions" as important for groupings. Indeed, enlarging the number of variables (dimensions) provides a more specific analysis of the differences between managerial perceptions of strategic competitive dimensions. These in turn might allow a clearer distinction to be made about the specific nature of competitive behaviour and the pursuit of competitive advantage.

This latter point regarding the number of variables (dimensions) to be tested led to the dimension list being extended for the wider population study, from which conclusions about specific strategic groupings were to be formed. In this respect the initial 19-dimension list was lengthened to 26 dimensions, using the pilot respondents as an "expert panel".

The expert panel was convened, consisting of four managers who participated in the Repertory Grid Technique, to test the comprehensiveness of the list of key dimensions. The review was a preface to the wider survey. The pilot study listed Location as a dimension which, when reviewed, was expanded to reflect National and Regional Geographic spread. Free Trade Penetration was added to specifically differentiate outlet channels, together with Wholesaling, Distribution, Diversification, Innovation and Management Structure. This process increased the number of key dimensions from 19 to 26 for the wider survey.

The wider survey of 53 respondents (strategists) from 36 firms was generated from the initial list of 101 companies from the ICC database (see page 173). The enhanced key dimension list combined with the full survey respondents provided a 26x53 data matrix. The analysis, results and conclusions from the descriptive statistics, that were provided using the Miniplan Version II package, are discussed in the concluding chapter which follows, chapter 6.

Chapter 6 Managerial Perceptions and Strategic Groups

The Factor Solution

Porter's strategic group concept rests on the competitive dimensions listed on the managerial perception questionnaire (Appendix II page 3, page 154). As discussed in Chapter 4, nine of the strategic dimensions recommended by Porter for identifying strategic groups were elicited from the laddering procedure in the repertory grid technique.

The emergence and inclusion of these dimensions has some significance for the testing of the hypothesis in this thesis. Incorporating Porter's dimensions enables the assumption of homogeneity along Porteresque lines to be more thoroughly scrutinised, utilising manager's perceptions of these dimensions as the test for homogeneity.

The pilot study and the subsequent development of the 26-dimension questionnaire, indicated that managers could relate to the dimensions derived as important to competitiveness in their industry. The factor solution to the principal components analysis of the database (26 dimensions x 53 managers, Appendix XVIII) produced three factors that accounted for a significant proportion of the variances of the original set. This three-factor solution explains 40.7 per cent of the variance in the data.

Analysing the factors in terms of the variable (dimension) factor loadings, where the loadings are > 0.50, gives the following factor index:

Figure 15. The Factor loadings of the wider survey data

Factor 1:	V1, V3, V14, V16, V20, V23, 24:
Factor 2:	V2, V7, V8, V10, V18:
Factor 3:	V4, V25, V26:

The communality of the variables (dimensions) in terms of the factor loadings are shown in Table 13, together with the percentage of variance accounted for by each of the three retained factors.

Table 13: Communality of Variables.

Variable Dimension		Communality	Factor	Eigen Value	Rotated Pct of Variance	Cum Pct
V1	National Geographical spread	0.454	1	6.2656	15.9	15.9
V2	Regional Geographical spread	0.309	2	2.2423	13.0	28.9
V3	Innovation	0.527	3	2.0678	11.8	40.7
V4	Free Trade Penetration	0.456				
V7	Distribution	0.574				
V8	Management Structure	0.508				
V10	Quality	0.580				
V14	Economies of Scale	0.293				
V16	Horizontal Integration	0.387				
V18	Pay and Salaries	0.528				
V20	Organisational Efficiency	0.545				
V23	Market Share	0.334				
V24	Process Technology	0.484				
V25	Discounts	0.623				
V26	Brewery Loan	0.667				

The Rotated Factor Analysis

Communalities can range from 0 to 1, with 0 indicating that the factors explain none of the variance and 1 indicating that all of the variance is explained by the factor solution. The factor loadings and the communalities indicate an observable correlation between the variables (dimensions) due to the sharing of the common retained factors and hence can be used to indicate the correlation between the variables (dimensions) and the clusters. The rotated factor diagram, Figure 16, illustrates the correlation between the cluster members, the common factors and the factor loadings.

In the variance rotation solution (Figure 16), the closer the cluster symbols to the extremity of the axis or to their intersection, then the closer the scores of the members to the factor solution. For example, members 1, 4 and 28 represented by the key symbol O in Figure 16, are spatially positioned positively to factor 1 and this provides further evidence of the efficacy of the cluster solution. The spatial clustering of the members on the Varimax rotation reinforces the cluster analysis.

As can be seen from Figure 17 the total cluster solution produces 27 clusters and these correspond with the cluster members shown in Figure 16.

The rotated factor loadings shown in the Factor Analysis, Appendix XIX, simplifies the structure of the factor matrix by producing a matrix where each factor has some non-zero loadings for some of the variables. This helps to interpret the factors and enables the factors to be differentiated from each other. Rotation does not affect the goodness of fit of a factor solution. Thus, although the factor matrix changes (as can be seen in Appendix XIX) the communality and the percentage of total variance explained by the factor solution does not change.

However, the percentage of variance accounted for by each of the factors does change. Rotation redistributes the explained variance for the individual factors. The most commonly used Varimax rotation has been utilised for the rotated analysis of the factor loadings. This enhances the interpretability of the factors and produces a redistribution of the variance explained by the factor solution, as shown in Figure 16.

For example, if we look more closely at the effect of the rotation of Factors 1 and 2 in Figure 16, we can see that the Varimax rotation produces a simple structure. This structure clusters the group members in relation to the factor loadings such that clusters of members with positive loadings occur near the ends of the axes and at their intersection.

Members clustering near the origin of the plot (0,0) have small loadings on the factors. Variables that are not near the axes are explained by both factors. If a simple structure has been achieved, there should be few, if any, members with large loadings on more than one factor.

From Figure 16, it can be seen that the number of groupings with more than one member (clusters:1,3,4,5,6,7,9,11,16,17,19,20,22), cluster in relative proximity consistent with the factor loadings. This is what we would expect to find when the clusters formed were meaningful in relation to the factor analysis and the factor solution, when these are taken together. Thus, the principle components and the factor analyses validate the significance of the group data produced through the clustering procedure.

The Cluster Analysis and the Factor Solution

27 groups have been formed from the cluster analysis (see Appendix XX). Figure 17, lists the clusters and the membership groupings. It can be seen that there are 13 clusters containing more than one member, with cluster 5 containing eight members. These clusters have been formed on the basis of managerial perceptions and represent groupings of manager's cognition's of key strategic dimensions. They are in fact maps of cognitive strategic groups, rather than industrial sector or structural groups.

Moreover, they are cognitive strategic groups, which illustrate heterogeneity across the sample, rather than homogeneity, which reflects firms' structural configurations. These groups differ significantly on both the strategic dimensions identified as being important to competitiveness

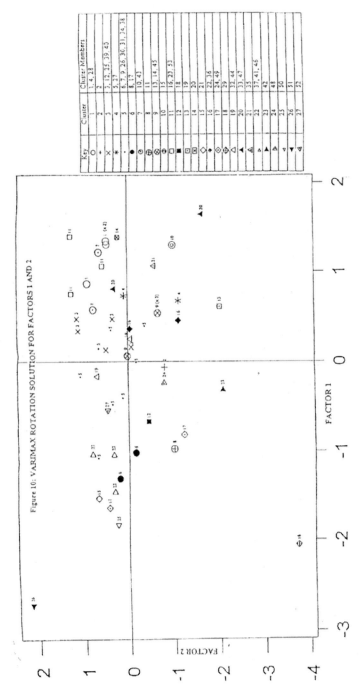

Figure 16. Varimax rotation solution for factors 1 and 2

Cluster	Firms		Cluster	Firms
Cluster 1			Cluster 12	
1	George Gale &Co		18	Brent Walker Breweries
4	Guinness Brewery Int.			
28	Bass		Cluster 13	
			19	Adnams Brewery
Cluster 2				
2	George Gale &Co		Cluster 14	
			20	Taylor Walker
Cluster 3				
3	George Gale &Co		Cluster 15	
12	Elgood & Sons		21	Mansfield Brewery
25	Morrells Brewery			
29	Scottish & Newcastle		Cluster 16	
40	Ruddles Brewery		22	Alloa Brewery Company
			36	Vaux Breweries
Cluster 4				
5	Guinness Brewery Int.		Cluster 17	
27	Peach Malt		24	Morrells Brewer
			40	Allied Breweries
Cluster 5				
6	Marston, Thompson & Evershed		Cluster 18	
7	Marston, Thompson & Evershed		29	Aston Manor
9	Alloa Brewery Company			
26	Maclay and Company		Cluster 19	
30	Aston Manor		32	Hook Norton Brewery Co
31	Aston Manor		44	HB Clark & Company
34	Whitbread Beer Company			
38	Cornish Brewery Company		Cluster 20	
			33	Frederick Robinson Ltd
Cluster 6			47	McMullen and Sons
8	Marston, Thompson & Evershed			
17	Moorhouse Brewery		Cluster 21	
			35	Whitbread Beer Company
Cluster 7				
10	Guiness		Cluster 22	
43	Broughton Brewer		27	SH Ward & Company
			41	Mauldons Brewery
Cluster 8			46	Jennings Brothers
11	Guinness Brewery Int.			
			Cluster 23	
Cluster 9			42	Mitchells of Lancaster
13	Kings & Barnes			
14	Kings & Barnes		Cluster 24	
45	Federation Brewery		48	Bellhaven Brewing Company
Cluster 10			Cluster 25	
15	Carlsberg Tetley		50	Wolverhampton & Dudley Brewery
Cluster 11			Cluster 26	
16	Morland & Co		51	Hall Woodhouse
23	Morrells Brewery			
53	Frederick Robinson Ltd		Cluster 27	
			52	Hall Woodhouse

Cluster members correspond with Respondents' listed in Appendix XVII page 161

Figure 17. Cluster Members

and on resource commitments related to the scale, scope, capacity and vertical and horizontal integration, of the group member's respective firms.

In these groupings it is evident that smaller and medium sized regional brewers cluster with large national companies along the same strategic dimension. Thus, the hypothesis H_1 (Chapter 5) that managers' perceptions of key strategic dimensions are homogeneous within strategic groups, can be rejected. Alternatively, the null hypothesis H_{01}, that managers' perceptions of key strategic dimensions indicate heterogeneity within strategic groups, can be accepted.

Indeed, if we examine the firms in the sample in terms of the construction of strategic groups along key dimensions utilised by Porter (1980), it is evident that the disparity, between strategists' perceptions of strategic dimensions and firms clustered using Porters method, is considerable. Figure 16, illustrates the "strategic groupings" of firms in the sample using the dimensions of competitive scope versus the number of brands as the vector coordinates.

Strategic Groups versus Cognitive groups

As we might expect, the dimensions used in Figure 18 result in the kind of "strategic groupings" Porter (and others) has identified in his studies. However, these groupings represent outcomes based on the structure-performance-conduct paradigm propounded by Porter and developed in his influential theories of position and market power (1980, 1985). It is not unreasonable to argue that we could predict these groupings, since the dimensions on which they are based reflect the configuration of resources. On this basis, what emerge are "structural groups" rather than strategic groups. The clusters indicate how firms are configured in ways which reflect linkages and resources, but they do not reflect the interconnectedness of emergent solutions involving transformation, competitive innovation, competencies and emergent strategy in competitive behaviour; nor do they reflect cognitive strategic groups.

Similarly, using the national and selected regional brewers in the industry sample, we can construct a "strategic group" map based on brands versus capital intensity, along Porteresque lines. Capital intensity represents the amount of capital invested relative to the flow of output produced (Buzzell and Gale, 1987). This is the method most commonly used to measure capital intensity, and is the measure adopted by Porter and represented by the ratio of capital employed to sales in Figure 19. The concurrence between the groups in Figures 18 and 19 is predictable, since capital intensity versus number of brands reflects similar structure linkages to groups clustered on this basis of scope considerations and brands.

While Figures 18 and 19 illustrate homogeneity in the clusters using Porters method, when contrasted with the clusters formed in Figure 17, based on managers' perceptions of strategic dimensions, we can see the discrepancy. The prescriptive assumption that managers within "strategic groups" will have homogeneous perceptions of key dimensions is contested by the reality of the clusters formed on the basis of managerial cognitions. For example, from Figure 17 the tightest cluster, cluster 1, contains respondents from three firms, George Gale, Guinness Brewery International and Bass, who cluster in different "strategic groups" based on Porters method. Similarly, cluster 3 in Figure 17, also contains heterogeneous members drawn from local, regional and national brewers. Cluster 5, the largest cluster in Figure 17, is similarly heterogeneous with respondents from small local brewers combining with larger regional and national brewers. There is in fact a juxtaposition between Porter's "strategic groups" and the "cognitive group" based on managerial perceptions.

Heterogeneity within Firms

As we have seen from the analysis of "strategic groups" versus "cognitive groups", there is a discrepancy between the assumption of homogeneous perceptions of key dimensions and the reality of those perceptions. Strategic groups, as formulated using the prescriptive methodology, do not reflect managers shared perceptions of the importance of the same competitive dimensions. Similarly, the cluster solution (Figure 17) of managerial perceptions indicates that managers within the same firms do not necessarily share the same perceptions of competitive strategic dimensions.

For example, Marston, Thompson and Evershed, one of the larger regional brewers with a turnover of £212.4 million in 1998 marketing six brands, provided three of the respondents. Two of these clustered together in cluster 5, while the third grouped with cluster 6. While these respondent's clusters ranked consecutively in the cluster solution, the distance between their perceptions of strategic dimensions was nevertheless dissimilar enough to confine them to different groups.

Of the 36 firms in the sample, only one firms' entire respondent's clustered in the same group (i.e. King and Barnes, cluster 9) in the cluster solution. Respondents from the same firm's did cluster together, but not the entire number of respondents from those firms (e.g. Marston, Thompson and Evershed (x2) cluster 5; Aston Manor (x2) cluster 5); and as can be seen from Figure 17, this only occurred in 2 out of the 27 clusters.

It is not unreasonable to argue that if respondents from the same "strategic group", constructed on the basis of prescriptive methods, do not cluster together, then we might expect respondents from the same firms not to cluster together. This view can be defended on the grounds that the dynamism of emergent strategy will reflect a cognitive dissonance between strategists, as individual knowledge and judgement combine in the reconciliation between abstraction and practical reality.

As suggested in chapter 3, strategists' knowledge and judgement and ultimately their learning and memory, are intimately bound up with their particular contexts of activity and experience. Hence, heterogeneity within firms in relation to the strategic dimensions is likely to reflect this. This view presents a major challenge to the content-driven approach to strategic groups – which focuses on the development of competitive superiority through the configuration of resources and linkages and which remains largely dominated by notions of equilibrium and control.

Strategic Change and Complexity

As discussed in Chapter 2, Stacey (1993) has suggested that organisations operate paradoxically. On the one hand, the centripetal forces of convergence and integration in the pursuit of stability, act like a vortex pulling-in on the organisation to create an unstable state. On the other hand, the centrifugal forces generated by diverse innovation, pushes the organisation progressively further from stability to the point where it descends in chaos.

This entropic state is most readily managed where changes and transformation are recognised as associated with non-equilibrium conditions and random developments. Adaptation to this complexity is achieved through a "dissipative structure" (Macintosh and Mclean, 1999:301) whereby, at the point of entropy, attention is focussed on the non-linearity and interconnectedness of emergent solutions, which emanate from the range of broad possibilities expressed through the differential cognitions of managers.

In the writer's view, the evidence provided by the clusters of managerial perceptions of strategic dimensions concurs with the notions of dissipative structures and complexity theory, since the synthesis to which they refer allows for the temporal coexistence of spatially contradictory perceptions within the organisation.

In an industry sector where environmental turbulence, brought about by regulation, precipitated both strategic innovation and corporate renewal across the industry, it is more likely that, at the 'edge of chaos', we will find the coexistence of contradictory perceptions. The use of a cognitive lens perspective in this research, as a means of investigating so called 'cognitive strategic groups', provides us with a valuable insight into the juxtaposition between the prescriptive groups formed in Figures 18 and 19, and the realities of managers' perceptions of strategic dimensions as shown in the cognitive groupings in Figure 17.

Moreover, these findings present us with the challenge to understand strategic change as the synthesis and integration of process and content that calls for a new paradigm which is de-coupled from existing mind-sets. Economic rationality and resourced based thinking must be linked with learning theory, tacit knowledge, and cognitive dimensions, in a dynamic view of strategy which accepts that organisations are not only complex and adaptive, but that their complexity and adaptiveness can itself change with new unstable conditions. In this respect it is now necessary to describe how the strategists in our sample from the Brewing industry, perceived the strategy for adapting to the conditions resulting from the environmental changes instigated by the Beer Orders.

The Three Factor Solution

Figure 15 and Table 13 summarised the three factor solution and the strategic dimensions represented in the factor loadings. These factors represent the overall strategic direction of the respondents in the sample, on the basis of their perceptions of key strategic dimensions. This orientation has to be described and interpreted in the light of the strategic direction the industry actually followed in the post Beer Order period, and a comparison made between this direction and that discussed in Chapter 4.

The Beer Orders forced the orientation of the sector towards greater concentration and importantly, differentiation in both products and services. Differentiation through innovation and branding aimed at creating discrete choices to market segments paralleled the development of increased market power based on oligopolistic market structures. Strategically, the sector product-market space exhibited horizontally differentiated competition, characterized by close substitutability coefficients. Similarly, in combatting the advantages of localised monopoly power, location became a key feature in characterising consumers' utility.

In the historiography of the UK Brewing Industry, scale and scope has played a major role in the strategy of industry concentration and consolidation that has characterised the industry. Notwithstanding the recent growth in entrepreneurial small brewing developments in, for example, the craft brewers, the oligopolistic nature of industry competition reflects the historical trend of developing scope and scale in the pursuit of market power objectives. The subsequent focus on branding and market segmentation has been driven by the evolution of the strategy and structure dynamics that have dominated the industry since the nineteenth century. This dominant strategy has cloaked the perceptions of strategic decision-makers in the industry and notwithstanding the divergence of managerial perceptions across the industry, the hybrid strategy of cost-leadership, market share differentiation continues to reinforce the structure considerations, as this research demonstrates.

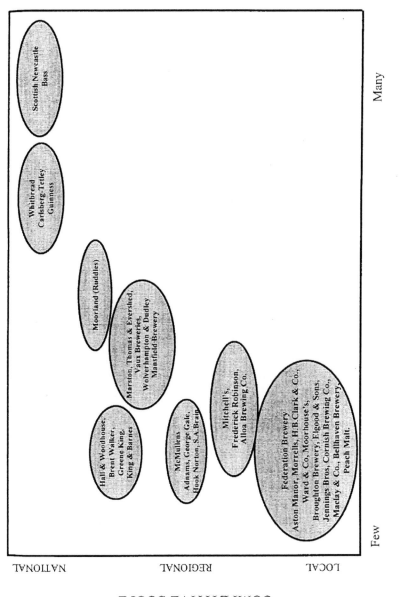

NUMBER of BRANDS
Figure: 11 "Strategic Groups" clustered using Porters Methodology.

Figure 18. Strategic Group Clusters

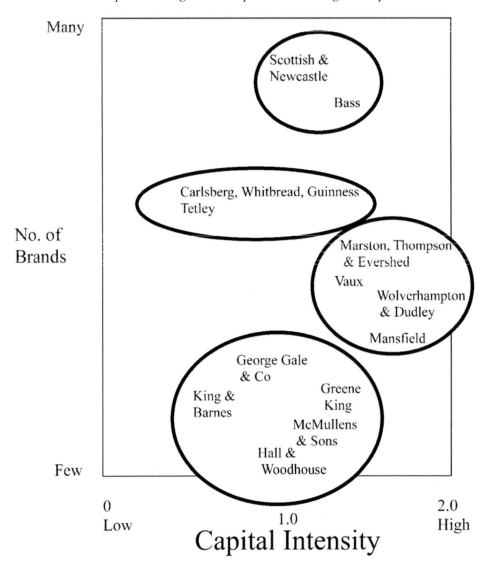

Figure 19. Brand and Capital Intensity. National and Selected Regional Brewers

Describing the Three Factor Solution

Factor 1: Loadings, V24, V1, V16, V20, V23, V3, V14

This factor can be interpreted as cost leadership through a market share/product differentiation strategy. The dimension that load on this factor are concerned with process technology (V24), national geographical spread (V1), horizontal integration (V16), organisational efficiency (V20), Market Share (V23), innovation (V3) and economies of scale (V14).

Vertical integration (V21), which we may have anticipated as associated with a cost leadership strategy in an industry with a high degree of concentration, actually loaded negatively on this factor (-0.035). This negative loading is entirely consistent with the actual strategic orientation following the Beer Orders which were implemented to radically reduce the vertical integration of the large national brewers. Moreover, this negative loading also suggests that cost leadership per se is not perceived as a mutually exclusive strategy in this industry. This could be interpreted as indicating that vertical integration is not a mobility barrier and indeed that the degree of vertical integration is now unrelated to market share strategy in this industry. This latter conclusion is supported by the PIMS (Profit Impact of Market Strategy) findings (Buzzell and Gale, 1987), where the payoff from a strategy of vertical integration varies in industries according to the market and competitive conditions.

The differentiated market share strategy leading to cost leadership, runs counter to Porters "generic" positioning strategies in that the mutually exclusive nature of "cost leadership", "differentiation" and "focus" as suggested by Porter, is overturned. More will be said about this in greater detail later in this chapter.

Factor 2: Loadings, V8, V18, V10, V7, V2.

This can be regarded as the "retail" factor and a competitive advantage underpinning the product differentiation cost leadership strategy. The competitive advantage emanates from merchandising based on the quality and efficient management of distribution at regional level. While service (V17) does not quite attain the loading criteria of >0.5, it nevertheless loads positively on this factor with a loading of 0.482 consistent with the significance of retailing.

The dimension loading on this factor are Management structure (V8), Pay and Salaries (V18), Quality (V10), Distribution (V7) and Regional Geographical spread (V2). Regional presence and penetration is a significant factor in this industry, with efficient distribution and the operation of regional public houses a key area of competition.

Factor 3: Loadings, V26, V25, V4

This factor can be interpreted as "financial leverage". The importance of the "on-trade" and the "off-trade", following the regulation of the tied-house system of distribution in 1991, has had a significant impact on firm rivalry. Brewery loans (V26) has a loading of 0.813 on this factor, while the discount (V25) loading is 0.780. These combined with free trade penetration (V4) indicate the importance of a strategy concerned with maintaining market share and competing for distribution outlets via the public houses. This factor underpins differentiation and retail competitiveness in describing a coherent strategy from the factor solution and the dimension loadings.

The three-factor solution reflects the perceived critical success factors of a component strategy, which can be summarised as follows;

Factor 1: Cost leader/product brand differentiator
Factor 2: Retail distribution
Factor 3: Financial leverage.

The key dimensions loading on these Factors and representing the strategic orientation of managers, through their perception of the importance of these dimensions to competitiveness in the industry, can be summarised as follows:

Factors	Strategic Dimensions
Factor 1:	Process Technology; National Geographical Spread; Horizontal Integration; Organisation Efficiency; Market Share; Innovation; Economies of Scale.
Factor 2:	Management Structure; Pay & Salaries; Quality; Distribution; Regional Geographical Spread
Factor 3:	Brewery Loans; Discounts; Free Trade Penetration.

Figure 20. Dimensions of a Three Factor Generic Strategy

Interpreting the Three-Factor Strategy

Factor 1: Cost Leader/Product Brand Differentiator

Product development and diversification have been a major factor in the industry in the last decade. The introduction of the Beer Orders dramatically altered the pattern of public house ownership, resulting in a strategic emphasis on product branding and positioning linked to new directions in retailing. The Free Trade developments, which followed, witnessed a flurry of new products linked to differentiation and product scope in the industry. The division between draught lagers and traditional dark draught beers saw a period in which lagers' volume share of the market reached approximately 70 per cent in 1997/8, from a position of less than 7 percent in the 1970's.

The emphasis on differentiation through product branding and positioning attempted to mirror consumer segment preferences and the characteristics that coincided with these preferences. In this, the differentiation strategy moved away from not merely defining consumption in broad product-market terms, but aimed to identify discrete choices where particular characteristics provided utility to consumers and paved a way to brand reinforcement. The discrete choice differentiation strategy was a response to the markets signal that the representative customer approach (where the assumption is that all customers are the same) was no longer valid and that the marginal consumer surplus could be enhanced by the bundling and packaging of products that enabled the consumers' reservation price to accommodate more extensive premium pricing. Allied to this was the focus on location as an important dimension in the discrete segmentation of the market and the trend towards *localisation* in representing the markets ideal preferences in the product-market space interface.

As a consequence of the discrete choice strategy, the industry sector moved increasingly to an oligopolistic structure reflecting horizontal product differentiation, matched on the supply-side with increasing economies of scale through firm concentration and a cloning effect in market space.

Factor 2: Retail Distribution

The retail distribution factor is dominated by two aspects, namely, the off-trade involving the supply and share of volume to non-traditional retailers such as the large grocery multinationals and chains (e.g., Tesco), and the on-trade through tied and free-trade public houses. The off-trade now accounts for approximately 33 per cent of the volume, with the on-trade remaining the major volume channel. In terms of value, the on-trade remains the dominant channel in spite of the growing volume share taken by the off-trade.

The continued dominance of the on-trade means that beer has its own unique distribution and delivery systems (the barrel itself requires special treatment). Within the £11.6 billion on-trade market, draught beer accounts for 88.8 per cent of the volume consumed and reinforces the cost dimension linked with Factor 1. With an estimated 58,000 public house outlets in the U.K., together with brewers other retail outlets and independents operating a further 6,800 wine bars and other on trade outlets, the importance of scope and segmentation also support the brand differentiation dimensions in Factor 1.

The four majors, Scottish Courage, Whitbread, Bass and Carlsberg Tetley, operate some 15,000 outlets or 26 per cent of the total on-trade. The licensed club sector which comprises approximately 3,800 outlets, also plays an important part in beer sales for the national and regional operators.

The supermarket/grocery trade accounts for 73 per cent of the beer off-trade with the consequent result that pressure on independent and specialist off-licenses has resulted in considerable concentration with two companies dominating this sector through Victoria Wine (Allied) and Threshers (Whitbread).

Factor 3: Financial Leverage

As discussed above, product development and diversification has been a large factor in the industry in the last decade. Free trade (V4) developments with a loading of 0.588, together with discounts (V25) with a high loading of 0.780 and brewery loans (V26) with a high loading of 0.813, suggest that new product development, linked to the achievement of segmentation and brand differentiation, has also been linked with retail penetration through competitive financial incentives. The product developments in the form of fashionable brands and their positioning with younger consumers, together with technological innovations in canned beers, have placed a greater emphasis on meeting retailer margins to gain penetration, while at the same time premium pricing to fund brand positioning.

The improvement in canned beers has led to the introduction of better draught products. Subsequently there has been a resurgence of interest in stouts and ales, both in public houses and in the off trade. For those brewers who misjudged the premium lager boom, but with specialisation in dark cast-conditioned beers, the drive to compete with premium lagers has placed an emphasis on developing stronger ties with the free trade sector. This has placed a greater emphasis on financial leverage to the retail sector through discounts and brewing loans in an attempt to regain their position.

The Extended Factor Solution

The principle component analysis extracted three factors that have Eiganvalues greater than 2.0, the third factor having an Eiganvalue of 2.0678, as can be seen in Table 14. The Eiganvalues are the ratios of the between-groups to within-groups sum of squares. Large Eiganvalues are associated with "good" functions and the three factor solution explains 40.7 per cent of the total variance of the 26 variables for the sample of 53 managers.

The three factors retained are significant by the amount of variance they explain. However, if we alter the criteria for determining the number of "significant" factors we can account for a greater amount of the variance. Thus, if we adopt the criteria that factors with an Eiganvalue greater than 1 should be included, we extend the factor solution to nine factors.

In the proximity ranking of factors, those with Eiganvalues less than 1 are likely to be the result of single variables. The Scree Plot shown in Appendix XXII, page 190, indicates the distinct break between the steep slope of the large factors and the gradual trailing off of the rest of the factors. From the Scree plot, we can see that a nine-factor model with Eiganvalues >1 would be justified in accounting for a greater proportion of the variance for the communality examined. The addition of six more factors increases the amount of variance explained to 73.4 per cent. Table 14, summarises the percentage of total variance explained and the Eiganvalues of the nine-factor solution.

The inclusion of six additional factors in an extended solution provides evidence of the supporting dimensions underpinning the main three factor strategy, Figure 20. Indeed, the significance of the extended factor solution is that it provides further evidence of the integration of Porter's dimensions in managers' perceptions of key dimensions. This has relevance for the clusters formed since, as we have seen in Figures 18 and 19, the assumed homogeneity of Porter's strategic groups is called into question by the heterogeneity of the cognitive groups in Figure 17.

Table 14: The Extended Factor Solution

Factor	Eiganvalue	Pct Variance	Cum. Variance
F1	6.2656	24.10	24.10
F2	2.2423	8.60	32.70
F3	2.0678	8.00	40.70
F4	1.8180	7.00	47.70
F5	1.5429	6.00	53.70
F6	1.4924	5.70	59.40
F7	1.3389	5.10	64.50
F8	1.2213	4.70	69.20
F9	1.0819	4.20	73.40

Having identified this contradiction, there remains an additional analysis and comparison to be made with the position school. This is between the strategic orientation of the clusters, which are borne out by the actual strategic dimension taken by the industry and Porter's "generic strategies", which in theory emphasises the mutual exclusivity of several aspects of the composite three factor solution strategy.

The Three Factor Strategy and Porters "Generic Strategies"

Porter suggests that his notion of strategic groups "captures the essential strategic differences among firms in an industry" (Porter, 1980: 129). These differences, according to Porter, lead to a relatively small number of strategic groups being formed. These strategic groups mirror broad characteristics such as, extensive integration, broad product lines and high volume. Others reflect specialisation and uniqueness with selective distribution, high pricing and superior quality.

Porters strategic group positioning dovetails logically with his three generic strategies of, overall cost leadership; differentiation; and focus. The three generic strategies are "alternative, viable approaches to dealing with the competitive forces" (Porter, 1980:41). Porter argues that a firm, which fails to develop its strategy in at least one of the three directions, will find itself in the strategic position of being "stuck in the middle". The potential inconsistencies involved for those firms who "flip back and forth among the generic strategies", results in an approach which, Porter argues, "is almost always doomed to failure" (Porter, 1980:42). Porter links these propositions in a u-shaped relationship between profitability and market share as illustrated in Figure 15.

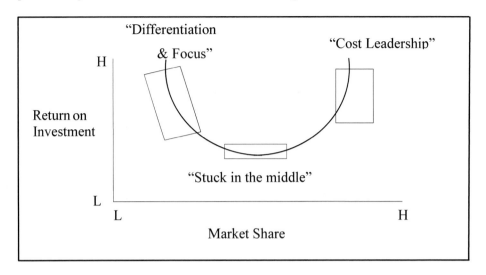

Figure 21. The mutually exclusive "Generic Strategy" position

From the interpretation of Factor 1 it is clear that cost leadership/product differentiation is a strategy widely perceived by a range of strategists across the industry. For example, it can be seen from the cluster members (cognitive groups page 131) in relation to the rotated factor solution, Figure 16, that the tightest cluster, cluster 1 (1, 4, 28), representing George Gale and Company, Guinness Brewing International and Bass, correlates positively with Factor 1 and the variable loadings.

Likewise, Cluster 3 (3, 12, 25, 39, 40) correlates positively with Factor 1. Cluster 3 is comprised of two regional firms Ruddles and Morrells and two regional locals, George Gale and Elgood. Moreover, Cluster 14 (20) represented by Taylor Walker as a single member cluster has a very positive correlation with Factor 1. Indeed, there are eleven clusters positively correlated to Factor 1 and the cost leadership/ differentiation strategy namely; 1, 7, 3, 11, 9, 10, 4, 20, 16, 14, 21.

Within these clusters range the perceptions of managers from firms in the top four in the industry: Bass, Guinness; Scottish Courage and Whitbread, as well as regional brewers such as Ruddles and locals such as Fredrick Robinson. Thus, what we can observe from this is that strategists, in opposition to Porter's broad characteristics, share the cost leadership/differentiator strategy and its strategic dimensions. Porter's characteristics would typify the essential strategic differences among firms in an industry on the basis of asset configurations and lead to a relatively small number of strategic groups.

Moreover, the combination of the cost leader differentiator strategy as indicated in this study can be explained by looking at the relationship between cost leadership and differentiation and highlighting the complementarity between them. This is in contrast to the otherwise mutually exclusive directions as suggested by the Porter Curve. It can be argued that differentiation leads to cost leadership through increasing the scope available to firms by facilitating a shift in their demand curve and through this shift, enabling them to drive down their long run average cost curves (Hill, 1988). Figure 22 illustrates this argument, as follows:

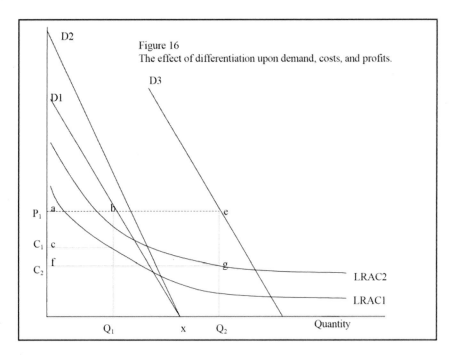

Figure 16
The effect of differentiation upon demand, costs, and profits.

Figure 22. The effect of differentiation upon demand, costs and profits

However, Figure 22, illustrates how differentiation can be used to provide industrywide scope by shifting a product/firms demand curve to the right (D3), while at the same time maintaining its price at the average industry level (P1). Differentiating the product will entail increased costs either in the form of research and development, materials, process technology, marketing or advertising, or a combination of these. Thus, the consequences of differentiating will be to increase the firms long run average cost curve ($LRAC_2$).

However, as can be seen, the utility of the differentiation will lead to greater demand with lower long run average costs ($LRAC_2$) per unit of output as indicated by the cost level C_2. Clearly this could lead to superior performance, which is what Porter suggests about differentiation in Figure 21. However, Porter's superior performance is based on premium pricing with relatively low market shares. The argument in Figure 22, clearly illustrates the possibility of cost leadership differentiation with relatively high market shares as well as low market shares.

Studies by Dess and Davies (1984) investigating the generic strategies as determinants of strategic group membership, and Bowman (1990) who examined managerial perceptions of the generic strategies, provide useful comparisons with this study. Dess and Davies found that when they compared the competitive factors derived from managers with those of "experts", with reference to the generic strategies, important differences emerged. There was little agreement between the managers and "experts" on factors related to differentiation, cost leadership and focus; a finding that would not have surprised Friedrich Hayek (1945) who argued that 'experts' were as "predictably irrational" as anyone drawn from the population and cautioned against their over-influence on decisions of resource allocation. Similarly, Bowman (1990:167) found that, "Managers' perceptions of competitive strategy are different from those of academics". Along similar lines, this study suggests that "academics" views about "cognitive strategic groups" based on assumptions of homogeneity of strategic dimensions, does not correspond with managerial reality nor the economic organisation of firms.

The argument propounded by Hill (1989) in relation to the Porter curve and the interrelatedness of cost leadership and differentiation, together with the findings of Dess and Davis (1984) and Bowman (1990), support the interpretations of this study of strategic groups and managerial perceptions. Similarly, this study suggests differences between the characteristics of strategic groups based on an analysis of asset configurations related to generic strategic directions, and those based on managers' perceptions of competitive strategic dimensions. Moreover, the evidence from this study indicates that cost leadership via product differentiation is a major realised strategy across the brewing industry; a strategy that is widely pursued by practitioners notwithstanding their "cognitive" differences about the strategic dimensions. In this context, Olsen (1971:2) has argued that "rational self-interested individuals will not act to achieve their own common or group interests" and that this is also the case "when there is unanimous agreement in a group about the common goal and the methods of achieving it". However, as Hayek alluded to, it is the coercion of the market in motivating large groups that results in the best use of resources, because it is the market that makes the best decisions since no one better can make the choices than the consumers themselves. In this argument the resonance with Adam Smith's '*Invisible Hand*' is clearly affirmed.

The data here indicates that cost leader differentiation is a widely perceived strategy across the industry. Moreover, it indicates that managers' perceptions of strategic dimensions are not homogeneous within strategic groups, as these are categorised in the Porteresque sense. What is also clear is that the cost leader-differentiation strategy is more commonly evident in this industry and that as a "generic strategy", at the level of the firm, strategists view this with different degrees of consensus, which reflects the perceptions of the different weightings within the competitive factors, and the firm as a composite of rational managerial individuals rather than an anthropomorphic group (of one form). The discrete choice differentiation strategy represents a *Nash Equilibrium* in an oligopolistic industry structure where the players (firms) cannot improve their payoffs given the other players strategy. The discrete choice cost leadership-differentiation strategy is a best response against the other players' differentiation strategy.

Discussion of the Results

Industry realignment is closely tied to external environmental change. Support for this proposition is strongly borne out in this study, on the basis of the amount of change in the U.K. brewing industry since 1991. An industry in transition, such as the one observed in this research, is likely to experience changes in its key dimensions of strategy.

The prescriptive notions of "strategic groups" implicitly assumes that, "groups of firms in an industry follow the same or similar strategy along the same strategic dimensions" (Porter, 1980:129). Thus, strategic group structure acts as a mid-point between industry structure and individual firm structure. Firms are assigned to a strategic group not only in a positional sense, but on the explicit assumption that their strategy is knowable by outsiders and as such, firms can be assigned unambiguously to a strategic group.

A corollary to this unambiguous assignment is that firms who do not follow a clear, constant strategy, are assumed to be reactors and misfits (Miles and Snow, 1978). Such firms have been described as "stuck in the middle" (Porter, 1980); they change strategic direction often or simply react to environmental events as they occur.

"Idiosyncratic" firms adopting strategies dramatically different from all others in an industry have been identified (Barney and Hoskinson, 1990). This has made it difficult to position them viz-a-viz other firms along common dimensions. Prescriptive researchers argue that these firms do not align with other firms; they do not compete in similar ways. Such firms may have a coherent strategy and that strategy may fit the industry, but it does not fit the cognitive maps of outsiders.

The cognitive maps of outsiders (researchers) can describe almost all other competitors within the industry on the basis of dimensions, which differentiate competitors. The so-called outliers are misaligned in this way since their radically different strategy appears mutually exclusive in the context of the industry and the mapping of strategic groups.

However, mental models reflect simple generalisations. We do not carry in our minds complete pictures of organisations, we carry assumptions, images and stories (Senge, 1990). Kelly's (1955) theory of personal construct psychology and our mental models, determine how we make sense of the world. Indeed, our mental models do more than this, as Senge has put it, they determine "how we take action" (1990:175). While our mental representations (Gardner, 1984) have congruency with our behaviour, our espoused theories do not (Argyris, 1982). The research in this book identifies the discrepancy between the mental representations of prescriptive theorists, and the congruency between strategists' mental maps of strategic dimensions and the strategic behaviour of the industry.

The clusters formed from an analysis of strategists perceptions of key strategic dimensions, differ significantly from strategic groups formed on the basis of "outsider" prescriptive dimensions. The analysis discussed above in this chapter yielded 27 cluster solutions from 53 respondent strategists. The results indicate that data based on managerial perceptions can provide a cognitive lens perspective of "strategic groups". Substantial differences emerge between these mental representations of the importance of key dimensions of strategy and the assumption of homogeneity of strategic dimensions in strategic group theory.

Instead of homogeneity among members of identified "strategic groups" in the prescriptive sense, what the results show is that there is heterogeneity both within firms and across firms in the industry. With the cognitive lens perspective, 13 clusters contained more than one member, with an additional 14 single member clusters. Moreover, the principal components and factor analyses showed that the 39 respondents contained in the 13 clusters, were unambiguously assigned to groups.

The cluster results show that 14 respondents do not have a strategic position which is shared. Moreover, respondents within the same firms did not assign to the same group across a number of clusters. For example, clusters 1, 2 and 3 each contained a respondent from the same firm. On the other hand, cluster 5 containing 8 members is made up of a pair of respondents from the same firm and 6 respondents from different firms.

Indeed, a striking result of the analysis is that none of the clusters of the respondents' firms (Figure 17) corresponds with the strategic group clusters formed using the prescriptive methodology (Figures 18 and 19). This would indicate that the null hypothesis H_0, "that managers' perceptions of key strategic dimensions are homogeneous within strategic groups", can be rejected with some confidence and that H_1 constitutes the assertion that can be accepted.

Conclusion

The results of this research suggest that the ontological status of strategic groups is very ambiguous. Indeed, the representation of strategic groups by academic researchers (Porter et al), is perhaps a gross oversimplification of the use of the term. What their mental representations provide is a clustering of firm characteristics in a structural sense, which is more representative of past performance than emergent competitive strategy. In this sense a more accurate description of these clusters would be met by the use of the term "structural groups".

Much of the existing research on strategic groups from the positional school perspective, could be regarded as portraying these observers as prisoners of their own thinking. The structure-performance-conduct paradigm, from which they develop the notion of strategic position and market power within an industry, owes much to the influencing assumption of equilibrium and the quest for stability in economic organisation. Indeed, the whole concept of competitive advantage, as propounded by the positioning school, and the focus on market power, paradoxically, reflects a view of strategic behaviour which is concerned with the pursuit of monopoly power as a strategy for achieving the ultimate stability. In this sense we might regard the preoccupation with position and market power as an anti-competitive outlook.

As an extended critique of the positioning school in relation to strategic groups we could translate entry barriers to signify moves to restrict the number of competitors in an industry, and mobility barriers as prescriptions designed to raise barriers to substitutes. Both reflect a school of thought concerned with defensive stability. The attraction of the concept of strategic groups is that it provides a method of summarising firms in terms of their characteristics, in industries that are heavily populated by many competitors. This is where the generalisations of the mental representations begin. This study argues and finds empirically, that in a changing industry, the concept of strategic groups disguises the rich diversity of strategy perceptions. Employing a cognitive lens perspective that concerns itself with managerial perceptions within firms in an industry, reveals the extent of this diversity.

Firms evolve in industries as complex non-linear dynamic organisations. As such, the specific nature of firms' strategic behaviour may have an underlying pattern, but may also be random and unpredictable. Industry competition reflects non-equilibrium, paradoxical forces and contradictions. Organisations who can sustain contradictions, through the on-going process of transformation management, will innovate and survive. The complexity of industry competition is mirrored in the diversity of managerial perceptions of strategy and with which, empirically, this study concurs.

Cognitive Consensus, Emergent Solutions and Realised Strategy

In this book attention has been drawn to the juxtaposition of cognitive groups across the brewing industry. In the dynamic conditions of industry competition, complexity and entropy would lead us to predict that such juxtapositions would be found. The cognitive lens perspective, as a research methodology, lends itself to the practical identification, within firms, of this temporal coexistence of spatially contradictory perceptions. Thus, it provides a practical tool in the process of transformation management.

As a practical management tool, the cognitive lens perspective can be utilised to create consensus from the broad range of possibilities and emergent solutions that are expressed through the differential cognitions of managers. Transforming entropy through a focus on the interconnectedness of emergent solutions can provide a powerful tool in the creation of realised strategy.

Directions for Future Research

This research has questioned the ontological status of strategic groups in their popularised form. Moreover, when the notion of strategic groups is reconceptualised as "cognitive strategic groups", several interesting research possibilities arise. Researchers could examine more closely the efficacy of this notion across industry sectors and the perspective of industry competition from a managerial perceptions standpoint.

The fact that this study found a strong congruence between the consensus of the three-factor strategy and firms' strategic behaviour in a post regulatory phase, suggests that this method may be a reliable and valid method of identifying overall future strategic directions. Moreover, by exploring the types of roles managers within firms play; it may be possible to clarify intrafirm dissimilarities along key dimensions, which enhance the transformation process.

Moreover, there is the potential to significantly refine the concept of strategic groups through a multi-industry research approach. This research could also explore any differences between industries, taking into consideration technological sophistication, levels of maturity and differences between industry sectors ranging from manufacturing to service.

Limitations of Cognitive Group Research

A problem with strategic groups in their prescriptive sense, is that they do not reflect the realities of the changing competitive environment. They are based on structural associations rather than perceived responses to actual competitive behaviour. While cognitive group research may overcome some of the structural bias towards the association of firms into strategic groups, it nevertheless faces the problem of scale in relation to the predictability of industry developments. Whilst the accuracy of managerial perceptions of strategic dimensions in this study undoubtedly relates more realistically with actual competitive strategies rather than the prediction of homogenous cognitive groups per se, the scale of research required to forecast future industry strategy remains a limiting factor.

At the level of the firm, utilising a cognitive lens perspective of manager's perceptions of competitive strategic dimensions may well assist in predicting realised strategy, if not strategic groups. Indeed, on the basis of this research, such a claim could have been made in relation to the exercise conducted with managers in Scottish and Newcastle. Their subsequent acquisition of a major brand (Courage) which gave them national geographical scope, linked with volume and distribution economies, could be discerned as a viable emergent strategy from the prior cognitive lens exercise.

However, since this study focussed on only one industry that faced a rather unique environmental challenge from regulation in terms of its historiography, the generalizability of the results must be interpreted with caution. To determine the generalizability of this approach, future research will be necessary in other industries, perhaps facing different environmental conditions.

The intensive methodology necessary to collect the data limits the extent of cognitive research across multiple industries. This limitation may be overcome by research that identifies an "optimal" number of subjects and firms across industries, which can then be regarded for study as a "cognitive community" (Porac et al, 1989; Reger and Huff, 1993). However, what must be cautioned is the view that "cognitive communities", while perhaps being able to be specific about firm prototypes in an industry, represent robust maps of managers understanding and by implications their agreement about strategic dimensions across the entire spectrum of industry competition. Extending the identification of prototypical firms to include assumptions that managers share common perceptions about strategic dimensions is more of a leap of faith than an approach that yields understanding of individuals' cognitive mapping.

PART IV Implications

Chapter 7 Strategic Management of a Third Kind: Towards a Paradigm of Strategy as Rationality, Fairness and Integration

Introduction

This book began with reference to the crucible of experience as the background against which the process of strategic management takes place. This process is informed by the cognitions of manager's; borne of experience tempered by the variability of choices and outcomes.

Theories of strategic management that attempt to differentiate between the object of study, namely strategy, and the organism of the object, the "strategist", blinker the researcher from the richness of the source of strategic behaviour. Thus, studies which ignore the strategist and elevate the strategy to the level of a theory or framework, have a tendency to limit our understanding and exploration of the here and now of the realities of this strategic behaviour. As such, much of the theorising becomes dogma. This dogma can constrain our empiricism and restrict our inclination for the freedom of exploration.

The word empirical means, based on observation and experiment, not theory, and comes from the Greek, *empeirikos*, meaning experience. Theories, by definition, are suppositions explaining something based on principles independent of the phenomena to be explained. But theories and empiricism have something in common, the explanations they provide must be derivable from, and related to, what has gone before. In this sense while we may live with their explanations, we must regard them as expendable; they are designed to be tested.

This book has attempted to test the theory of "strategic groups", from the empirical standpoint of the experience and cognitions of manager's as sources of strategic behaviour. It has explored the reality of strategic groups through the experience of "insiders". This exploration has been conducted from the point of view that strategic behaviour within competitive environments has more in common with the exercise of freedom, than the constrained attachment to economic paradigms. Such paradigms do not, in reality, mirror the search for freedom of movement in competitive behaviour, based on human experience. The theory of strategic groups by implication and assertion claims to provide point and direction for particular firms in specific industries. But theories, which attempt to explain firms' strategies without reference to the cognitions of strategists, by their very nature, cannot provide point and direction for entire groups within sectors. On this issue of theories, George Kelly, whose construct elicitation methodology played an important part in this research, has stated that, "theories are the thinking of men who seek freedom amid swirling events". Such theories require experience about certain realms of these events, so that the events themselves, from this prior experience, may be construed and paths followed which allow control and freedom of manoeuvre in the process. In this sense when we engage in theories of organisation strategy, we should attempt to redefine strategy as a strategy of persons, in the way that Kelly's personal construct theory redefined psychology as a psychology of persons (Bannister and Fransella, 1971).

Construct theory was deliberately stated in very broad terms in order to avoid the very limitations suggested above with regard to the narrowness of concepts such as strategic groups. In Kelly's terms the notion of a "theory" was to be reserved for structures of ideas that have a wide range of convenience, rather than being tied to one particular concept-phenomenon. In considering the notion of strategic groups, such a range of convenience is necessary so that we may ultimately explain strategic decisions that were perhaps not even envisaged prior to the point when they were constructed.

The research outlined in this book has identified "generic" strategic dimensions across an industry in contrast to the prescriptions of strategic group theory that assumes homogeneity among decision-makers within the same firms about key strategic dimensions. What it has indicated is that there is a strategy of persons in a particular industry that requires a new paradigm providing a range of convenience, which enables a more meaningful understanding of how strategy formulation and implementation operates in reality. Strategic dimensions denote the bridge between the discrete choices of the market and the organisation of strategy as a creative response. The remainder of this chapter will attempt to outline an approach towards such a paradigm.

Perfect Rationality

The notion of 'perfect rationality' in decision-making (promulgated most notably in economic theory) characterises perfection in human decision-making as an expressive proposition. However, simple heuristics play a significant role in human behaviour and in their decision-making; people do not exhibit perfect rationality but behave "predictably irrationally" (Ariely, 2010), due to a commingled fusion of bias, prejudice, misunderstanding, lack of knowledge, lack of ability, issues with data and a host of other behavioural influences that mitigate against expressive or prescriptive propositions. This results in the assumptions based on the rationality perspective, such as those held among scholars writing on strategic groups, eschewing the rather messy reality that strategic decision-makers do not conform with the neat characteristics of homogeneity, but have substantially different perceptions of strategic dimensions; even within the same organisations.

However, the developments of frameworks for decision-making based on heuristics that guide collective behaviour is a powerful influence on strategy. Indeed, the application of heuristics in the strategy making process, guiding decision-making, is a rational response and by its very nature manifests rational behaviour. Thus the application of heuristics may result in our decision-making being broadly right; although certain aspects may be precisely wrong (in a 'perfectly rational' sense).

In an analogous way, the merits of perfect rationality were alluded to by Friederick Hayek (1945) in his challenge to economic rationality when he disputed that scarcity was not the essence of the problems of economics. He argued that because market wants are elusive, that allocative decisions made by so-called experts were an imposition on the markets decisions (in terms of individuals' decisions) about what consumers themselves actually wanted. For Hayek, the problem faced by economics was not scarcity but how to secure the best use of resources to members of society (the market) for ends whose relative importance only they understood for themselves. In the Hayekian sense, the decisions of authorities could be just as 'predictably irrational' as the individuals they purported to influence/guide because being drawn from the population themselves, their decision-making was as defective as anyone else's and subject to the same irrational limitations (McKenzie and Lee, 2017).

The Hayekian insights serve to inform us of the apparent paradox displayed in the analysis of the data on the variability of the managerial cognitions between managers in the same firms and the overwhelming evidence from the Three Factor Solution. While individuals within the same firms did not cluster in any meaningfully prescriptive cognitive sense as often assumed in the literature on strategic groups, the importance of specific dimensions to strategy implementation was significantly clear and recognised in the factor loadings; the strategic emphasis was guided by the collective heuristics of the decision-makers.

What the factor loadings indicate is the utilisation of the knowledge of the key strategic dimensions emanating from the entire sample of decision-makers, rather than from any particular decision-maker or like-minded groups of decision-makers within firms. The utilisation of the knowledge regarding the strategic intent provided by the factor loadings, is a reflection of the best use of resources based on the importance of what the market wants. In this sense, the positional view of strategic management is determined by the market, rather than by allocations based on homogenous managerial cognitions from within the firms. Notwithstanding the diversity of managerial cognitions within firms, the heterogeneity in conjunction with the factor loadings exhibits an important feature of heuristic behaviour that has collectively served the human condition both defensively and pro-actively in evolution; namely, the phenomenon of herding.

The factor loadings mirror the 'herding' phenomenon characteristic of human behaviour. However, herding is not irrational behaviour-even when the protagonists do not have scientific data that affirms the herding behaviour. While herding has its risks, it undoubtedly may provide a simpler heuristic when uncertainty exists. Other members of the herd (firms) may be perceived to possess information or data that others do not, and abandoning the 'safety' of the herd may carry significantly higher risks.

Utilising the herding phenomenon in relation to the factor loadings highlights an interesting aspect of strategic groups in that they represent clusters of firms responding to markets, through a form of cooperation that manifests itself in the pursuit of similar strategic dimensions at the level of the industry. At the same time however, the firms in the group are viewed as competitors and often as direct competitors. In this sense they represent firms within markets with a common interest displayed through a dominant strategy. As in the discussion of differentiation strategy (Chapter 2), in a broad product-market sense where particular characteristics provide utility and discrete choices, the similarity of strategic dimensions that make groups identifiable mirrors the demand-side of these discrete characteristics. However, strategic groups do not fit with the classical notions of the 'common interest theory' of group behaviour.

Unlike the common interest theory of group behaviour, where the group has a life of its own (McKenzie and Lee, 2017), strategic groups comprise of individual firms who have a life of their own within the market. The structure and conditions of the market invokes a strategic response that may reflect firms' shared objectives in pursuing the same customers and in that sense strategic groups have a common interest, but they do not intend the same advantage in the way that common interest groups (for example, environmental pressure groups) have an incentive to work with others to pursue the same interest.

Certain examples may suggest that firms work together as common interest groups (for example, the soft drinks industry lobby against the imposition of a sugar tax), but as competitors they do not intend to maximise the groups welfare as a single entity as in the case of an environmental pressure group. Strategic group incumbents are competing with other firms along the same dimensions to maximise their own welfare. Firm's within strategic groups have their own rational self-interest that mitigates against them acting to achieve group interests. In this sense we might regard strategic groups as an example of 'club goods', where the common interest of the group does not yield private benefits as in the case of *private goods* (the slimming group) nor as benefits that are shared as in the case of *public goods* (the pavement shared between the road and your property), but as members of a group defined by their dominant strategy that reflects market conditions and industry evolution within the context of their rational self-interest. While the concept of mobility barriers (chapter 2) encourages the notion of firms existing within 'strategic groups' on the basis that group specific barriers act as a deterrent to competition from both external and internal industry competition, it distorts the realities of the industry structure that reflects the dominant strategy.

In the UK brewing case, strategic group identity emanates from the evolution of the dominant strategy and structure of the industry; not from the existence of the homogeneity of strategic dimensions of particular firms. In this respect the dominant strategy perspective (chapter 6) concurs with the Chandlerian view that oligopolistic structures are not inherently inefficient, but on the contrary evolve and adapt to the changes in market wants. Notwithstanding the growth in 'craft beers' in the UK, internalising market transactions through an oligopolistic structure has resulted in continued innovation in the industry. This structure is the response to a dominant strategy that continues to be evident among firms in other industries; automobiles, electronics, banking and finance, information technology, distribution and logistics, energy, pharmaceuticals and others where efficiencies through scope and scale reflect a rational response to market wants and contribute significantly to economic growth.

Strategy as Knowledge Creation

Strategist's cognition of key competitive dimensions is a function of their knowledge and learning, borne of experience. The weight placed on particular dimensions of competition reflects the knowledge that is stored in memory and which has been created by the assimilation of education and training, trial and error, action and reaction, lost opportunities, failures and successes, understanding and misunderstanding. Whether narrow or wide, managers' experience of strategizing is a process of knowledge creation. By its very nature this process is a commingled one and cannot represent the same experience for each individual, for it is also a process of conscious and subconscious influences.

Strategy as the Economics of Co-creation

To propound that strategizing is a straightforward rational process, based on analysing the environment, identifying strengths and weaknesses, and embarking on decisions to achieve goals, is to denigrate the process of strategy making in organisations. Strategy making in firms is a process of social organisation where people both shape and are shaped by the economics of co-creation. By this is meant the continual search for a means whereby the economics of internal organisation of the firm adapts to and influences changes in its environment.

This process does not necessarily entail competition by the firm with its environment, but co-operation. Competition is itself a social process, where one firms actions will be based on the knowledge of other firms developments in the same environment. Seeking adjustments to strategy as a result of this knowledge can be viewed as a form of co-creative co-operation within the context of adding to the adaptiveness of organisations with each other.

Indeed, even in terms of the economic rationality proposed by game theory, what we encounter in the propositions of the "Nash Equilibrium", is a recognition and tacit acknowledgement that this point is only reached as a result of the cognitive process of co-creative co-operation.

The adaptiveness of one organisation to the environment can create shared knowledge for another and as such forms part of that organisations own co-operation with the environment. Indeed, firms may exert control over the environment through this process of co-creative co-operation in a symbiotic fashion, which bears more resemblance to environmental socialisation than naked competition.

Such environmental socialisation is perhaps what Adam Smith actually meant when he referred to the "invisible hand" in economic activity. Markets can be viewed as "creations" in which organisations, operating within a legal framework with people who have knowledge of the market system, can bring about transactions of an appropriate level to make exchange competitively profitable.

The structure-performance-conduct paradigm explains the competitiveness of the firm in terms of the integration of its strategy and structure. However, what is being propounded here is a paradigm in which there is a distinct departure from the purely organisational concept of structure. What is being stressed here is the "inter-subjective dimension" of human organisation within the firm. There are parallels' to this paradigm. The harmonisation model of Japanese enterprise is based on a continuous extension of the concept of knowledge creation, assimilated and providing meaning to the process of work, which translates itself into competitive strategy. Success is built upon the integration of rational economic activity with an "inter-subjective dimension" to produce a new form of institutional economics. Within the context of the institutional economics of Japanese firms, the specificity of the "inter-subjective dimension" represents a difference in the degree of commitment to the paradigm. In particular industry cases, this commitment manifests itself in a strategic orientation that is a continuum of historical evolution.

While accepting Adam Smith's proposition that productivity depended on specialisation (in order to achieve low transaction costs), in elaborate systems of exchange, as found in modern industrial economies, low transaction costs are achieved through inter-organisational co-operation. The prescriptive assumption of homogeneity among decision-makers within strategic groups perhaps stems from the classic notion of rationality emanating from the classical economic perspective. This research indicates that to some extent this is true at the level of the industry sector where the influence of the competitive dynamics imposes a positional logic on the incumbents. Thus, while the evidence of heterogeneity in decision-making among individuals in the same firm and across firms is clear from the cluster analysis, the three factor strategy loadings (chapter 6) indicate a strong positional response to the strategic imperatives of the sector. In this respect the Porteresque prescription of strategy as denoting a particular response to the determinants of industry dynamics and structure represents a valid proposition. However, it is one that reflects decision-making based on heuristics that guide collective behaviour in the strategy process.

The Japanese Paradigm

Within the boundaries of specialisation, in the post-World War II era, the Japanese paradigm has enlarged the potential for human labour and inter-organisational collaboration by adopting an approach opposite to that traditionally pursued by western firms.

In the notion of competitive advantage in post-modern prescriptive theory, there is the suggestion that there is almost irreconcilable "social distance" between firms in a sector. Competition is perceived as recognisably adversarial. In this view, organisational institutional structure is responsible for the tendency of prohibitive social distance between firms. This notion is portrayed in the concept of strategic groups.

However, an analysis of the Japanese paradigm reveals that this model works meaningfully in antagonistic environments because the Japanese paradigm relies heavily by design on trusting interaction between trading entities. When trading behaviour is assumed to be dictated by market forces in the tradition of neo-classical economic theory, the application of the concept of trading opportunities is fairly simple. That is, give fair opportunities to competing agents in the market place, let them bid, and give contracts to those who bid the cheapest. From this understanding the classical mass production system perfected the phenomenon of the interchangeable supplier.

While western industrial economies were extending this concept to the market in the post-World War II era, Japanese firms worked on their own version of fair trading opportunities based on radically different principles. For example, together with the development of contract assembly and systems components outsourcing, which made it dysfunctional to rely on market prices, the Japanese developed the cost targeting method. This entailed the decomposition of complex cost structures and the identification, item by item, of parts and cost sensitive elements. In this exercise, assemblers and suppliers shared cost information. Instead of negotiating prices downstream, assemblers began to work at the possibility of reducing costs at source by means of joint problem solving projects based on the value analysis method. Using joint value engineering, suppliers became involved in assembler designs in order to reduce costs. Consequently, continuous cost reduction became systemised during the course of a product life cycle, and the 50/50 profit sharing principle between buyer and supplier was established.

The proceeding Japanese share of world trade was a testament to the success of this paradigm, which had at its roots a philosophy of co-creation and co-operation. By combining formerly laissez-faire trading patterns with strategies of knowledge creation and co-operation, Japanese firms disentangled the myths of economic rationality from the realities of the market and strategic management.

Strategy as Orchestral Management

Strategic analysis utilising rational frameworks such as Porters five forces framework, the so called generic strategies, matrix analysis, SWOT analysis, value chain analysis and so on, combined with detailed financial analysis, arguably represent fairly simple ways of informing organisations about actual and potential economic positions. While this form of analysis is useful and undoubtedly plays a role in the analysis of industry competition, the actual implementation of strategies to secure and maintain advantage in competitive environments is a humanistic process. What has been shown in this study is how a number of different dimensions can be stressed as more important than others by different managers within the same firm, as well as by managers across firms in the same sector. Even when managers can agree on decisions arrived at through rational economic analysis, the process of translating this agreement into strategic actions shifts the emphasis of implementation to a deeper level of human engagement. The process of this engagement produces encounters, which are rooted in non-rational influences and barriers.

This implementation activity is well recognised in the literature on strategic management, which offers a number of examples whereby the process of strategy implementation can be more effectively accommodated (Balogun, Hailey and Gustafsson, 2016). As a contribution to this implementation process, the cognitive lens approach adopted in this study provides a method of identifying both the dimensions of rational analysis and the deeper perceptual differences between managers, which require resolution in the process of effective implementation.

There is an assumption in the prescriptive analysis of strategic groups that suggests that managers can agree the rational dimensions; but what this study shows is that this is not the case. There is little chance of the process of implementation being successful, if the dimensions cannot be reconciled to form the basis of cooperation and a coherent strategy, which acknowledges and recognises the knowledge creation and learning inherent in the heuristics of diverse individuals shaped by a dominant strategy. This reconciliation of strategic dimensions is a crucial aspect of the effective transformation process in strategy implementation. To this extent, this study provides evidence of how managers in the brewing industry share cognitions of the importance of generic strategic dimensions across the industry, but do not share homogenous perceptions of dimensions within firms in the industry. This is not surprising, since their knowledge and experience of strategic dimensions at the level of the firm will be assimilated differently. However, they find convergence when it comes to the generic competitive strategies they actually pursue. This convergence is due to the influence of the evolutionary and historical strategy that has shaped the structure and heuristics of the industry in responding to market wants. In this regard, there is significant evidence that humans have genetically evolved to co-operate and work together for their own survival and economic welfare (Rubin, 2002;

Hirshleifer, 1999; Ridley, 2008) and indeed, that individuals would rather be regarded as co-operators, even when they are not.

The focus of strategic management lies in revitalising the organisation and in nurturing new developmental activities. Disharmony between the alliance of these two areas lies at the root of many failed enterprises.

The successful performance of an orchestra cannot be expected if there is a lack of co-ordination among its players, or if even one of them is out of tune with the rest. Likewise, while individual decision-makers in an organisation have their own identity as members of a managerial alliance, at the same time they are required to work with other parties in a co-operative and harmonious manner. It is people who make an organisation functional and the essence of strategic management is to orchestrate different alliances into an entity where harmonious revitalisation and development can take place.

Strategy as orchestral management requires horizontal networking as opposed to the reaffirmation of vertical relationships and co-ordination. As described above, a key element of the Japanese paradigm is the existence of mutual trust and confidence. Sustaining an organisation, through revitalisation and development, requires tuning, which harmonises the knowledge and activities of different parties based on a philosophy of trust and confidence. What might be termed the heart-to-heart association of different alliances, combined with a sharp sense of responsiveness to the co-creative competitive environment, lies at the core of this philosophy.

"Heart-to-heart" harmony in the autonomous, decentralised structure, interlinked by lateral alliances, can form and strengthen the sense of 'mutual trust and confidence' in organisations. Sharing this common philosophy is the enabling process of strategic transformation on a continuing basis and the process whereby strategy is creative and precise.

In developing this paradigm several factors contribute to influence the process. Firstly, participating members must be able to confirm that each party possesses specific advantages from which they can mutually benefit. Secondly, constant efforts are required to maintain and nurture mutual advantages and benefits. Thirdly, information has to be shared to upgrade the extent of mutual understanding. Intra-firm alliance begins with the sharing of information between top management, between middle management, and between teams and groups of employees. The accumulation of this effort will generate mutual trust and confidence. This stage will enable the "strategies of persons" to take stock of past experiences and decisions and confirm whether the philosophy and vision, as well as the strategic direction, remains valid or not under given circumstances. These processes epitomise strategy as orchestral management and can be illustrated in the following figure:

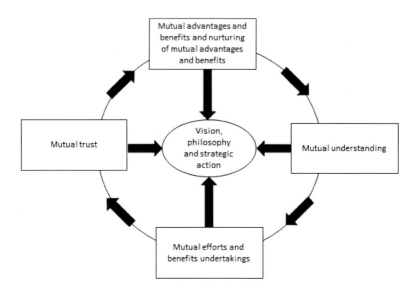

Figure 23. Orchestral management cycle and the formation of mutual trust

This process facilitates the creation and accumulation of knowledge and can be superimposed on Nonaka's (1995) content of knowledge creation, to produce a model of orchestral management, knowledge creation and strategy.

Rationality, Fairness and Integration

The orchestral management cycle and the formation of mutual trust is a knowledge creation process. The notion of orchestral management recognises the diversity of perceptions between individuals, in the process of reconciling these perceptions to form a coherent strategic response to competitive conditions. The links between orchestral management, knowledge creation and strategy require continued reinforcement in the ever present need to adjust to changes in these competitive conditions.

This reinforcement and motivation produce the dynamics of competitive behaviour, which, as has been suggested earlier (Chapter 3), provides a pattern in strategic-decision making within a context that at times appears random and chaotic. This inter-subjective dimension of human organisation reflects the search for freedom of movement in competitive behaviour, based on human experience. It is the process whereby thinking people seek freedom amid the swirling events of competition. It is not the 'orderly' adoption by individuals sharing a homogenous sense of a firm's strategy, as suggested by a prescriptive theory based on the rationality premise alone.

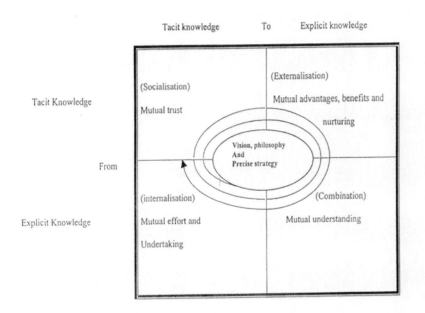

Figure 18: Orchestral management, knowledge creation and strategy

Rafferty,J. 1999

Figure 24. Orchestral management, knowledge creation and strategy

In the competitive environment inter and intra organisational relations are a long-standing product of socio-economic, technological, political and co-creative factors. Through this study, together with the writer's own experience and ongoing research, there has emerged three norms that at the generalised level, account for the successful strategic adaptation of firms to the competitive environment; namely, fairness, rationality and integration.

The process of orchestral management is a process of knowledge creation based on mutual trust and confidence. It is a process whereby fairness becomes the ethos within which alliances can be built for mutual advantage, in the same way that Japanese producers developed the system of "fair trading" through co-creative co-operation with suppliers.

The rationality of strategic change in essence refers to the context of strategy. Conventionally, this is divided into two parts; namely, the outer, economic, social and competitive context; and the inner, structure, culture and political context. In the popular literature on strategic change the context forms one apex of a triangular model whose two other points of reference are the content and the process. This model can be illustrated as follows:

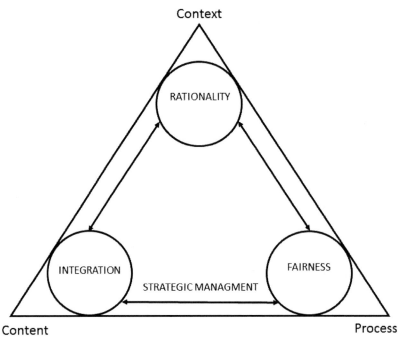

Rafferty J. *Strategic Groups and Management Perceptions* 1999

Figure 25. Context, Content and Process

Content refers to the areas of change under examination, for example, technology, manpower, products, scope and markets. The process refers to the actions, reactions and interactions of the organisation. However, this model is still lacking an understanding of the humanistic dimension of strategy as the integration of "strategies of persons". The above model stops short of explaining how the integration of the context, content and process actually takes place. The orchestral management, knowledge creation and strategy model illustrated in Figure 18 provides this missing link. The model provides the integrating mechanism whereby the successful reconciliation and co-ordination of strategic change takes place and can be illustrated as follows:

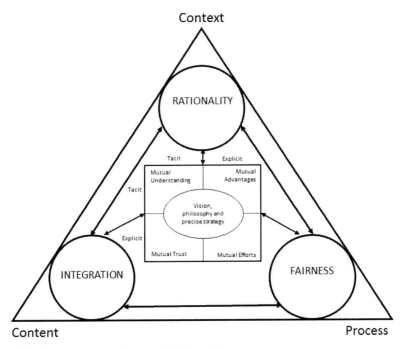

Rafferty J. *Strategic Groups and Management Perceptions* 1999

Figure 26. Strategic Management as Integration, Rationality and Fairness

This model provides an understanding of strategy as a humanistic process that is continually engaged in exercising freedom of movement amid changing competitive conditions. It represents the managerial corollary paradigm of Adam Smith's "invisible hand". The hidden strategy referred to in the quotation from Sun Tzu at the beginning of this book, is perhaps alluding to a managerial paradigm of strategy as orchestral management guided by the norms of rationality, fairness and integration. In this lies the success of organisations in shaping their competitive response, which in turn shapes the process of learning and knowledge creation within the firm. This notion of the "invisible hand" may at one level provide an explanation as to why, across an industry where there is a dominant generic strategy, some firms are more successful than others and why the notion of strategic groups, while attractive from a theoretical point of view, is nevertheless a somewhat misleading phenomenon in reality.

This book has explored the assumptions and realities underlying the notion of cognitive strategic groups. While it has been demonstrated that managers in a particular industry are capable of categorising firms on the basis of configurations that enable them to be grouped in a prototypical fashion (Reger and Huff, 1993), the same cannot be said of their individual cognitions when attempting to link perceptions of key strategic dimensions to strategic actions.

The assumption of homogeneity between perceptions of strategic dimensions at the level of firm cannot be relied upon. In this study, managers within the same firms have not shared group cognitions about strategic dimensions; there is a discrepancy between their perceptions of strategic dimensions at the level of the firm. However, the evolution of the industry reflects a congruency in strategic behaviour towards concentration and oligopoly, which serves to illustrate that it is not necessary for individuals within firms to share common perceptions of strategic dimensions in order to exhibit strategic decision-making that suggests group agreement and uniformity.

Managers cognitively frame their strategic decisions on their environment, borne of the evolution of strategy and structure in their industry. While at an individual level their preferences for specific competitive dimensions may differ widely within and across firms. At a strategic level, decision-making and the consistency informed by bounded rationality produces a heuristic response that is shaped by the historical links between strategy and structure. The decision criteria that has informed the scope and scale characteristics of the UK Brewing industry and that give it its oligopolistic structure, reflects a constraining effect of the dominant strategy of cost-leadership differentiation evident in this study.

The 'group' level identity emerges at the level of the industry because it is shaped by the evolution and heuristics of a strategy and structure that offers an economic response to the possibilities of optimising market wants. In the Chandlerian sense, managers shape the structure of their industry to reflect the strategies that offer efficiencies through scope and scale considerations. Notwithstanding the emergence of 'sub-structures' in the form of 'craft brewers' in the UK, the overriding scope and scale characteristics dramatize the concentration of the industry.

In this study, group level identities do not emerge as cognitive groups forming meaningful sub-structures (Petraf and Shanley, 1997). On the contrary, an industry-level cognitive identity emerges in terms of strategy and structure within the industry that gives coherence to firm actions. Managers within firms have weak identities and do not form cognitive strategic groups in any meaningful sense. The strong identity emerges across the industry in the form of a cognitive consensus about a dominant strategy that coalesces with a corresponding industry structure. At the level of the industry the evidence suggests a shared understanding, rather than a mutual understanding at the level of the firm; where sub-structures of firms possessing strategic group identities would be anticipated within the parameters of strategic group theory. Thus, "while the central characteristics of an organisation must be enduring" (Petraf and Shanley, 1997:166), so may the dominant strategy and structure of an industry provide an enduring degree of temporal stability and perceived continuity at the level of the industry.

Appendices

Appendix I The Strategic Dimensions

Elicited dimensions in the strategic dimensions questionnaire.

1. *National Geographical Spread:* the geographical spread of operations in terms of production and the markets served.
2. *Regional Geographical Spread:* the degree to which focus of operations in terms of product lines and customer segments plays an important role in competition.
3. *Innovation:* the degree to which technological leadership and technical and market innovations are seen as important versus following or imitation. Such innovations may include new product development, new financial arrangements with distribution channels etc.
4. *Free Trade Penetration:* the extent to which firms seek to develop brand identification with the ultimate consumer through the support of free trade distribution channels in selling their products.
5. *Diversification:* the degree of related diversification activities in terms of the importance of these as a percentage of total turnover.
6. *Wholesaling:* the extent to which imported brands are brewed and distribution through licensing agreements and the supply of own-label brands through major supermarket chains.
7. *Distribution:* the choice of distribution channels ranging from the off-trade and the on-trade through tied and free trade public houses.
8. *Management Structure*: the relationship with a parent company and the nature of this relationship in influencing the objectives with which the firm is managed and the resources available to it.
9. *Prices:* the firms' relative price position in the market.
10. *Quality:* the firm's product quality in terms of raw materials, specifications and adherence to beverage standards etc.
11. *Advertising:* the degree to which the firm seeks brand identification through advertising.
12. *Image:* the extent to which the firm seeks to develop brand identification through the presentation of a particular image to specific target customers segments.
13. *Product Range:* the degree to which the firm focuses on the width of its product line in terms of broad versus narrow.
14. *Economics of Scale:* the extent to which the firm seeks a low-cost position in production and distribution through investments in cost-minimising facilities and equipment.
15. *Product Brands:* the extent to which the firm seeks to develop brand

identification through differentiation rather than compete or price.

16. ***Horizontal Integration:*** the degree of horizontal integration in controlling and monitoring operating costs and securing distribution channels.

17. ***Service:*** the degree to which the firm provides ancillary services with its product line, such as training assistance, technical assistance, catering assistance and so on.

18. ***Pay and Salaries:*** the firm's relative position in the industry in providing competitive remuneration's to its employees.

19. ***Packaging:*** the extent to which packaging plays an important role in brand identification and distribution.

20. ***Organisational Efficiency***: the extent to which networks and information systems add value through cost effectiveness.

21. ***Vertical Integration:*** the extent of value added as reflected in the level of forward and backward integration adopted, including whether the firm has captive distribution channels or exclusive or owned retail outlets.

22. ***Outlet Mix:*** the extent to which the choice of distribution outlets ranging from company-owned channels to speciality outlets such as wine bars, licensed clubs and the grocery trade affect competitiveness.

23. ***Market Share:*** the degree to which market share of the geographical markets served affects competitiveness.

24. ***Process Technology:*** the extent to which process technology and quality go together.

25. ***Discounts:*** the degree to which product volume discounts affect distribution.

26. ***Brewery Loans:*** the extent to which financial leverage relationships with distribution channels influences product sales.

Appendix II: Questionnaire

Company: ……………………...…….. Position: ….…………….

These dimensions are of importance to competitive success in the Brewing Industry.

Please tick (☐) the column which best describes your personal view of the importance of each dimension to competitiveness in the industry.

	Strongly Agree	Agree	Neither agree or disagree	Disagree	Strongly disagree
National geographical spread	☐	☐	☐	☐	☐
Regional geographical spread	☐	☐	☐	☐	☐
Innovation	☐	☐	☐	☐	☐
Free trade penetration	☐	☐	☐	☐	☐
Diversification	☐	☐	☐	☐	☐
Wholesaling	☐	☐	☐	☐	☐
Distribution	☐	☐	☐	☐	☐
Management structure	☐	☐	☐	☐	☐
Prices	☐	☐	☐	☐	☐
Quality	☐	☐	☐	☐	☐
Advertising	☐	☐	☐	☐	☐
Image	☐	☐	☐	☐	☐
Product range	☐	☐	☐	☐	☐
Economies of scale	☐	☐	☐	☐	☐
Product brands	☐	☐	☐	☐	☐
Horizontal integration	☐	☐	☐	☐	☐
Service	☐	☐	☐	☐	☐
Pay and salaries	☐	☐	☐	☐	☐
Packaging	☐	☐	☐	☐	☐
Organisational efficiency	☐	☐	☐	☐	☐
Vertical integration	☐	☐	☐	☐	☐
Outlet mix	☐	☐	☐	☐	☐
Market share	☐	☐	☐	☐	☐
Process technology	☐	☐	☐	☐	☐
Discounts	☐	☐	☐	☐	☐
Brewery loans	☐	☐	☐	☐	☐

Appendix III: The Repertory Grid

Appendix IV: Construct Elements

ELEMENTS	RANDOM NUMBER
WATNEYS	1
GREENE KING	2
AYLESBURY BREWING	3
WHITBREADS	4
SCOTTISH & NEWCASTLE	5
RUDDLES	6
COURAGE	7

Appendix V: Triads of Elements

CODE	TRIAD RANDOM COMBINATION	CODE	TRIAD RANDOM COMBINATION
A	1 2 6	AA	1 2 3
B	1 5 6	BB	1 2 6
C	1 2 4	CC	3 5 6
D	1 3 4	DD	1 3 6
E	4 5 6	EE	1 3 7
F	4 5 7	FF	2 4 5
G	1 4 6		
H	2 5 7		
I	3 4 7		
J	3 4 5		
K	2 3 6		
L	4 5 7		
M	2 3 7		
N	4 6 7		
O	1 4 5		
P	2 5 6		
Q	3 6 7		
R	3 4 7		
S	3 4 6		
T	2 4 5		
U	2 3 4		
V	1 5 6		
W	1 3 5		
X	3 5 6		
Y	1 4 7		
Z	2 5 7		

Appendix VI

METHOD OF CONSTRUCT ELICITATION

MINIMUM CONTEXT CARD FORM

IN WHAT WAYS ARE TWO OF THE THREE COMPANIES SIMILAR AND
IN WHAT WAY IS THE THIRD DISSIMILAR FROM THE OTHER TWO?

Appendix VII Triad of Elements

TRIAD OF ELEMENTS

ORDER OF SHOWING TRIADS:

<u>RESPONDENTS</u>

CODE

L	FF	EE	N	D	L
M	AA	W	D	L	S
N	P	A	X	I	DD
J	U	R	BB	V	P
D	C	FF	O	Q	W
V	Q	T	V	CC	H
U	A	J	H	A	C
K	Y	B	Y	X	FF
I	BB	Z	P	E	B
C	K	I	G	U	J

Appendix VIII Strategic Dimensions

Pilot Study

Rated Order Grid

	STRONGLY AGREE	AGREE	NEITHER AGREE NOR DISAGREE	DISAGREE	STRONGLY DISAGREE
Location					
Prices					
Quality					
Advertising					
Image					
Product Range					
Economy of Scale					
Product Brand					
Horiz Integ.					
Service					
Pay					
Packaging					
Org Effect					
Vert Integ.					
Outlet Mix					
Market Share					
Process Tec					
Discounts					
Loans					

Please tick (☐) the column which best describes your view of the importance of each dimension to competitiveness in this industry.

Appendix IX: Summary of Pilot Variables

GET FILE = PILOT1
The SPSS/PC system file is read from file PILOT1
The file was created at 10:54:56 and is titled SPSS/PC+
The SPSS/PC+ system file contains
       15 bases, each consisting of
       22 variables (including system variables)
       22 variables will be used in this session.

This procedure was completed at 14:30:34 SPSS/PC:DESCRIBE ALL.

Number of Valid Observations (Listwise) = 15.00

Variable	Mean	Std Dev	Minimum	Maximum	N	Label
LO	3.80	1.08	2	5	15	Location
PR	4.13	.99	2	5	15	Price
QU	4.07	.88	3	5	15	Quality
AD	3.53	1.30	1	5	15	Advertising
IM	3.67	.90	2	5	15	Image
PRR	2.87	.99	1	5	15	Product Ran
ES	3.40	1.18	2	5	15	Econ Scale
PRB	3.53	.92	2	5	15	Prod Brand
HOI	2.67	.62	2	4	15	Hor Integ
SE	2.80	.56	2	4	15	Service
PAY	2.60	.99	1	4	15	Pay
PA	3.60	.91	1	5	15	Packaging
OE	3.60	.77	3	5	15	Org Eff
VI	2.13	.92	1	3	15	Vert Int
OM	2.87	.98	1	4	15	Outlet Mix
MS	3.27	.77	2	4	15	Mkt Share
PT	3.53	.92	2	5	15	Proc Tech
DI	2.87	.78	1	5	15	Discounts
L	3.00	.78	2	4	15	Loans

This procedure was completed at 14:31:49 SPSS/PC:

Appendix X: Hierarchical Cluster Analysis
Page 1 Hierarchical Cluster Analysis

Clustering of Pilot Study: Measure = Euclidean Method = Between Group Average Data Information: 15 unweighted cases accepted 0 cases rejected because of missing value
Euclidean measure used:
1. Agglomeration method specified. Euclidean Dissimilarity Coefficient Matrix

Case	1	2	3	4
2	7.2111			
3	7.1414	5.9161		
4	7.0711	5.2915	5.7446	
5	7.2111	6.3246	4.5826	5.0990
6	5.4772	6.2346	7.1414	6.3246
7	8.000	6.282	7.0000	5.0990
8	7.2111	0.0	5.9161	5.2915
9	7.6811	6.8557	7.0711	5.3852
Case	1	2	3	4
10	6.4.31	6.4031	5.8310	3.3166
11	6.0828	6.5574	6.6332	4.3589
12	7.8740	6.0000	4.7958	5.6569
13	5.2915	5.0990	4.5826	4.4721
14	7.1414	5.5678	4.4721	4.3589
15	7.2111	6.3246	5.3852	4.8990
Case	5	6	7	8
6	5.8310			
7	6.1644	7.3485		
8	6.3246	6.3246	6.9282	
9	6.4031	7.9373	4.1231	6.8557
10	4.3589	5.9161	5.7446	6.4031
11	5.0000	6.0828	4.3589	6.5574
12	4.2426	6.4807	7.0711	6.0000
13	3.7417	4.2426	5.6569	5.0990
14	4.7958	6.8557	4.5826	5.5678
15	3.1623	5.6569	5.8310	6.3246
Case	9	10	11	12
10	6.3246			
11	4.8990	4.0000		
12	7.9373	5.0000	6.0828	
13	5.9161	4.3589	4.1231	4.0000
14	5.2915	4.6904	4.8990	4.1231
14	6.2450	3.3166	4.7958	4.4721
Case	13	14		
14	4.3589			
15	4.0000	4.7958		

Appendix X page 2

Agglomeration Schedule using Average Linkage (Between Groups)

Clusters Combined				Stage Cluster 1st Appears Next		
Stage	Cluster 1	Cluster 2	Coefficient	Cluster 1	Cluster 2	Stage
1	2	8	0.0	0	0	0
2	5	15	3.162278	0	0	4
3	4	10	3.316625	0	0	7
4	5	13	3.870829	2	0	8
5	12	14	4.123106	0	0	8
6	7	9	4.123106	0	0	13
7	4	11	4.179450	3	0	9
8	5	12	4.444223	4	5	9
9	4	5	4.740760	7	8	10
10	3	4	5.253381	0	9	12
11	1	6	5.477226	0	0	14
12	2	3	5.942671	1	10	13
13	2	7	6.115854	12	6	14
14	1	2	6.692207	11	13	0

Cluster Membership of Cases using Average Linkage (Between Groups)

		Number of Clusters								
Label	Case	10	9	8	7	6	5	4	3	2
	1	1	1	1	1	1	1	1	1	1
	2	2	2	2	2	2	2	2	2	2
	3	3	3	3	3	3	3	3	2	2
	4	4	4	4	4	4	3	3	2	2
	5	5	5	5	5	4	3	3	2	2
	6	6	6	6	6	5	4	1	1	1
	7	7	7	7	7	6	5	4	3	2
	8	2	2	2	2	2	2	2	2	2
	9	8	7	7	7	6	5	4	3	2
	10	4	4	4	4	4	3	3	2	2
	11	9	8	4	4	4	3	3	2	2
	12	10	9	8	5	4	3	3	2	2
	13	5	5	5	5	4	3	3	2	2
	14	10	9	8	5	4	3	3	2	2
	15	5	5	5	5	4	3	3	2	2

Appendix X page 3

Rescaled Distance Cluster Combine

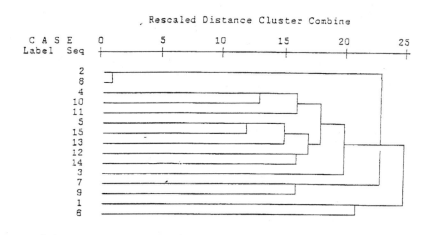

This procedure was completed at 14:28:28

Appendix XI Results from Pilot

Page 1 Results from Pilot

MTB > Cluo C21-C39;
SUBC> Complete;
SUBC> Cut 65;
SUBC> Dendrogram; SUBC> Ydist; SUBC> Member c40.

Hierarchical Cluster Analysis of Observations

Euclidean Distance, Complete Linkage

Amalgamation Steps

Step	Number of clusters	Similarity level	Distance level	Clusters joined		New cluster	Number of Obs in new cluster
1	14	100.00	0.000	2	8	2	2
2	13	60.47	3.162	5	15	5	2
3	12	58.54	3.317	4	10	4	2
4	11	50.00	4.000	12	14	12	2
5	10	50.00	4.000	5	13	5	3
6	9	48.46	4.123	7	9	7	2
7	8	45.51	4.359	4	11	4	3
8	7	40.05	4.796	3	12	3	3
9	6	36.26	5.099	4	5	4	6
10	5	31.53	5.477	1	6	1	2
11	4	25.00	6.000	2	3	2	5
12	3	19.96	6.403	4	7	4	8
13	2	1.57	7.874	1	2	1	7
14	1	0.00	8.000	1	4	1	15

Final Partition

Number of clusters: 14

	Number of observations	Within cluster sum of squares	Average distance from centroid	Maximum distance from centroid
Cluster1	1	0.000	0.000	0.000
Cluster2	2	0.000	0.000	0.000
Cluster3	1	0.000	0.000	0.000
Cluster4	1	0.000	0.000	0.000
Cluster5	1	0.000	0.000	0.000
Cluster6	1	0.000	0.000	0.000
Cluster7	1	0.000	0.000	0.000
Cluster8	1	0.000	0.000	0.000
Cluster9	1	0.000	0.000	0.000
Cluster10	1	0.000	0.000	0.000
Cluster11	1	0.000	0.000	0.000
Cluster12	1	0.000	0.000	0.000
Cluster13	1	0.000	0.000	0.000
Cluster14	1	0.000	0.000	0.000

Cluster Centroids

Variable	Cluster1	Cluster2	Cluster3	Cluster4	Cluster5
C21	3.0000	5.0000	5.0000	4.0000	5.0000
C22	2.0000	4.0000	5.0000	4.0000	5.0000
C23	3.0000	3.0000	5.0000	4.0000	5.0000
C24	5.0000	2.0000	4.0000	3.0000	4.0000
C25	4.0000	3.0000	3.0000	2.0000	4.0000
C26	4.0000	3.0000	5.0000	2.0000	3.0000
C27	4.0000	5.0000	3.0000	2.0000	4.0000
C28	5.0000	4.0000	4.0000	4.0000	3.0000
C29	4.0000	3.0000	3.0000	2.0000	2.0000
C30	3.0000	3.0000	4.0000	3.0000	3.0000
C31	3.0000	4.0000	3.0000	2.0000	1.0000

Appendix XI Page 2

C32	1.0000	4.0000	3.0000	4.0000	4.0000
C33	4.0000	5.0000	4.0000	4.0000	3.0000
C34	3.0000	3.0000	3.0000	1.0000	3.0000
C35	4.0000	1.0000	3.0000	2.0000	3.0000
C36	2.0000	4.0000	3.0000	3.0000	3.0000
C37	4.0000	5.0000	3.0000	4.0000	2.0000
C38	1.0000	3.0000	5.0000	3.0000	3.0000
C39	2.0000	3.0000	4.0000	2.0000	3.0000

Variable	Cluster6	Cluster7	Cluster8	Cluster9	Cluster10
C21	3.0000	2.0000	2.0000	4.0000	3.0000
C22	2.0000	4.0000	5.0000	4.0000	4.0000
C23	3.0000	4.0000	4.0000	5.0000	3.0000
C24	5.0000	1.0000	2.0000	4.0000	4.0000
C25	4.0000	4.0000	2.0000	4.0000	4.0000
C26	4.0000	2.0000	1.0000	3.0000	2.0000
C27	5.0000	2.0000	4.0000	2.0000	2.0000
C28	4.0000	2.0000	2.0000	4.0000	2.0000
C29	3.0000	3.0000	3.0000	2.0000	2.0000
C30	3.0000	3.0000	3.0000	2.0000	2.0000
C31	1.0000	3.0000	4.0000	2.0000	3.0000
C32	4.0000	4.0000	3.0000	4.0000	3.0000
C33	3.0000	3.0000	3.0000	4.0000	3.0000
C34	2.0000	1.0000	1.0000	1.0000	2.0000
C35	2.0000	4.0000	4.0000	2.0000	3.0000
C36	4.0000	4.0000	2.0000	2.0000	3.0000
C37	4.0000	3.0000	3.0000	3.0000	3.0000
C38	1.0000	3.0000	3.0000	2.0000	2.0000
C39	4.0000	3.0000	3.0000	2.0000	2.0000

Variable	Cluster11	Cluster12	Cluster13	Cluster14	Grand centrd
C21	5.0000	4.0000	3.0000	4.0000	3.8000
C22	5.0000	4.0000	5.0000	5.0000	4.1333
C23	5.0000	4.0000	5.0000	5.0000	4.0667
C24	5.0000	5.0000	3.0000	4.0000	3.5333
C25	5.0000	4.0000	5.0000	5.0000	3.7333
C26	3.0000	3.0000	2.0000	3.0000	2.8667
C27	3.0000	4.0000	2.0000	4.0000	3.4000
C28	4.0000	3.0000	4.0000	4.0000	3.5333
C29	2.0000	3.0000	3.0000	2.0000	2.6667
C30	2.0000	3.0000	3.0000	2.0000	2.8000
C31	2.0000	2.0000	3.0000	2.0000	2.6000
C32	5.0000	3.0000	4.0000	4.0000	3.6000
C33	5.0000	4.0000	4.0000	3.0000	3.8000
C34	3.0000	2.0000	3.0000	1.0000	2.1333
C35	3.0000	3.0000	3.0000	2.0000	2.6667
C36	4.0000	4.0000	3.0000	3.0000	3.2000
C37	4.0000	4.0000	4.0000	2.0000	3.5333
C38	4.0000	3.0000	4.0000	3.0000	2.8667
C39	4.0000	3.0000	4.0000	3.0000	3.0000

Distances Between Cluster Centroids

	Cluster1	Cluster2	Cluster3	Cluster4	Cluster5
Cluster1	0.0000	7.2111	7.1414	7.0711	7.2111
Cluster2	7.2111	0.0000	5.9161	5.2915	6.3246
Cluster3	7.1414	5.9161	0.0000	5.7446	4.5826
Cluster4	7.0711	5.2915	5.7446	0.0000	5.0990
Cluster5	7.2111	6.3246	4.5826	5.0990	0.0000
Cluster6	5.4772	6.3246	7.1414	6.3246	5.8310
Cluster7	8.0000	6.9282	7.0000	5.0990	6.1644
Cluster8	7.6811	6.8557	7.0711	5.3852	6.4031
Cluster9	6.4031	6.4031	5.8310	3.3166	4.3589
Cluster10	6.0828	6.5574	6.6332	4.3589	5.0000
Cluster11	7.8740	6.0000	4.7958	5.6569	4.2426
Cluster12	5.2915	5.0990	4.5826	4.4721	3.7417
Cluster13	7.2111	5.8310	4.7958	4.8990	4.8990
Cluster14	7.2111	6.3246	5.3852	4.8990	3.1623

Appendix XI Page 3

	Cluster6	Cluster7	Cluster8	Cluster9	Cluster10
Cluster1	5.4772	8.0000	7.6811	6.4031	6.0828
Cluster2	6.3246	6.9282	6.8557	6.4031	6.5574
Cluster3	7.1414	7.0000	7.0711	5.8310	6.6332
Cluster4	6.3246	5.0990	5.3852	3.3166	4.3589
Cluster5	5.8310	6.1644	6.4031	4.3589	5.0000
Cluster6	0.0000	7.3485	7.9373	5.9161	6.0828
Cluster7	7.3485	0.0000	4.1231	5.7446	4.3589
Cluster8	7.9373	4.1231	0.0000	6.3246	4.8990
Cluster9	5.9161	5.7446	6.3246	0.0000	4.0000
Cluster10	6.0828	4.3589	4.8990	4.0000	0.0000
Cluster11	6.4807	7.0711	7.9373	5.0000	6.0828
Cluster12	4.2426	5.6569	5.9161	4.3589	4.1231
Cluster13	6.9282	4.6904	5.7446	4.7958	5.0000
Cluster14	5.6569	5.8310	6.2450	3.3166	4.7958

	Cluster11	Cluster12	Cluster13	Cluster14
Cluster1	7.8740	5.2915	7.2111	7.2111
Cluster2	6.0000	5.0990	5.8310	6.3246
Cluster3	4.7958	4.5826	4.7958	5.3852
Cluster4	5.6569	4.4721	4.8990	4.8990
Cluster5	4.2426	3.7417	4.8990	3.1623
Cluster6	6.4807	4.2426	6.9282	5.6569
Cluster7	7.0711	5.6569	4.6904	5.8310
Cluster8	7.9373	5.9161	5.7446	6.2450
Cluster9	5.0000	4.3589	4.7958	3.3166
Cluster10	6.0828	4.1231	5.0000	4.7958
Cluster11	0.0000	4.0000	4.0000	4.4721
Cluster12	4.0000	0.0000	4.4721	4.0000
Cluster13	4.0000	4.4721	0.0000	4.6904
Cluster14	4.4721	4.0000	4.6904	0.0000

```
MTB > PCA C21-C39;
SUBC>  GScree.
```

Appendix XII Pilot Study Dendogram

PILOT

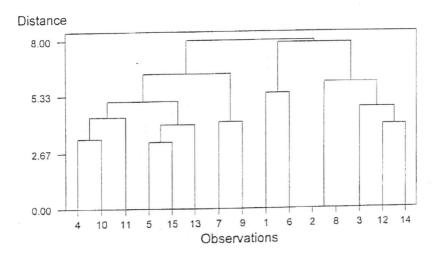

Appendix XIII Pilot Principal Components Analysis

```
MTB > PCA C21-C39;
SUBC>   NComponents 3;
SUBC>   Scores c41-c43;
SUBC>  GScree.
```

Principal Component Analysis

Eigenanalysis of the Correlation Matrix

Eigenvalue	4.5126	3.9573	2.9971	2.2596	1.5883	1.1943
Proportion	0.238	0.208	0.158	0.119	0.084	0.063
Cumulative	0.238	0.446	0.604	0.722	0.806	0.869

Eigenvalue	0.7522	0.6180	0.3957	0.2942	0.2187	0.1407
Proportion	0.040	0.033	0.021	0.015	0.012	0.007
Cumulative	0.908	0.941	0.962	0.977	0.989	0.996

Eigenvalue	0.0714	0.0000	0.0000	0.0000	0.0000	-0.0000
Proportion	0.004	0.000	0.000	0.000	0.000	-0.000
Cumulative	1.000	1.000	1.000	1.000	1.000	1.000

Eigenvalue	-0.0000
Proportion	-0.000
Cumulative	1.000

Variable	PC1	PC2	PC3
C21	-0.256	0.331	0.044
C22	0.178	0.353	-0.265
C23	0.197	0.368	0.058
C24	-0.063	0.066	0.505
C25	0.046	0.193	0.325
C26	-0.291	0.062	0.308
C27	-0.293	-0.079	0.036
C28	-0.309	0.072	0.243
C29	-0.240	-0.318	-0.080
C30	-0.197	-0.101	-0.205
C31	-0.101	-0.172	-0.435
C32	0.037	0.385	-0.119
C33	-0.343	0.145	-0.137
C34	-0.337	0.105	0.028
C35	0.234	-0.163	0.029
C36	-0.208	0.172	-0.110
C37	-0.365	-0.090	-0.166
C38	-0.008	0.349	-0.305
C39	-0.145	0.257	-0.062

```
MTB >
```

Appendix XIV: Scree Plot Pilot

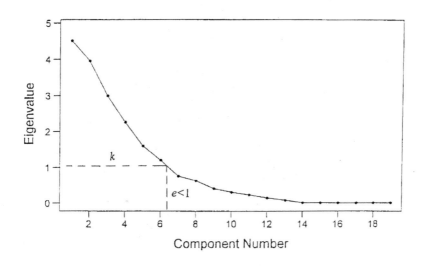

Appendix XV Factors 1 and 2: Rotated Factor Diagram

PILOT

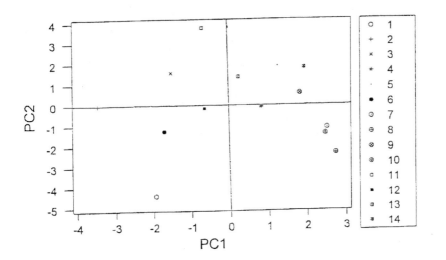

Appendix XVI Factors 1 and 3: Rotated Factor Diagram

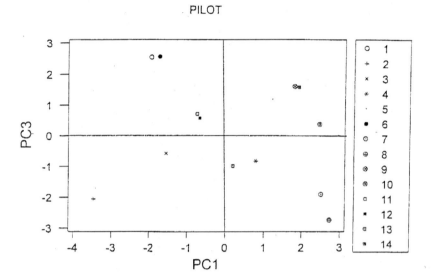

PILOT

Appendix XVII: Main Survey Dimensions Matrix
(26 Dimensions x 53 Respondents)

Main Survey Dimensions Matrix
(26 Dimensions x 53 Respondents)

Strategic Dimensions	MI	MA	AVER	STDEV
Nat. geograph. spread	1	5	3.45	1.15
Reg. geograph. spread	2	5	4.02	0.91
Free trade	2	5	3.77	0.89
Innovation	2	5	4.28	0.79
Diversification	1	5	2.74	1.02
Wholesaling	1	5	3.75	1.02
Distribution	2	5	4.09	0.93
Mgmt structure	2	5	3.98	0.95
Prices	2	5	4.09	0.86
Quality	2	5	4.77	0.54
Advertising	2	5	4.15	0.74
Image	1	5	4.51	0.72
Prod. range	1	5	4.08	0.92
Econs. of scale	1	5	4.00	1.00
Prod. brands	2	5	4.28	0.79
Hor. integration	1	5	2.94	1.06
Service	2	5	4.55	0.67
Pay and salaries	2	5	3.55	0.70
Packaging	2	5	3.83	0.85
Org. efficiency	2	5	4.34	0.65
Vert. integration	1	5	3.62	1.00
Outlet mix	2	5	3.57	0.80
Market share	1	5	3.89	0.97
Process technology	2	5	3.62	0.84
Discounts	2	5	3.60	0.88
Brewery loans	1	5	3.55	1.01

5= Strongly agree
4= Agree
3= Neither agree nor disagree
2= Disagree
1= Strongly disagree

189

Appendix XVIII Full Survey Cluster Analysis
Page 1: Full Survey Cluster Analysis

Euclidean Distance, Complete Linkage

Amalgamation Steps

Step	Number of clusters	Similarity level	Distance level	Clusters joined		New cluster	Number of Obs in new cluster
1	52	100.00	0.000	13	14	13	2
2	51	80.75	2.646	3	12	3	2
3	50	75.88	3.317	25	39	25	2
4	49	75.88	3.317	30	38	30	2
5	48	74.80	3.464	16	53	16	2
6	47	74.80	3.464	37	41	37	2
7	46	74.80	3.464	1	28	1	2
8	45	73.77	3.606	9	34	9	2
9	44	72.78	3.742	3	40	3	3
10	43	72.78	3.742	6	7	6	2
11	42	71.83	3.873	16	23	16	3
12	41	70.90	4.000	6	30	6	4
13	40	70.01	4.123	22	36	22	2
14	39	70.01	4.123	9	26	9	3
15	38	70.01	4.123	1	4	1	3
16	37	69.14	4.243	13	45	13	3
17	36	69.14	4.243	5	27	5	2
18	35	68.29	4.359	24	49	24	2
19	34	68.29	4.359	37	46	37	3
20	33	68.29	4.359	10	43	10	2
21	32	68.29	4.359	6	31	6	5
22	31	66.67	4.583	33	47	33	2
23	30	66.67	4.583	8	17	8	2
24	29	65.88	4.690	32	44	32	2
25	28	65.88	4.690	3	25	3	5
26	27	65.12	4.796	6	9	6	8
27	26	63.63	5.000	21	24	21	3
28	25	63.63	5.000	18	22	18	3
29	24	63.63	5.000	1	16	1	6
30	23	62.20	5.196	3	10	3	7
31	22	60.16	5.477	13	18	13	6
32	21	58.85	5.657	3	32	3	9
33	20	57.59	5.831	37	48	37	4
34	19	57.59	5.831	15	20	15	2
35	18	56.36	6.000	2	21	2	4
36	17	56.36	6.000	1	6	1	14
37	16	55.16	6.164	19	42	19	2
38	15	52.86	6.481	11	50	11	2
39	14	52.86	6.481	3	5	3	11
40	13	51.75	6.633	13	19	13	8
41	12	51.20	6.708	8	11	8	4
42	11	49.60	6.928	15	33	15	4
43	10	47.55	7.211	2	51	2	5
44	9	47.55	7.211	1	15	1	18
45	8	45.57	7.483	3	13	3	19
46	7	42.26	7.937	1	3	1	37
47	6	41.36	8.062	1	37	1	41
48	5	40.02	8.246	8	52	8	5
49	4	35.35	8.888	2	8	2	10
50	3	30.61	9.539	2	35	2	11
51	2	24.41	10.392	1	2	1	52
52	1	0.00	13.748	1	29	1	53

Final Partition

Number of clusters: 27

	Number of observations	Within cluster sum of squares	Average distance from centroid	Maximum distance from centroid
Cluster1	3	14.000	2.153	2.309

Appendix XVIII Page 2

Cluster2	1	0.000	0.000	0.000
Cluster3	5	28.000	2.340	2.757
Cluster4	2	9.000	2.121	2.121
Cluster5	8	56.375	2.639	3.013
Cluster6	2	10.500	2.291	2.291
Cluster7	2	9.500	2.179	2.179
Cluster8	1	0.000	0.000	0.000
Cluster9	3	12.000	1.886	2.828
Cluster10	1	0.000	0.000	0.000
Cluster11	3	14.000	2.158	2.309
Cluster12	1	0.000	0.000	0.000
Cluster13	1	0.000	0.000	0.000
Cluster14	1	0.000	0.000	0.000
Cluster15	1	0.000	0.000	0.000
Cluster16	2	8.500	2.062	2.062
Cluster17	2	9.500	2.179	2.179
Cluster18	1	0.000	0.000	0.000
Cluster19	2	11.000	2.345	2.345
Cluster20	2	10.500	2.291	2.291
Cluster21	1	0.000	0.000	0.000
Cluster22	3	16.667	2.346	2.667
Cluster23	1	0.000	0.000	0.000
Cluster24	1	0.000	0.000	0.000
Cluster25	1	0.000	0.000	0.000
Cluster26	1	0.000	0.000	0.000
Cluster27	1	0.000	0.000	0.000

Cluster Centroids

Variable	Cluster1	Cluster2	Cluster3	Cluster4	Cluster5
C101	5.0000	2.0000	3.6000	4.0000	3.8750
C102	4.0000	4.0000	3.8000	3.0000	4.3750
C103	5.0000	4.0000	4.4000	3.5000	3.8750
C104	5.0000	4.0000	3.6000	4.0000	4.2500
C105	2.6667	5.0000	2.6000	4.0000	3.6250
C106	4.0000	2.0000	4.2000	4.0000	4.5000
C107	4.0000	2.0000	4.2000	3.5000	4.6250
C108	4.3333	4.0000	4.4000	3.5000	4.3750
C109	4.3333	4.0000	4.2000	5.0000	4.1250
C110	5.0000	5.0000	5.0000	4.5000	4.7500
C111	4.6667	4.0000	4.2000	5.0000	3.8750
C112	5.0000	5.0000	4.6000	5.0000	4.1250
C113	4.3333	4.0000	4.2000	4.5000	4.1250
C114	4.0000	5.0000	3.6000	5.0000	3.7500
C115	5.0000	3.0000	4.0000	5.0000	4.5000
C116	4.0000	4.0000	3.0000	2.0000	3.1250
C117	5.0000	5.0000	4.4000	4.0000	4.6250
C118	4.3333	3.0000	4.0000	4.0000	3.3750
C119	5.0000	2.0000	4.2000	4.0000	3.8750
C120	5.0000	4.0000	4.6000	4.5000	4.3750
C121	3.6667	4.0000	3.2000	2.5000	3.8750
C122	3.6667	3.0000	3.8000	3.0000	3.7500
C123	4.0000	2.0000	3.8000	3.5000	4.0000
C124	4.0000	3.0000	4.2000	3.5000	3.6250
C125	3.3333	4.0000	3.4000	3.5000	4.0000
C126	4.0000	3.0000	2.6000	2.0000	4.2500

Variable	Cluster6	Cluster7	Cluster8	Cluster9	Cluster10
C101	2.5000	3.5000	4.0000	4.0000	5.0000
C102	4.5000	4.0000	2.0000	4.3333	3.0000
C103	3.0000	5.0000	4.0000	4.0000	4.0000
C104	3.0000	4.5000	4.0000	5.0000	5.0000
C105	2.0000	1.5000	1.0000	4.0000	5.0000
C106	4.0000	2.5000	4.0000	4.3333	3.0000
C107	3.5000	4.5000	4.0000	3.6667	3.0000
C108	3.5000	5.0000	3.0000	4.3333	3.0000
C109	2.0000	4.0000	2.0000	5.0000	5.0000
C110	4.5000	5.0000	4.0000	5.0000	5.0000
C111	3.5000	4.0000	4.0000	4.6667	5.0000

191

Appendix XVIII Page 3

C112	4.5000	5.0000	4.0000	5.0000	5.0000
C113	3.0000	4.5000	2.0000	5.0000	5.0000
C114	2.5000	4.5000	4.0000	5.0000	5.0000
C115	4.5000	4.5000	3.0000	4.6667	5.0000
C116	2.0000	2.5000	3.0000	2.6667	4.0000
C117	5.0000	4.5000	4.0000	4.0000	5.0000
C118	3.5000	4.0000	4.0000	3.0000	3.0000
C119	2.0000	4.5000	4.0000	4.3333	4.0000
C120	4.0000	4.5000	4.0000	4.6667	4.0000
C121	2.5000	3.0000	2.0000	4.6667	2.0000
C122	3.0000	4.0000	2.0000	3.0000	5.0000
C123	4.0000	4.5000	2.0000	4.3333	5.0000
C124	3.5000	4.5000	3.0000	4.3333	3.0000
C125	2.0000	2.0000	4.0000	5.0000	3.0000
C126	2.5000	2.5000	4.0000	5.0000	3.0000

Variable	Cluster11	Cluster12	Cluster13	Cluster14	Cluster15
C101	4.0000	2.0000	3.0000	3.0000	1.0000
C102	4.3333	5.0000	3.0000	5.0000	5.0000
C103	4.6667	3.0000	3.0000	4.0000	4.0000
C104	5.0000	4.0000	5.0000	3.0000	4.0000
C105	3.6667	2.0000	3.0000	3.0000	2.0000
C106	4.6667	4.0000	4.0000	4.0000	3.0000
C107	5.0000	5.0000	2.0000	2.0000	4.0000
C108	5.0000	3.0000	2.0000	5.0000	4.0000
C109	4.6667	5.0000	5.0000	3.0000	4.0000
C110	5.0000	5.0000	5.0000	5.0000	5.0000
C111	5.0000	5.0000	3.0000	4.0000	3.0000
C112	5.0000	5.0000	5.0000	5.0000	3.0000
C113	5.0000	4.0000	4.0000	4.0000	4.0000
C114	5.0000	5.0000	5.0000	5.0000	4.0000
C115	5.0000	5.0000	5.0000	4.0000	3.0000
C116	4.0000	3.0000	3.0000	5.0000	1.0000
C117	5.0000	3.0000	5.0000	5.0000	5.0000
C118	4.3333	3.0000	2.0000	4.0000	4.0000
C119	4.6667	3.0000	3.0000	3.0000	3.0000
C120	5.0000	4.0000	4.0000	5.0000	4.0000
C121	3.6667	3.0000	3.0000	2.0000	4.0000
C122	4.3333	2.0000	4.0000	5.0000	4.0000
C123	4.6667	4.0000	5.0000	4.0000	3.0000
C124	4.0000	3.0000	4.0000	5.0000	3.0000
C125	4.3333	3.0000	5.0000	3.0000	4.0000
C126	4.3333	3.0000	5.0000	3.0000	4.0000

Variable	Cluster16	Cluster17	Cluster18	Cluster19	Cluster20
C101	4.0000	2.0000	2.0000	3.0000	4.5000
C102	4.5000	4.0000	2.0000	4.0000	4.5000
C103	4.0000	3.5000	2.0000	3.5000	3.5000
C104	4.0000	4.0000	2.0000	4.5000	4.5000
C105	2.0000	3.5000	2.0000	3.0000	2.5000
C106	2.5000	4.0000	2.0000	2.0000	2.0000
C107	4.5000	4.5000	2.0000	4.0000	3.5000
C108	2.5000	2.5000	2.0000	4.5000	3.5000
C109	4.0000	3.5000	5.0000	4.5000	5.0000
C110	5.0000	4.5000	2.0000	5.0000	4.5000
C111	4.0000	4.0000	2.0000	3.0000	4.5000
C112	4.5000	4.0000	2.0000	3.5000	5.0000
C113	4.0000	4.0000	2.0000	4.0000	3.5000
C114	5.0000	3.5000	2.0000	3.5000	4.0000
C115	4.5000	4.0000	2.0000	4.0000	4.5000
C116	3.5000	2.5000	2.0000	3.0000	5.0000
C117	5.0000	4.5000	2.0000	5.0000	5.0000
C118	3.0000	3.0000	2.0000	4.0000	4.0000
C119	3.5000	3.0000	2.0000	4.0000	4.0000
C120	4.5000	3.5000	2.0000	4.5000	4.5000
C121	4.5000	4.5000	2.0000	3.0000	5.0000
C122	2.5000	3.0000	2.0000	3.5000	4.0000
C123	5.0000	3.0000	2.0000	4.5000	5.0000
C124	4.0000	3.0000	2.0000	3.5000	4.5000

Appendix XVIII Page 4

C125	3.5000	3.0000	2.0000	3.0000	4.0000
C126	3.5000	3.0000	2.0000	3.0000	4.0000

Variable	Cluster21	Cluster22	Cluster23	Cluster24	Cluster25
C101	5.0000	1.6667	4.0000	2.0000	4.0000
C102	5.0000	4.3333	3.0000	2.0000	4.0000
C103	5.0000	2.3333	2.0000	3.0000	3.0000
C104	5.0000	5.0000	5.0000	4.0000	5.0000
C105	5.0000	2.3333	2.0000	1.0000	1.0000
C106	2.0000	4.0000	3.0000	4.0000	3.0000
C107	2.0000	4.6667	4.0000	4.0000	5.0000
C108	5.0000	4.3333	3.0000	4.0000	4.0000
C109	5.0000	4.0000	2.0000	5.0000	3.0000
C110	5.0000	5.0000	4.0000	5.0000	5.0000
C111	5.0000	4.3333	5.0000	5.0000	5.0000
C112	3.0000	4.6667	4.0000	5.0000	5.0000
C113	5.0000	4.6667	5.0000	5.0000	2.0000
C114	5.0000	2.6667	4.0000	2.0000	2.0000
C115	3.0000	4.3333	5.0000	5.0000	2.0000
C116	1.0000	2.3333	2.0000	5.0000	1.0000
C117	3.0000	4.6667	4.0000	5.0000	4.0000
C118	3.0000	3.6667	2.0000	3.0000	3.0000
C119	3.0000	4.0000	3.0000	4.0000	4.0000
C120	5.0000	4.3333	4.0000	4.0000	4.0000
C121	5.0000	3.3333	5.0000	2.0000	5.0000
C122	5.0000	3.6667	4.0000	4.0000	3.0000
C123	3.0000	4.0000	3.0000	2.0000	4.0000
C124	3.0000	3.0000	4.0000	4.0000	2.0000
C125	3.0000	4.3333	4.0000	5.0000	2.0000
C126	3.0000	4.3333	4.0000	5.0000	4.0000

Variable	Cluster26	Cluster27	Grand centrd
C101	1.0000	5.0000	3.4528
C102	5.0000	3.0000	4.0189
C103	4.0000	2.0000	3.7736
C104	4.0000	4.0000	4.2830
C105	3.0000	3.0000	2.7358
C106	5.0000	5.0000	3.7547
C107	5.0000	5.0000	4.0943
C108	5.0000	5.0000	3.9811
C109	4.0000	5.0000	4.0943
C110	5.0000	4.0000	4.7736
C111	3.0000	3.0000	4.1509
C112	5.0000	5.0000	4.5094
C113	3.0000	1.0000	4.0755
C114	5.0000	5.0000	4.0000
C115	4.0000	3.0000	4.2830
C116	1.0000	1.0000	2.9434
C117	5.0000	5.0000	4.5472
C118	5.0000	3.0000	3.5472
C119	4.0000	4.0000	3.8302
C120	3.0000	5.0000	4.3396
C121	5.0000	5.0000	3.6226
C122	3.0000	4.0000	3.5660
C123	1.0000	5.0000	3.8868
C124	1.0000	3.0000	3.6226
C125	4.0000	3.0000	3.6038
C126	3.0000	1.0000	3.5472

Distances Between Cluster Centroids

	Cluster1	Cluster2	Cluster3	Cluster4	Cluster5
Cluster1	0.0000	7.0000	3.2455	4.7434	3.2906
Cluster2	7.0000	0.0000	5.9833	5.9582	5.9015
Cluster3	3.2455	5.9833	0.0000	3.6194	2.7619
Cluster4	4.7434	5.9582	3.6194	0.0000	4.4106
Cluster5	3.2906	5.9015	2.7619	4.4106	0.0000
Cluster6	6.9462	6.8739	4.9649	6.1847	5.6083

Appendix XVIII Page 5

Cluster7	4.0104	7.1239	3.1859	4.9749	4.7120
Cluster8	6.6332	7.5498	5.7271	6.5192	6.2512
Cluster9	3.9016	7.0238	4.4347	5.2757	3.5111
Cluster10	4.8305	8.1854	5.0990	5.6125	5.6194
Cluster11	2.8087	7.2572	4.0579	5.1478	3.2652
Cluster12	6.0828	6.6332	4.8374	4.7434	4.9828
Cluster13	6.2981	6.4807	6.0828	5.8737	5.2752
Cluster14	5.5377	5.9161	4.6043	6.1237	5.4155
Cluster15	6.9522	6.0000	5.1962	6.6708	5.1067
Cluster16	4.4253	6.1847	4.2485	5.2202	4.0716
Cluster17	5.9231	5.0744	4.2367	4.9244	3.9310
Cluster18	12.0277	9.5394	10.0000	9.9247	10.5275
Cluster19	4.6368	5.6125	3.4205	4.8477	3.7521
Cluster20	3.9476	6.5765	4.8010	6.0622	4.5087
Cluster21	7.0946	6.4807	6.6783	6.5192	6.4868
Cluster22	5.3437	6.6667	4.2400	5.5327	3.6546
Cluster23	6.4031	7.0711	5.8481	6.1237	5.2515
Cluster24	6.4291	7.8102	5.9330	7.1063	6.1505
Cluster25	7.2111	8.5440	6.3875	7.7782	6.4675
Cluster26	8.0208	7.2111	6.7676	7.3144	6.5634
Cluster27	7.6594	8.8882	6.4187	6.6708	6.6203

	Cluster6	Cluster7	Cluster8	Cluster9	Cluster10
Cluster1	6.9462	4.0104	6.6332	3.9016	4.8305
Cluster2	6.8739	7.1239	7.5498	7.0238	8.1854
Cluster3	4.9649	3.1859	5.7271	4.4347	5.0990
Cluster4	6.1847	4.9749	6.5192	5.2757	5.6125
Cluster5	5.6083	4.7120	6.2512	3.5111	5.6194
Cluster6	0.0000	5.8310	6.0208	7.3428	6.7268
Cluster7	5.8310	0.0000	6.9101	5.2361	5.4544
Cluster8	6.0208	6.9101	0.0000	6.9041	6.7823
Cluster9	7.3428	5.2361	6.9041	0.0000	5.8023
Cluster10	6.7268	5.4544	6.7823	5.8023	0.0000
Cluster11	7.9110	5.0083	7.9791	3.8586	5.6862
Cluster12	5.6789	5.5453	6.8557	5.0990	6.5574
Cluster13	7.1589	7.1239	7.5498	5.0990	5.9161
Cluster14	5.9372	5.4544	7.6158	6.8069	5.8310
Cluster15	5.5902	5.8949	6.8557	6.1101	8.0623
Cluster16	5.8310	4.5277	6.5000	3.7749	5.6789
Cluster17	4.4159	5.7879	5.9791	5.4848	6.7639
Cluster18	8.4410	10.9430	8.6023	11.8462	11.6619
Cluster19	5.1720	3.7081	6.5192	5.4924	6.3640
Cluster20	7.3824	5.2915	7.6322	4.6098	6.2650
Cluster21	8.8459	7.0534	9.5394	7.1647	8.6603
Cluster22	5.4493	5.4645	6.6916	4.5947	6.4893
Cluster23	6.2650	6.5383	6.5574	4.9666	6.2450
Cluster24	7.6974	7.3314	6.9282	6.5574	6.9282
Cluster25	6.2650	6.6895	6.4807	7.0475	8.1240
Cluster26	7.5000	7.7942	7.8102	7.7460	9.5394
Cluster27	7.5664	7.2629	8.2462	7.8951	8.3666

	Cluster11	Cluster12	Cluster13	Cluster14	Cluster15
Cluster1	2.8087	6.0828	6.2981	5.5377	6.9522
Cluster2	7.2572	6.6332	6.4807	5.9161	6.0000
Cluster3	4.0579	4.8374	6.0828	4.6043	5.1962
Cluster4	5.1478	4.7434	5.8737	6.1237	6.6708
Cluster5	3.2652	4.9828	5.2752	5.4155	5.1067
Cluster6	7.9110	5.6789	7.1589	5.9372	5.5902
Cluster7	5.0083	5.5453	7.1239	5.4544	5.8949
Cluster8	7.9791	6.8557	7.5498	7.6158	6.8557
Cluster9	3.8586	5.0990	5.0990	6.8069	6.1101
Cluster10	5.6862	6.5574	5.9161	5.8310	8.0623
Cluster11	0.0000	6.1644	6.4291	5.8023	7.0711
Cluster12	6.1644	0.0000	6.3246	6.8557	6.0000
Cluster13	6.4291	6.3246	0.0000	6.7082	6.7823
Cluster14	5.8023	6.8557	6.7082	0.0000	7.0000
Cluster15	7.0711	6.0000	6.7823	7.0000	0.0000
Cluster16	5.2520	4.5000	5.3151	6.1847	5.8523
Cluster17	6.3574	4.3301	5.9791	6.6895	4.3301

Appendix XVIII Page 6

Cluster18	13.1276	9.6437	10.4403	11.3137	9.2195
Cluster19	5.3697	5.4314	5.9582	5.5227	4.5277
Cluster20	4.8563	6.3443	5.8523	6.0208	7.0887
Cluster21	7.3937	8.2462	8.3666	7.9373	7.0711
Cluster22	5.1854	4.8074	5.8119	6.6416	4.4472
Cluster23	6.9761	6.3246	6.1644	7.6811	6.4807
Cluster24	6.8557	7.0000	6.7082	7.3485	7.5498
Cluster25	8.3865	7.0000	8.7750	9.1652	6.5574
Cluster26	7.9162	6.9282	9.0554	8.8882	5.2915
Cluster27	7.9791	7.8102	8.4261	8.7178	8.0623

	Cluster16	Cluster17	Cluster18	Cluster19	Cluster20
Cluster1	4.4253	5.9231	12.0277	4.6368	3.9476
Cluster2	6.1847	5.0744	9.5394	5.6125	6.5765
Cluster3	4.2485	4.2367	10.0000	3.4205	4.8010
Cluster4	5.2202	4.9244	9.9247	4.8477	6.0622
Cluster5	4.0716	3.9310	10.5275	3.7521	4.5087
Cluster6	5.8310	4.4159	8.4410	5.1720	7.3824
Cluster7	4.5277	5.7879	10.9430	3.7081	5.2915
Cluster8	6.5000	5.9791	8.6023	6.5192	7.6322
Cluster9	3.7749	5.4848	11.8462	5.4924	4.6098
Cluster10	5.6789	6.7639	11.6619	6.3640	6.2650
Cluster11	5.2520	6.3574	13.1276	5.3697	4.8563
Cluster12	4.5000	4.3301	9.6437	5.4314	6.3443
Cluster13	5.3151	5.9791	10.4403	5.9582	5.8523
Cluster14	6.1847	6.6895	11.3137	5.5227	6.0208
Cluster15	5.8523	4.3301	9.2195	4.5277	7.0887
Cluster16	0.0000	4.5277	10.4523	4.2131	3.7417
Cluster17	4.5277	0.0000	8.4705	4.5552	6.1237
Cluster18	10.4523	8.4705	0.0000	9.2466	11.3248
Cluster19	4.2131	4.5552	9.2466	0.0000	4.6637
Cluster20	3.7417	6.1237	11.3248	4.6637	0.0000
Cluster21	7.4330	7.1937	11.2694	6.5955	7.5664
Cluster22	5.4186	4.2655	10.3333	4.2361	5.8618
Cluster23	5.3151	4.8734	10.1489	6.2048	6.3443
Cluster24	7.3655	6.8374	10.7703	6.7454	6.9462
Cluster25	6.5765	5.9791	9.7980	6.4420	7.3655
Cluster26	8.0156	5.7228	11.0000	7.2457	8.9582
Cluster27	7.2284	7.1937	10.7703	6.8920	7.8262

	Cluster21	Cluster22	Cluster23	Cluster24	Cluster25
Cluster1	7.0946	5.3437	6.4031	6.4291	7.2111
Cluster2	6.4807	6.6667	7.0711	7.8102	8.5440
Cluster3	6.6783	4.2400	5.8481	5.9330	6.3875
Cluster4	6.5192	5.5327	6.1237	7.1063	7.7782
Cluster5	6.4868	3.6546	5.2515	6.1505	6.4675
Cluster6	8.8459	5.4493	6.2650	7.6974	6.2650
Cluster7	7.0534	5.4645	6.5383	7.3314	6.6895
Cluster8	9.5394	6.6916	6.5574	6.9282	6.4807
Cluster9	7.1647	4.5947	4.9666	6.5574	7.0475
Cluster10	8.6603	6.4893	6.2450	6.9282	8.1240
Cluster11	7.3937	5.1854	6.9761	6.8557	8.3865
Cluster12	8.2462	4.8074	6.3246	7.0000	7.0000
Cluster13	8.3666	5.8119	6.1644	6.7082	8.7750
Cluster14	7.9373	6.6416	7.6811	7.3485	9.1652
Cluster15	7.0711	4.4472	6.4807	7.5498	6.5574
Cluster16	7.4330	5.4186	5.3151	7.3655	6.5765
Cluster17	7.1937	4.2655	4.8734	6.8374	5.9791
Cluster18	11.2694	10.3333	10.1489	10.7703	9.7980
Cluster19	6.5955	4.2361	6.2048	5.7454	6.4420
Cluster20	7.5664	5.8618	6.3443	6.9462	7.3655
Cluster21	0.0000	8.0277	7.4833	10.3441	8.4261
Cluster22	8.0277	0.0000	5.3333	5.2387	6.0093
Cluster23	7.4833	5.3333	0.0000	7.0000	6.5574
Cluster24	10.3441	5.2387	7.0000	0.0000	8.8318
Cluster25	8.4261	6.0093	6.5574	8.8318	0.0000
Cluster26	8.9443	6.3596	8.4853	9.1104	7.8102
Cluster27	8.6603	7.7531	8.1854	10.3923	6.9282

Appendix XVIII Page 7

```
                 Cluster26    Cluster27
Cluster1          8.0208       7.6594
Cluster2          7.2111       8.8882
Cluster3          6.7676       6.4187
Cluster4          7.3144       6.6708
Cluster5          6.5634       6.6203
Cluster6          7.5000       7.5664
Cluster7          7.7942       7.2629
Cluster8          7.8102       8.2462
Cluster9          7.7460       7.8951
Cluster10         9.5394       8.3666
Cluster11         7.9162       7.9791
Cluster12         6.9282       7.8102
Cluster13         9.0554       8.4261
Cluster14         8.8882       8.7178
Cluster15         5.2915       8.0623
Cluster16         8.0156       7.2284
Cluster17         5.7228       7.1937
Cluster18        11.0000      10.7703
Cluster19         7.2457       6.8920
Cluster20         8.9582       7.8262
Cluster21         8.9443       8.6603
Cluster22         6.3596       7.7531
Cluster23         8.4853       8.1854
Cluster24         9.1104      10.3923
Cluster25         7.8102       6.9282
Cluster26         0.0000       8.0623
Cluster27         8.0623       0.0000
```

```
MTB > Cluo  C101-C126;
SUBC>    Complete;
SUBC>    Cut 65;
SUBC>    Dendrogram;
SUBC>    Member c131.
```

Hierarchical Cluster Analysis of Observations

Euclidean Distance, Complete Linkage

Amalgamation Steps

Step	Number of clusters	Similarity level	Distance level	Clusters joined		New cluster	Number of Obs in new cluster
1	52	100.00	0.000	13	14	13	2
2	51	80.75	2.646	3	12	3	2
3	50	75.88	3.317	25	39	25	2
4	49	75.88	3.317	30	38	30	2
5	48	74.80	3.464	16	53	16	2
6	47	74.80	3.464	37	41	37	2
7	46	74.80	3.464	1	28	1	2
8	45	73.77	3.606	9	34	9	2
9	44	72.78	3.742	3	40	3	3
10	43	72.78	3.742	6	7	6	2
11	42	71.83	3.873	16	23	16	3
12	41	70.90	4.000	6	30	6	4
13	40	70.01	4.123	22	36	22	2
14	39	70.01	4.123	9	26	9	3
15	38	70.01	4.123	1	4	1	3
16	37	69.14	4.243	13	45	13	3
17	36	69.14	4.243	5	27	5	2
18	35	68.29	4.359	24	49	24	2
19	34	68.29	4.359	37	46	37	3
20	33	68.29	4.359	10	43	10	2
21	32	68.29	4.359	6	31	6	5
22	31	66.67	4.583	33	47	33	2
23	30	66.67	4.583	8	17	8	2
24	29	65.88	4.690	32	44	32	2
25	28	65.88	4.690	3	25	3	5

Appendix XVIII Page 8

26	27	65.12	4.796	6	9	6	8
27	26	63.63	5.000	21	24	21	3
28	25	63.63	5.000	18	22	18	3
29	24	63.63	5.000	1	16	1	6
30	23	62.20	5.196	3	10	3	7
31	22	60.16	5.477	13	18	13	6
32	21	58.85	5.657	3	32	3	9
33	20	57.59	5.831	37	48	37	4
34	19	57.59	5.831	15	20	15	2
35	18	56.36	6.000	2	21	2	4
36	17	56.36	6.000	1	6	1	14
37	16	55.16	6.164	19	42	19	2
38	15	52.86	6.481	11	50	11	2
39	14	52.86	6.481	3	5	3	11
40	13	51.75	6.633	13	19	13	8
41	12	51.20	6.708	8	11	8	4
42	11	49.60	6.928	15	33	15	4
43	10	47.55	7.211	2	51	2	5
44	9	47.55	7.211	1	15	1	18
45	8	45.57	7.483	3	13	3	19
46	7	42.26	7.937	1	3	1	37
47	6	41.36	8.062	1	37	1	41
48	5	40.02	8.246	8	52	8	5
49	4	35.35	8.888	2	8	2	10
50	3	30.61	9.539	2	35	2	11
51	2	24.41	10.392	1	2	1	52
52	1	0.00	13.748	1	29	1	53

Final Partition

Number of clusters: 27

	Number of observations	Within cluster sum of squares	Average distance from centroid	Maximum distance from centroid
Cluster1	3	14.000	2.153	2.309
Cluster2	1	0.000	0.000	0.000
Cluster3	5	28.000	2.340	2.757
Cluster4	2	9.000	2.121	2.121
Cluster5	8	56.375	2.639	3.013
Cluster6	2	10.500	2.291	2.291
Cluster7	2	9.500	2.179	2.179
Cluster8	1	0.000	0.000	0.000
Cluster9	3	12.000	1.886	2.828
Cluster10	1	0.000	0.000	0.000
Cluster11	3	14.000	2.158	2.309
Cluster12	1	0.000	0.000	0.000
Cluster13	1	0.000	0.000	0.000
Cluster14	1	0.000	0.000	0.000
Cluster15	1	0.000	0.000	0.000
Cluster16	2	8.500	2.062	2.062
Cluster17	2	9.500	2.179	2.179
Cluster18	1	0.000	0.000	0.000
Cluster19	2	11.000	2.345	2.345
Cluster20	2	10.500	2.291	2.291
Cluster21	1	0.000	0.000	0.000
Cluster22	3	16.667	2.346	2.667
Cluster23	1	0.000	0.000	0.000
Cluster24	1	0.000	0.000	0.000
Cluster25	1	0.000	0.000	0.000
Cluster26	1	0.000	0.000	0.000
Cluster27	1	0.000	0.000	0.000

Cluster Centroids

Variable	Cluster1	Cluster2	Cluster3	Cluster4	Cluster5
C101	5.0000	2.0000	3.6000	4.0000	3.8750
C102	4.0000	4.0000	3.8000	3.0000	4.3750
C103	5.0000	4.0000	4.4000	3.5000	3.8750

Appendices

Appendix XVIII Page 9

C104	5.0000	4.0000	3.6000	4.0000	4.2500
C105	2.6667	5.0000	2.6000	4.0000	3.6250
C106	4.0000	2.0000	4.2000	4.0000	4.5000
C107	4.0000	2.0000	4.2000	3.5000	4.6250
C108	4.3333	4.0000	4.4000	3.5000	4.3750
C109	4.3333	4.0000	4.2000	5.0000	4.1250
C110	5.0000	5.0000	5.0000	4.5000	4.7500
C111	4.6667	4.0000	4.2000	5.0000	3.8750
C112	5.0000	5.0000	4.6000	5.0000	4.1250
C113	4.3333	4.0000	4.2000	4.5000	4.1250
C114	4.0000	5.0000	3.6000	5.0000	3.7500
C115	5.0000	3.0000	4.0000	5.0000	4.5000
C116	4.0000	4.0000	3.0000	2.0000	3.1250
C117	5.0000	5.0000	4.4000	4.0000	4.6250
C118	4.3333	3.0000	4.0000	4.0000	3.3750
C119	5.0000	2.0000	4.2000	4.0000	3.8750
C120	5.0000	4.0000	4.6000	4.5000	4.3750
C121	3.6667	4.0000	3.2000	2.5000	3.8750
C122	3.6667	3.0000	3.8000	3.0000	3.7500
C123	4.0000	2.0000	3.8000	3.5000	4.0000
C124	4.0000	3.0000	4.2000	3.5000	3.6250
C125	3.3333	4.0000	3.4000	3.5000	4.0000
C126	4.0000	3.0000	2.6000	2.0000	4.2500

Variable	Cluster6	Cluster7	Cluster8	Cluster9	Cluster10
C101	2.5000	3.5000	4.0000	4.0000	5.0000
C102	4.5000	4.0000	2.0000	4.3333	3.0000
C103	3.0000	5.0000	4.0000	4.0000	4.0000
C104	3.0000	4.5000	4.0000	5.0000	5.0000
C105	2.0000	1.5000	1.0000	2.0000	1.0000
C106	4.0000	2.5000	4.0000	4.0000	5.0000
C107	3.5000	4.5000	4.0000	4.3333	3.0000
C108	3.5000	5.0000	3.0000	3.6667	3.0000
C109	2.0000	4.0000	2.0000	4.3333	3.0000
C110	4.5000	5.0000	4.0000	5.0000	5.0000
C111	3.5000	4.0000	4.0000	4.6667	5.0000
C112	4.5000	5.0000	4.0000	5.0000	5.0000
C113	3.0000	4.5000	2.0000	5.0000	5.0000
C114	2.5000	4.5000	4.0000	5.0000	5.0000
C115	4.5000	4.5000	3.0000	4.6667	5.0000
C116	2.0000	2.5000	3.0000	2.6667	4.0000
C117	5.0000	4.5000	4.0000	4.0000	5.0000
C118	3.5000	4.0000	4.0000	3.0000	3.0000
C119	2.0000	4.5000	4.0000	4.3333	4.0000
C120	4.0000	4.5000	4.0000	4.6667	4.0000
C121	2.5000	3.0000	2.0000	4.6667	2.0000
C122	3.0000	4.0000	2.0000	3.0000	5.0000
C123	4.0000	4.5000	2.0000	4.3333	5.0000
C124	3.5000	4.5000	3.0000	4.3333	3.0000
C125	2.0000	2.0000	4.0000	5.0000	3.0000
C126	2.5000	2.5000	4.0000	5.0000	3.0000

Variable	Cluster11	Cluster12	Cluster13	Cluster14	Cluster15
C101	4.0000	2.0000	3.0000	3.0000	1.0000
C102	4.3333	5.0000	3.0000	5.0000	5.0000
C103	4.6667	3.0000	3.0000	4.0000	4.0000
C104	5.0000	4.0000	5.0000	3.0000	4.0000
C105	3.6667	2.0000	3.0000	3.0000	2.0000
C106	4.6667	4.0000	4.0000	4.0000	3.0000
C107	5.0000	5.0000	2.0000	2.0000	4.0000
C108	5.0000	3.0000	2.0000	5.0000	4.0000
C109	4.6667	5.0000	5.0000	3.0000	4.0000
C110	5.0000	5.0000	5.0000	5.0000	5.0000
C111	5.0000	5.0000	3.0000	4.0000	3.0000
C112	5.0000	5.0000	5.0000	5.0000	3.0000
C113	5.0000	4.0000	4.0000	4.0000	4.0000
C114	5.0000	5.0000	5.0000	5.0000	4.0000
C115	5.0000	5.0000	5.0000	4.0000	3.0000
C116	4.0000	3.0000	3.0000	5.0000	1.0000

198

Appendix XVIII Page 10

C117	5.0000	3.0000	5.0000	5.0000	5.0000
C118	4.3333	3.0000	2.0000	4.0000	4.0000
C119	4.6667	3.0000	3.0000	3.0000	3.0000
C120	5.0000	4.0000	4.0000	5.0000	4.0000
C121	3.6667	3.0000	3.0000	2.0000	4.0000
C122	4.3333	2.0000	4.0000	5.0000	4.0000
C123	4.6667	4.0000	5.0000	4.0000	3.0000
C124	4.0000	3.0000	4.0000	5.0000	3.0000
C125	4.3333	3.0000	5.0000	3.0000	4.0000
C126	4.3333	3.0000	5.0000	3.0000	4.0000

Variable	Cluster16	Cluster17	Cluster18	Cluster19	Cluster20
C101	4.0000	2.0000	2.0000	3.0000	4.5000
C102	4.5000	4.0000	2.0000	4.0000	4.5000
C103	4.0000	3.5000	2.0000	3.5000	3.5000
C104	4.0000	4.0000	2.0000	4.5000	4.5000
C105	2.0000	3.5000	2.0000	3.0000	2.5000
C106	2.5000	4.0000	2.0000	2.0000	2.0000
C107	4.5000	4.5000	2.0000	4.0000	3.5000
C108	2.5000	2.5000	2.0000	4.5000	3.5000
C109	4.0000	3.5000	5.0000	4.5000	5.0000
C110	5.0000	4.5000	2.0000	5.0000	4.5000
C111	4.0000	4.0000	2.0000	3.0000	4.5000
C112	4.5000	4.0000	2.0000	3.5000	5.0000
C113	4.0000	4.0000	2.0000	4.0000	3.5000
C114	5.0000	3.5000	2.0000	3.5000	4.0000
C115	4.5000	4.0000	2.0000	4.0000	4.5000
C116	3.5000	2.5000	2.0000	3.0000	5.0000
C117	5.0000	4.5000	2.0000	5.0000	5.0000
C118	3.0000	3.0000	2.0000	4.0000	4.0000
C119	3.5000	3.0000	2.0000	4.0000	4.5000
C120	4.5000	3.5000	2.0000	4.5000	4.0000
C121	4.5000	4.5000	2.0000	3.0000	5.0000
C122	2.5000	3.0000	2.0000	3.5000	4.0000
C123	5.0000	3.0000	2.0000	4.5000	5.0000
C124	4.0000	3.0000	2.0000	3.5000	4.5000
C125	3.5000	3.0000	2.0000	3.0000	4.0000
C126	3.5000	3.0000	2.0000	3.0000	4.0000

Variable	Cluster21	Cluster22	Cluster23	Cluster24	Cluster25
C101	5.0000	1.6667	4.0000	2.0000	4.0000
C102	5.0000	4.3333	3.0000	2.0000	4.0000
C103	5.0000	2.3333	2.0000	3.0000	3.0000
C104	5.0000	5.0000	5.0000	4.0000	5.0000
C105	5.0000	2.3333	2.0000	1.0000	1.0000
C106	2.0000	4.0000	3.0000	4.0000	3.0000
C107	2.0000	4.6667	4.0000	4.0000	5.0000
C108	5.0000	4.3333	3.0000	4.0000	4.0000
C109	5.0000	4.0000	2.0000	5.0000	3.0000
C110	5.0000	5.0000	4.0000	5.0000	5.0000
C111	5.0000	4.3333	5.0000	5.0000	5.0000
C112	3.0000	4.6667	4.0000	5.0000	5.0000
C113	5.0000	4.6667	5.0000	5.0000	2.0000
C114	5.0000	2.6667	4.0000	2.0000	2.0000
C115	3.0000	4.3333	5.0000	5.0000	2.0000
C116	1.0000	2.3333	2.0000	5.0000	1.0000
C117	3.0000	4.6667	4.0000	5.0000	4.0000
C118	3.0000	3.6667	2.0000	3.0000	3.0000
C119	3.0000	4.0000	3.0000	4.0000	4.0000
C120	5.0000	4.3333	4.0000	4.0000	4.0000
C121	5.0000	3.3333	5.0000	2.0000	5.0000
C122	5.0000	3.6667	4.0000	4.0000	3.0000
C123	3.0000	4.0000	3.0000	2.0000	4.0000
C124	3.0000	3.0000	4.0000	4.0000	2.0000
C125	3.0000	4.3333	4.0000	5.0000	2.0000
C126	3.0000	4.3333	4.0000	5.0000	4.0000

Variable	Cluster26	Cluster27	Grand centrd
C101	1.0000	5.0000	3.4528

Appendix XVIII Page 11

C102	5.0000	3.0000	4.0189
C103	4.0000	2.0000	3.7736
C104	4.0000	4.0000	4.2830
C105	3.0000	3.0000	2.7358
C106	5.0000	5.0000	3.7547
C107	5.0000	5.0000	4.0943
C108	5.0000	5.0000	3.9811
C109	4.0000	5.0000	4.0943
C110	5.0000	4.0000	4.7736
C111	3.0000	3.0000	4.1509
C112	5.0000	5.0000	4.5094
C113	3.0000	1.0000	4.0755
C114	5.0000	5.0000	4.0000
C115	4.0000	3.0000	4.2830
C116	1.0000	1.0000	2.9434
C117	5.0000	5.0000	4.5472
C118	5.0000	3.0000	3.5472
C119	4.0000	4.0000	3.8302
C120	3.0000	5.0000	4.3396
C121	5.0000	5.0000	3.6226
C122	3.0000	4.0000	3.5660
C123	1.0000	5.0000	3.8868
C124	1.0000	3.0000	3.6226
C125	4.0000	3.0000	3.6038
C126	3.0000	1.0000	3.5472

Distances Between Cluster Centroids

	Cluster1	Cluster2	Cluster3	Cluster4	Cluster5
Cluster1	0.0000	7.0000	3.2455	4.7434	3.2906
Cluster2	7.0000	0.0000	5.9833	5.9582	5.9015
Cluster3	3.2455	5.9833	0.0000	3.6194	2.7619
Cluster4	4.7434	5.9582	3.6194	0.0000	4.4106
Cluster5	3.2906	5.9015	2.7619	4.4106	0.0000
Cluster6	6.9462	6.8739	4.9649	6.1847	5.6083
Cluster7	4.0104	7.1239	3.1859	4.9749	4.7120
Cluster8	6.6332	7.5498	5.7271	6.5192	6.2512
Cluster9	3.9016	7.0238	4.4347	5.2757	3.5111
Cluster10	4.8305	8.1854	5.0990	5.6125	5.6194
Cluster11	2.8087	7.2572	4.0579	5.1478	3.2652
Cluster12	6.0828	6.6332	4.8374	4.7434	4.9828
Cluster13	6.2981	6.4807	6.0828	5.8737	5.2752
Cluster14	5.5377	5.9161	4.6043	6.1237	5.4155
Cluster15	6.9522	6.0000	5.1962	6.6708	5.1067
Cluster16	4.4253	6.1847	4.2485	5.2202	4.0716
Cluster17	5.9231	5.0744	4.2367	4.9244	3.9310
Cluster18	12.0277	9.5394	10.0000	9.9247	10.5275
Cluster19	4.6368	5.6125	3.4205	4.8477	3.7521
Cluster20	3.9476	6.5765	4.8010	6.0622	4.5087
Cluster21	7.0946	6.4807	6.6783	6.5192	6.4868
Cluster22	5.3437	6.6667	4.2400	5.5327	3.6546
Cluster23	6.4031	7.0711	5.8481	6.1237	5.2515
Cluster24	6.4291	7.8102	5.9330	7.1063	6.1505
Cluster25	7.2111	8.5440	6.3875	7.7782	6.4675
Cluster26	8.0208	7.2111	6.7676	7.3144	6.5634
Cluster27	7.6594	8.8882	6.4187	6.6708	6.6203

	Cluster6	Cluster7	Cluster8	Cluster9	Cluster10
Cluster1	6.9462	4.0104	6.6332	3.9016	4.8305
Cluster2	6.8739	7.1239	7.5498	7.0238	8.1854
Cluster3	4.9649	3.1859	5.7271	4.4347	5.0990
Cluster4	6.1847	4.9749	6.5192	5.2757	5.6125
Cluster5	5.6083	4.7120	6.2512	3.5111	5.6194
Cluster6	0.0000	5.8310	6.0208	7.3428	6.7268
Cluster7	5.8310	0.0000	6.9101	5.2361	5.4544
Cluster8	6.0208	6.9101	0.0000	6.9041	6.7823
Cluster9	7.3428	5.2361	6.9041	0.0000	5.8023
Cluster10	6.7268	5.4544	6.7823	5.8023	0.0000

Appendix XVIII Page 12

Cluster11	7.9110	5.0083	7.9791	3.8586	5.6862
Cluster12	5.6789	5.5453	6.8557	5.0990	6.5574
Cluster13	7.1589	7.1239	7.5498	5.0990	5.9161
Cluster14	5.9372	5.4544	7.6158	6.8069	5.8310
Cluster15	5.5902	5.8949	6.8557	6.1101	8.0623
Cluster16	5.8310	4.5277	6.5000	3.7749	5.6789
Cluster17	4.4159	5.7879	5.9791	5.4848	6.7639
Cluster18	8.4410	10.9430	8.6023	11.8462	11.6619
Cluster19	5.1720	3.7081	6.5192	5.4924	6.3640
Cluster20	7.3824	5.2915	7.6322	4.6098	6.2650
Cluster21	8.8459	7.0534	9.5394	7.1647	8.6603
Cluster22	5.4493	5.4645	6.6916	4.5947	6.4893
Cluster23	6.2650	6.5383	6.5574	4.9666	6.2450
Cluster24	7.6974	7.3314	6.9282	6.5574	6.9282
Cluster25	6.2650	6.6895	6.4807	7.0475	8.1240
Cluster26	7.5000	7.7942	7.8102	7.7460	9.5394
Cluster27	7.5664	7.2629	8.2462	7.8951	8.3666

	Cluster11	Cluster12	Cluster13	Cluster14	Cluster15
Cluster1	2.8087	6.0828	6.2981	5.5377	6.9522
Cluster2	7.2572	6.6332	6.4807	5.9161	6.0000
Cluster3	4.0579	4.8374	6.0828	4.6043	5.1962
Cluster4	5.1478	4.7434	5.8737	6.1237	6.6708
Cluster5	3.2652	4.9828	5.2752	5.4155	5.1067
Cluster6	7.9110	5.6789	7.1589	5.9372	5.5902
Cluster7	5.0083	5.5453	7.1239	5.4544	5.8949
Cluster8	7.9791	6.8557	7.5498	7.6158	6.8557
Cluster9	3.8586	5.0990	5.0990	6.8069	6.1101
Cluster10	5.6862	6.5574	5.9161	5.8310	8.0623
Cluster11	0.0000	6.1644	6.4291	5.8023	7.0711
Cluster12	6.1644	0.0000	6.3246	6.8557	6.0000
Cluster13	6.4291	6.3246	0.0000	6.7082	6.7823
Cluster14	5.8023	6.8557	6.7082	0.0000	7.0000
Cluster15	7.0711	6.0000	6.7823	7.0000	0.0000
Cluster16	5.2520	4.5000	5.3151	6.1847	5.8523
Cluster17	6.3574	4.3301	5.9791	6.6895	4.3301
Cluster18	13.1276	9.6437	10.4403	11.3137	9.2195
Cluster19	5.3697	5.4314	5.9582	5.5227	4.5277
Cluster20	4.8563	6.3443	5.8523	6.0208	7.0887
Cluster21	7.3937	8.2462	8.3666	7.9373	7.0711
Cluster22	5.1854	4.8074	5.8119	6.6416	4.4472
Cluster23	6.9761	6.3246	6.1644	7.6811	6.4807
Cluster24	6.8557	7.0000	6.7082	7.3485	7.5498
Cluster25	8.3865	7.0000	8.7750	9.1652	6.5574
Cluster26	7.9162	6.9282	9.0554	8.8882	5.2915
Cluster27	7.9791	7.8102	8.4261	8.7178	8.0623

	Cluster16	Cluster17	Cluster18	Cluster19	Cluster20
Cluster1	4.4253	5.9231	12.0277	4.6368	3.9476
Cluster2	6.1847	5.0744	9.5394	5.6125	6.5765
Cluster3	4.2485	4.2367	10.0000	3.4205	4.8010
Cluster4	5.2202	4.9244	9.9247	4.8477	6.0622
Cluster5	4.0716	3.9310	10.5275	3.7521	4.5087
Cluster6	5.8310	4.4159	8.4410	5.1720	7.3824
Cluster7	4.5277	5.7879	10.9430	3.7081	5.2915
Cluster8	6.5000	5.9791	8.6023	6.5192	7.6322
Cluster9	3.7749	5.4848	11.8462	5.4924	4.6098
Cluster10	5.6789	6.7639	11.6619	6.3640	6.2650
Cluster11	5.2520	6.3574	13.1276	5.3697	4.8563
Cluster12	4.5000	4.3301	9.6437	5.9582	6.3443
Cluster13	5.3151	5.9791	10.4403	5.5227	6.0208
Cluster14	6.1847	6.6895	11.3137	4.5277	7.0887
Cluster15	5.8523	4.3301	9.2195	4.2131	3.7417
Cluster16	0.0000	4.5277	10.4523	4.5552	6.1237
Cluster17	4.5277	0.0000	8.4705	9.2466	11.3248
Cluster18	10.4523	8.4705	0.0000	9.2466	11.3248
Cluster19	4.2131	4.5552	9.2466	0.0000	4.6637
Cluster20	3.7417	6.1237	11.3248	4.6637	0.0000
Cluster21	7.4330	7.1937	11.2694	6.5955	7.5664

Appendix XVIII Page 13

Cluster22	5.4186	4.2655	10.3333	4.2361	5.8618
Cluster23	5.3151	4.8734	10.1489	6.2048	6.3443
Cluster24	7.3655	6.8374	10.7703	6.7454	6.9462
Cluster25	6.5765	5.9791	9.7980	6.4420	7.3655
Cluster26	8.0156	5.7228	11.0000	7.2457	8.9582
Cluster27	7.2284	7.1937	10.7703	6.8920	7.8262

	Cluster21	Cluster22	Cluster23	Cluster24	Cluster25
Cluster1	7.0946	5.3437	6.4031	6.4291	7.2111
Cluster2	6.4807	6.6667	7.0711	7.8102	8.5440
Cluster3	6.6783	4.2400	5.8481	5.9330	6.3875
Cluster4	6.5192	5.5327	6.1237	7.1063	7.7782
Cluster5	6.4868	3.6546	5.2515	6.1505	6.4675
Cluster6	8.8459	5.4493	6.2650	7.6974	6.2650
Cluster7	7.0534	5.4645	6.5383	7.3314	6.6895
Cluster8	9.5394	6.6916	6.5574	6.9282	6.4807
Cluster9	7.1647	4.5947	4.9666	6.5574	7.0475
Cluster10	8.6603	6.4893	6.2450	6.9282	8.1240
Cluster11	7.3937	5.1854	6.9761	6.8557	8.3865
Cluster12	8.2462	4.8074	6.3246	7.0000	7.0000
Cluster13	8.3666	5.8119	6.1644	6.7082	8.7750
Cluster14	7.9373	6.6416	7.6811	7.3485	9.1652
Cluster15	7.0711	4.4472	6.4807	7.5498	6.5574
Cluster16	7.4330	5.4186	5.3151	7.3655	6.5765
Cluster17	7.1937	4.2655	4.8734	6.8374	5.9791
Cluster18	11.2694	10.3333	10.1489	10.7703	9.7980
Cluster19	6.5955	4.2361	6.2048	6.7454	6.4420
Cluster20	7.5664	5.8618	6.3443	6.9462	7.3655
Cluster21	0.0000	8.0277	7.4833	10.3441	8.4261
Cluster22	8.0277	0.0000	5.3333	5.2387	6.0093
Cluster23	7.4833	5.3333	0.0000	7.0000	6.5574
Cluster24	10.3441	5.2387	7.0000	0.0000	8.8318
Cluster25	8.4261	6.0093	6.5574	8.8318	0.0000
Cluster26	8.9443	6.3596	8.4853	9.1104	7.8102
Cluster27	8.6603	7.7531	8.1854	10.3923	6.9282

	Cluster26	Cluster27
Cluster1	8.0208	7.6594
Cluster2	7.2111	8.8882
Cluster3	6.7676	6.4187
Cluster4	7.3144	6.6708
Cluster5	6.5634	6.6203
Cluster6	7.5000	7.5664
Cluster7	7.7942	7.2629
Cluster8	7.8102	8.2462
Cluster9	7.7460	7.8951
Cluster10	9.5394	8.3666
Cluster11	7.9162	7.9791
Cluster12	6.9282	7.8102
Cluster13	9.0554	8.4261
Cluster14	8.8882	8.7178
Cluster15	5.2915	8.0623
Cluster16	8.0156	7.2284
Cluster17	5.7228	7.1937
Cluster18	11.0000	10.7703
Cluster19	7.2457	6.8920
Cluster20	8.9582	7.8262
Cluster21	8.9443	8.6603
Cluster22	6.3596	7.7531
Cluster23	8.4853	8.1854
Cluster24	9.1104	10.3923
Cluster25	7.8102	6.9282
Cluster26	0.0000	8.0623
Cluster27	8.0623	0.0000

MTB >

202

Appendix XIX: Full Survey Similarity Dendogram

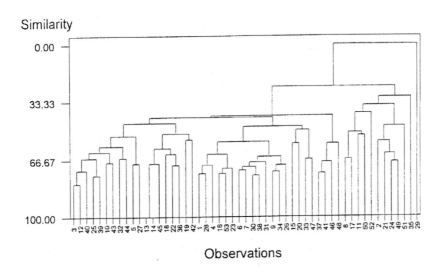

Appendix XX: Dendogram Full Survey Centroids Distance

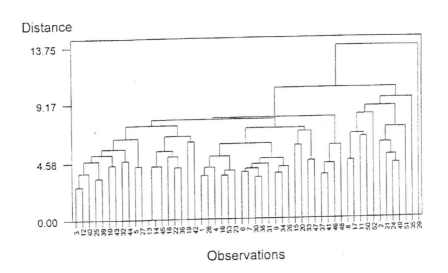

Appendix XXI: Screen Plot of Full Data Set

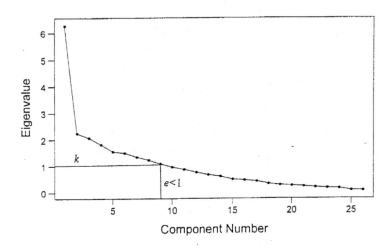

Appendix XXII Principal Component Analysis Full Survey
Page 1 Principal Component Analysis Full Survey

```
MTB > PCA C101-C126;
SUBC>   Scores c151.
```

Principal Component Analysis

Eigenanalysis of the Correlation Matrix

Eigenvalue	6.2656	2.2423	2.0678	1.8180	1.5429	1.4924
Proportion	0.241	0.086	0.080	0.070	0.059	0.057
Cumulative	0.241	0.327	0.407	0.477	0.536	0.593
Eigenvalue	1.3389	1.2213	1.0819	0.9638	0.8644	0.7562
Proportion	0.051	0.047	0.042	0.037	0.033	0.029
Cumulative	0.645	0.692	0.734	0.771	0.804	0.833
Eigenvalue	0.6635	0.5968	0.4888	0.4545	0.4109	0.3269
Proportion	0.026	0.023	0.019	0.017	0.016	0.013
Cumulative	0.858	0.881	0.900	0.918	0.933	0.946
Eigenvalue	0.2780	0.2494	0.2223	0.1902	0.1628	0.1473
Proportion	0.011	0.010	0.009	0.007	0.006	0.006
Cumulative	0.957	0.966	0.975	0.982	0.988	0.994
Eigenvalue	0.0794	0.0737				
Proportion	0.003	0.003				
Cumulative	0.997	1.000				

Variable	PC1	PC2	PC3	PC4	PC5	PC6
C101	-0.185	0.073	-0.332	-0.120	-0.325	-0.231
C102	-0.134	-0.224	0.200	-0.179	0.391	-0.274
C103	-0.211	-0.275	-0.196	-0.014	0.059	-0.074
C104	-0.221	0.240	0.100	-0.189	-0.244	0.104
C105	-0.061	-0.123	-0.086	-0.441	0.232	0.217
C106	-0.127	-0.083	0.305	0.173	-0.068	0.148
C107	-0.134	-0.137	0.451	0.025	-0.168	-0.249
C108	-0.173	-0.362	0.111	-0.141	-0.177	0.298
C109	-0.112	-0.011	-0.106	-0.307	0.041	0.111
C110	-0.269	-0.153	0.187	0.007	0.211	-0.078
C111	-0.220	0.218	-0.028	0.105	-0.233	-0.034
C112	-0.208	0.016	0.061	0.276	-0.002	-0.257
C113	-0.258	0.144	-0.019	0.011	0.277	0.185
C114	-0.157	0.093	-0.240	-0.233	0.037	-0.199
C115	-0.254	0.174	0.003	0.238	0.080	0.010
C116	-0.199	0.120	-0.226	0.273	0.210	0.083
C117	-0.194	-0.134	0.120	0.167	0.280	0.008
C118	-0.165	-0.399	0.014	0.098	-0.165	0.174
C119	-0.272	-0.072	0.019	0.066	-0.364	-0.041
C120	-0.282	-0.124	-0.071	-0.045	-0.149	-0.002
C121	-0.082	0.090	0.186	-0.451	0.000	-0.388
C122	-0.191	-0.042	-0.156	-0.131	-0.051	0.399
C123	-0.206	0.028	-0.180	-0.024	-0.025	-0.231
C124	-0.219	0.004	-0.297	0.144	0.246	-0.094
C125	-0.177	0.376	0.230	-0.139	0.075	0.222
C126	-0.175	0.379	0.271	-0.034	0.052	0.123

Variable	PC7	PC8	PC9	PC10	PC11	PC12
C101	0.050	0.028	0.116	0.006	-0.366	0.037
C102	0.052	0.157	-0.176	-0.002	-0.040	0.028
C103	-0.266	0.055	-0.339	-0.059	-0.190	0.150
C104	0.150	0.093	-0.071	-0.212	0.326	0.202
C105	-0.241	-0.125	0.273	0.034	-0.179	-0.084
C106	-0.171	-0.138	0.376	0.369	-0.290	0.249
C107	0.048	-0.188	-0.049	0.243	-0.107	-0.024
C108	0.134	0.117	-0.002	0.055	-0.093	-0.248
C109	-0.067	-0.585	-0.117	0.143	0.381	-0.211
C110	-0.019	0.221	-0.022	0.021	0.251	-0.043
C111	-0.298	0.360	-0.059	0.055	0.053	-0.300
C112	-0.170	-0.050	0.328	-0.114	0.217	-0.482
C113	-0.163	0.168	-0.244	0.281	0.168	0.152
C114	-0.329	0.006	0.281	-0.129	0.071	0.223
C115	-0.193	-0.055	0.106	0.054	0.080	0.422
C116	0.028	-0.196	-0.113	-0.254	-0.296	-0.203

Appendix XXII Page 2

C117	0.247	-0.066	0.332	-0.449	0.028	0.073
C118	-0.114	-0.097	-0.165	-0.361	0.020	0.146
C119	-0.040	-0.294	-0.227	-0.098	-0.015	0.070
C120	0.056	0.151	0.121	0.196	0.112	-0.146
C121	0.014	0.074	0.000	-0.166	-0.198	-0.033
C122	0.271	0.292	0.217	0.004	-0.042	0.001
C123	0.519	-0.136	0.098	0.178	0.159	0.217
C124	0.226	-0.084	-0.119	0.311	-0.170	-0.164
C125	-0.036	-0.214	0.033	-0.090	-0.131	-0.111
C126	0.155	0.036	-0.233	-0.093	-0.271	-0.051

Variable	PC13	PC14	PC15	PC16	PC17	PC18
C101	-0.074	0.037	-0.151	-0.011	0.242	0.072
C102	-0.217	-0.325	0.136	-0.275	0.284	-0.019
C103	0.265	0.183	-0.074	0.240	0.292	0.011
C104	-0.101	-0.005	-0.234	0.264	0.334	0.065
C105	-0.393	-0.004	-0.329	0.092	-0.003	0.128
C106	0.091	0.143	0.211	-0.129	0.382	0.024
C107	-0.109	-0.115	-0.125	0.372	-0.271	-0.287
C108	0.065	-0.383	-0.061	0.158	-0.035	-0.104
C109	-0.041	0.125	0.222	-0.074	0.152	-0.046
C110	0.197	0.293	-0.109	-0.162	0.030	-0.288
C111	-0.313	-0.096	0.099	0.000	0.032	-0.067
C112	0.081	-0.133	0.131	0.104	0.202	0.291
C113	-0.035	0.041	0.072	0.259	-0.075	0.112
C114	0.426	-0.362	0.035	0.007	-0.168	-0.314
C115	-0.340	-0.097	0.008	-0.073	-0.280	0.103
C116	-0.260	0.065	0.038	-0.084	0.023	-0.518
C117	-0.011	0.211	-0.125	0.275	-0.016	0.066
C118	-0.036	-0.213	0.094	-0.301	-0.179	0.328
C119	0.000	0.153	0.141	0.038	-0.101	-0.034
C120	0.056	0.320	-0.384	-0.447	-0.246	0.020
C121	-0.082	0.314	0.371	0.026	-0.266	0.179
C122	0.020	0.084	0.531	0.097	-0.082	-0.112
C123	-0.096	-0.222	0.019	-0.139	0.116	-0.063
C124	0.191	-0.081	-0.021	0.181	-0.208	0.366
C125	0.309	-0.142	-0.099	-0.120	-0.108	0.026
C126	0.157	-0.082	-0.087	-0.208	0.114	0.135

Variable	PC19	PC20	PC21	PC22	PC23	PC24
C101	-0.238	0.533	-0.013	-0.217	-0.036	0.088
C102	-0.043	0.160	-0.245	0.222	0.238	-0.185
C103	0.287	-0.062	-0.025	0.116	-0.272	-0.220
C104	0.063	-0.288	0.018	-0.103	0.212	-0.237
C105	-0.174	-0.212	0.208	-0.253	-0.110	0.080
C106	0.013	-0.240	-0.073	-0.166	0.115	0.025
C107	0.018	0.023	-0.136	0.074	-0.310	-0.013
C108	0.237	0.139	0.212	-0.290	0.305	0.065
C109	0.222	0.227	-0.088	-0.150	-0.155	0.011
C110	-0.366	0.076	0.488	-0.172	-0.154	-0.054
C111	-0.067	-0.148	-0.247	-0.067	-0.272	-0.058
C112	0.053	0.005	0.183	0.153	0.037	0.071
C113	-0.192	0.093	-0.214	-0.141	0.167	0.491
C114	0.092	-0.116	-0.064	0.050	0.067	0.174
C115	0.315	0.312	0.312	-0.018	0.017	-0.284
C116	0.074	-0.223	0.022	-0.179	0.168	0.026
C117	0.050	0.175	-0.341	-0.031	-0.051	0.137
C118	-0.174	-0.166	-0.073	-0.239	-0.263	0.099
C119	-0.296	-0.000	0.101	0.495	0.388	0.091
C120	0.288	-0.056	-0.310	0.127	0.153	0.006
C121	0.135	-0.180	0.091	-0.289	0.111	0.019
C122	-0.004	0.096	-0.007	0.310	-0.200	-0.162
C123	-0.082	-0.275	0.051	-0.014	-0.252	0.150
C124	-0.064	-0.205	0.059	-0.074	0.086	-0.248
C125	-0.317	0.095	-0.221	-0.073	-0.039	-0.411
C126	0.307	0.045	0.220	0.233	-0.231	0.402

Variable	PC25	PC26
C101	-0.186	-0.005
C102	-0.101	0.069
C103	0.216	-0.246
C104	-0.312	0.054
C105	0.027	-0.004
C106	-0.012	0.125

Appendix XXII Page 3

C107	-0.313	-0.068
C108	0.297	-0.009
C109	-0.042	0.201
C110	-0.030	0.148
C111	0.324	0.349
C112	-0.132	-0.343
C113	-0.045	-0.285
C114	-0.108	0.199
C115	0.087	-0.026
C116	-0.180	-0.159
C117	0.231	0.275
C118	-0.242	-0.025
C119	0.224	0.141
C120	-0.090	-0.138
C121	0.097	-0.107
C122	-0.231	-0.086
C123	0.372	-0.251
C124	-0.153	0.385
C125	0.214	-0.287
C126	-0.074	0.190

MTB >

Appendix XXIII Full Survey Factor Analysis
Page 1 Full Survey Factor Analysis

```
MTB > Factor C101-C126;
SUBC>    NFactors 3;
SUBC>    VMax;
SUBC>    Correlation.
```

Factor Analysis

Principal Component Factor Analysis of the Correlation Matrix

Unrotated Factor Loadings and Communalities

Variable	Factor1	Factor2	Factor3	Communality
C101	-0.463	0.109	-0.477	0.454
C102	-0.336	-0.336	0.288	0.309
C103	-0.528	-0.412	-0.281	0.527
C104	-0.552	0.360	0.144	0.456
C105	-0.154	-0.184	-0.124	0.073
C106	-0.318	-0.124	0.438	0.309
C107	-0.335	-0.205	0.648	0.574
C108	-0.434	-0.542	0.159	0.508
C109	-0.281	-0.016	-0.152	0.103
C110	-0.674	-0.230	0.269	0.580
C111	-0.551	0.327	-0.040	0.412
C112	-0.520	0.024	0.087	0.279
C113	-0.645	0.215	-0.028	0.464
C114	-0.392	0.139	-0.345	0.293
C115	-0.636	0.260	0.005	0.472
C116	-0.499	0.179	-0.326	0.387
C117	-0.486	-0.201	0.173	0.307
C118	-0.413	-0.598	0.021	0.528
C119	-0.681	-0.108	0.027	0.476
C120	-0.707	-0.186	-0.102	0.545
C121	-0.205	0.135	0.268	0.132
C122	-0.478	-0.063	-0.224	0.283
C123	-0.516	0.042	-0.258	0.334
C124	-0.549	0.005	-0.426	0.484
C125	-0.444	0.563	0.331	0.623
C126	-0.439	0.567	0.390	0.667
Variance	6.2656	2.2423	2.0678	10.5757
% Var	0.241	0.086	0.080	0.407

Rotated Factor Loadings and Communalities
Varimax Rotation

Variable	Factor1	Factor2	Factor3	Communality
C101	0.671	-0.046	0.034	0.454
C102	0.006	0.549	0.081	0.309
C103	0.538	0.449	-0.191	0.527
C104	0.314	0.103	0.588	0.456
C105	0.182	0.157	-0.123	0.073
C106	-0.096	0.457	0.302	0.309
C107	-0.239	0.618	0.367	0.574
C108	0.150	0.691	-0.086	0.508
C109	0.304	0.093	0.038	0.103
C110	0.266	0.646	0.304	0.580
C111	0.441	0.042	0.464	0.412
C112	0.306	0.300	0.309	0.279
C113	0.490	0.178	0.438	0.464
C114	0.531	-0.046	0.094	0.293
C115	0.464	0.156	0.482	0.472
C116	0.595	-0.009	0.182	0.387
C117	0.204	0.482	0.183	0.307
C118	0.229	0.657	-0.210	0.528
C119	0.451	0.453	0.259	0.476
C120	0.554	0.465	0.148	0.545
C121	-0.035	0.134	0.336	0.132
C122	0.490	0.199	0.059	0.283
C123	0.548	0.128	0.131	0.334
C124	0.688	0.097	0.030	0.484
C125	0.121	-0.016	0.780	0.623
C126	0.077	0.005	0.813	0.667

Appendix XXIII Page 2

```
Variance        4.1419        3.3538        3.0800        10.5757
% Var           0.159         0.129          0.118          0.407

Factor Score Coefficients

Variable    Factor1       Factor2       Factor3
C101          0.219        -0.100        -0.057
C102         -0.073         0.199        -0.003
C103          0.141         0.115        -0.162
C104          0.025        -0.036         0.191
C105          0.053         0.044        -0.078
C106         -0.118         0.162         0.101
C107         -0.191         0.236         0.132
C108         -0.025         0.245        -0.094
C109          0.083        -0.004        -0.024
C110         -0.024         0.189         0.050
C111          0.087        -0.066         0.132
C112          0.029         0.056         0.070
C113          0.089        -0.020         0.108
C114          0.167        -0.086        -0.018
C115          0.079        -0.028         0.130
C116          0.173        -0.086         0.007
C117         -0.011         0.143         0.019
C118          0.018         0.230        -0.149
C119          0.063         0.099         0.025
C120          0.108         0.097        -0.031
C121         -0.064         0.033         0.128
C122          0.128         0.012        -0.043
C123          0.148        -0.026        -0.016
C124          0.208        -0.048        -0.069
C125         -0.044        -0.069         0.295
C126         -0.064        -0.058         0.311

MTB >
```

Appendix XXIV Full Survey data Display

```
MTB > print c131-c134

Data Display

Row   C131      C132       C133       C134

  1     1     1.34054    0.47264   -0.51880
  2     2    -0.06041   -0.79737   -0.65174
  3     3     0.47164    0.34599   -0.86776
  4     1     0.86816    0.89421    0.24875
  5     4     0.67808   -1.11617   -0.31485
  6     5    -0.16795    1.06126    0.60851
  7     5     0.14848    0.64865    0.27950
  8     6    -1.01239   -0.14438   -1.00538
  9     5    -0.40316    0.12525    0.49229
 10     7     0.57687    0.76672   -1.00110
 11     8    -0.96811   -1.00715   -0.29111
 12     3     0.16730   -0.07217   -0.69679
 13     9     0.54092   -0.66295    1.88599
 14     9     0.54092   -0.66295    1.88599
 15    10     1.30071   -0.99986    0.25096
 16    11     1.06084    0.57086    0.47117
 17     6    -1.29993    0.21166   -1.41074
 18    12    -0.66866   -0.43249    0.48023
 19    13     0.61033   -2.02820    1.26637
 20    14     1.38522    0.23022   -1.62173
 21    15    -1.52084    0.68690   -0.31209
 22    16     0.45841   -1.11871    0.45590
 23    11     0.75187    1.24583    1.26717
 24    17    -1.63012    0.44397    0.38173
 25     3     0.33897    1.10354   -0.65607
 26     5    -1.06960    0.68926    0.74040
 27     4     0.73358    0.09617   -0.85437
 28     1     1.30297    0.46367    0.34680
 29    18    -2.05631   -3.73897   -2.51184
 30     5     0.39869   -0.36553   -0.24461
 31     5     0.35302    0.38453    0.06243
 32    19    -0.16535    0.69126   -1.66183
 33    20     0.81230    0.31339    0.07787
 34     5    -0.47795    0.35350    0.32945
 35    21     1.06785   -0.57359   -1.19669
 36    16     0.36581   -0.04364   -0.07772
 37    22    -1.45194    0.32539    0.60275
 38     5    -0.00464   -0.16494    0.61058
 39     3     0.47441    1.12631   -0.76872
 40     3     0.13550    0.49195   -1.11302
 41    22    -1.02996    0.81081    1.22240
 42    23    -0.31717   -2.08424    1.55859
 43     7     1.21431    0.64234   -1.51362
 44    19     0.25956   -0.04810   -0.34453
 45     9     0.06825    0.02532    1.21677
 46    22    -1.03935    0.34712    1.97992
 47    20     1.64763   -1.63665    0.28418
 48    24    -0.23464   -0.78502    1.59818
 49    17    -0.81166   -1.22315   -0.26196
 50    25    -1.82307    0.25277    0.19178
 51    26    -2.70892    2.15659    0.00757
 52    27    -0.54093    0.46509   -1.24101
 53    11     1.38994    1.26307    0.33383

MTB >
```

BIBLIOGRAPHY and REFERENCES

Abell D F and Hammond J S (1979), Strategic Market Planning: Problems and Analytical Approaches. Prentice-Hall International.

Ackoff R L (1970), A Concept of Corporate Planning. John Wiley and Sons.

Allen P M (1988) Dynamics Models of Evolving Systems. System Dynamics Review, 4, Summer, pp. 109-130

Argysis C (1982), Reasoning, Learning and Action: Individual and Organizational. San Francisco: Jossey-Bass.

Argysis C and Schon D (1978), Organizational Learning: A Theory of Action Perspective. Reading M A. Addison-Wesley.

Ariely D (2010), Predictably Irrational, Revised and Expanded Edition: The Hidden Forces that Shape Our Decisions, New York: HarperCollins.

Bain, J. S. (1956), Barriers to New Competition: Their Character and Consequences in Manufacturing Industries. Harvard University Press, Cambridge.

Balogun, J., Hailey, V. H. and Gustafsson, S, (2016). Exploring Strategic Change. Pearson

Bannister D & Fransella F (1986), Inquiring Man: The Psychology of Personal Constructs. Croom Helm (3rd ed).

Barr P S, Stimpert J L and Huff A S (1992), Cognitive Change, Strategic Action and Organizational Renewal. Strategic Management Journal, 13, pp.15-36.

Barney J B and Hoskisson R E (1990), Strategic Groups: Untested Assertions and Research Proposals. Managerial and Decision Economics, 11, pp. 187-198.

Bartlett C A (1983), MNCs: get off the reorganization merry-go-round. Harvard Business Review, March-April, pp. 138–146.

Bartlett C A and Ghoshal S (1989), Managing Across Borders: The Transnational Solution, Harvard Business School Press, Boston M.A.

Békésy G v (1957), The Ear. in, Physiological Psychology: Readings from the Scientific American, (1972) San Francisco, W H Freeman & Co.

Besanko D, Dranove D and Shanley M (1996), Economics of Strategy. John Wiley & Sons, New York.

Best M H, (1990), The New Competition: Institutions of Industrial Restructuring. Polity Press, Cambridge.

Best M H, (2001), The New Competitive Advantage: The Renewal of American Industry. Oxford University Press.

Boeker W (1991), Organizational Strategy: An ecological perspective. Academy of Management Journal, Vol.34, No.3, pp. 613-635.

Bowman C C (1991), Perceptions of Competitive Strategy: Realised Strategy, Consensus and Performance. Unpublished PhD Thesis, School of Management, Cranfield Institute of Technology.

Bresser R K F, Dunbar R L M and Jithernranathan T (1994), Competitive and Collective strategies: An empirical examination of strategic groups. Advances in Strategic Management, Vol. 10B, pp. 187-211.

Briggs A (1974), The Age of Improvement. Longman.

Brozen Y (1971), Bain's concentration and rates of return revisited. Journal of Law and Economics, Vol. 14, pp.351–369.

Buzzell R D, Gale B T and Sultan R G M (1975) Market Share: A key to profitability. Harvard Business Review, January –February, pp. 97-106.

Buzzell R D and Gale B T (1987), The Pims Principles – Linking Strategy to Performance. New York: Free Press

Caves R E (1980), Industrial organization, corporate strategy, and structure: a survey. Journal of Economic Literature, Vol. 18, No. 1, pp. 64–92.

Caves R E and Ghemawat P (1992), Identifying Mobility Barriers. Strategic Management Journal. Vol. 13, No.1, pp. 1-12.

Caves R E and Porter M E (1977), From entry barriers to mobility barriers: conjectural decisions and contrived deterrence to new competition. Quarterly Journal of Economics, Vol. 26, pp. 113-14O.

Caves R E and Porter M E (1977), From entry barriers to mobility barriers. Quarterly Journal of Economics, May, pp. 241-261.

Caves R E and Porter M E (1977), Market structure, oligopoly and stability of market shares. Journal of Industrial Economics, Vol. 26, No. 4, pp. 289–313.

Chandler A D (1962), Strategy and Structure: Chapters in the History of the American Industrial Enterprise. Cambridge, MA. MIT Press.
The Visible Hand: The Managerial Revolution in American Business. Harvard University Press, 1977.
Scale and Scope: The Dynamics of Industrial Capitalism. Harvard University Press, 1990.

Charniak E and McDermott D (1985), Introduction to Artificial Intelligence. Reading, Massachusetts, Addison Wesley.

Child J and Smith C (1987), The context and process of organisational transformation – Cadbury Limited in its Sector. Journal of Management Studies, 24, pp. 565–593.

Chrisman J J, Hofer C W and Boulton W R (1988), Towards a system for classifying business strategies. Academy of Management Review, Vol. 13, No. 3, pp. 413–428.

Clarke R (1985), Industrial Economics. Basil Blackwell.

Clarke, Davies and Watson (1984), The profitability - concentration relation: market power or efficiency? Journal of Industrial Economics Vol. 34, pp. 435-45O.

Collins and Preston (1969), Price-cost margins and industry structure. Review of Economics and Statistics, Vol. 51, pp. 271–286.

Collins A M and Quillian M R (1969), Retrieval time form Semantic Memory. Journal of Verbal Learning and Verbal Behaviour, No.8 pp. 240–247.

Cool K O (1985), Strategic Group Formation and Strategic Skills: A longitudinal Analysis of the U.S. Pharmaceutical Industry, 1963-1982. Unpublished doctoral dissertation, Purdue University.

Cool K O and Dierickx I (1993), Rivalry, Strategic Groups and Firm Profitability: Strategic Management Journal, Vol.14, No.1, January

Cool K O and Schendel D E (1987), Strategic Group Formation and Performance: The case of the U.S. Pharmaceutical Industry, 1963-1982, Management Science, Vol. 33, No. 9, pp. 11O2–1124.

Cool K O and Schendel D E (1988), Performance Differences among Strategic Group Members. Strategic Management Journal, Vol. 9, pp. 2O7–223.

Cosier R A and Rechner P L (1985), Inquiry Method Effects on Performance in a Simulated Business Environment. Organisational Behaviour and Human Decision Processes. Vol.36, pp. 79-95.

Cowley P R (1988), Market Structure and Business Performance: an evaluation of buyer/seller power in the PIMS database. Strategic Management Journal Vol. 9, pp.

271– 278.

Cowling and Waterson (1976), Price-cost Margins and Market Structure. Economica, Vol. 43, pp. 267–274.

Curry and George (1983), Industrial concentration: a survey. Journal of Industrial Economics Vol. 31, pp. 2O3–255.

Cyert R and March J (1963), A Behavioural Theory of the Firm. Englewood Cliffs, N J: Prentice-Hall.

Day D L W, De Sarbo W S and Oliva T A (1987), Strategy maps: a spatial representation of intra-industry competitive strategy. Management Science Vol. 33, No. 12, pp. 1534– 1551.

Daniels K, de Chernatony L and Johnson G (1992), Paper presented to the British Academy of Management Conference, Bradford September.

Demsetz H (1973), Industrial structure, market rivalry and public policy. Journal of Law and Economics, Vol. 6, pp. 64–92.

Demsetz H (1982), Barriers to entry. The American Economic Review, Vol. 72, pp. 47–57.

Dess G G (1987), Consensus on Strategy Formulation and Organizational Performance: Competitors in a Fragmented Industry. Strategic Management Journal, Vol.8, pp. 259277.

Dess G G & Davies P S (1984), Porter's (1980) Generic Strategies as Determinants of Strategic Group Membership and Organizational Performance. Academy of Management Journal, Vol.27, No.3, pp. 467-488.

Dillon W R & Goldstein (1984), M, Multivariate analysis: Methods and Applications. John Wiley & Sons.

Di Maggio P J and Powell W W (1983), The Iron Cage Revisited: Institutional Isomorphism and Collective Rationality in Organizational Fields. American Sociological Review, 48(2), pp.147-160.

Dunn W N, Cahill G, Dukes M J and Ginsberg A (1986), The Policy Grid: A cognitive methodology for assessing policy dynamics: In Dunn W N (ed), Policy Analysis: Perspectives, Concepts and Methods. JAI Press, New York, pp.355-375.

Dutton J E, Fahey L and Narayanan V K (1983), Toward understanding strategic issues diagnosis: Strategic Management Journal, 4, pp.307-324.

Everitt B S (1974), Cluster Analysis. London: Heineman Educational Books.

Everitt B S and Dunn G (1991), Applied Multivariate Data Analysis. London, Edward Arnold.

Figenbaum A (1987), Dynamic aspects of strategic groups and competitive strategy: Concepts and empirical examination in the insurance industry. Unpublished doctoral dissertation, University of Illinois at Urbana-Champaign.

Figenbaum A and Thomas H (1990), Strategic Groups and Performance: The U.S. insurance industry, 1970-1984. Strategic Management Journal, 11, pp.197-215.

Fombrun C J and Zajac E J (1987), Structural and perceptual influences on intra-industry stratification. Academy of Management Journal, Vol.30, No.1, pp.33-50.

Fransella F & Bannister D (1977), A Manual for Repertory Grid Technique. New York, Academic Press.

Galbraith C, Merrill G B and Morgan G (1994), Bilateral Strategic Groups: The Market for Nontactical Navy Information Systems. Strategic Management Journal, Vol.15, No.8, pp. 613-626.

Bibliography

Galbraith C and Schendel D E (1983), An Empirical Analysis of Strategy Types. Strategic Management Journal, Vol. 4, No.2, pp. 153–173.

Gardner H (1984), The Mind's New Science, New York: Basic Books.

Ghemawat P (1999), Strategy and the Business Landscape, Addison Wesley.

Ginsburg A and Abrahamson E (1991), Champions of Change and Strategic Shifts: The role of internal and external change advocates. Journal of Management Studies, 28, pp. 173-190.

Glaser B G & Strauss A L (1967) The Discovery of Grounded Theory: Strategies for qualitative research, Weidenfeld & Nicolson, London

Green P E (1977), A new approach to market segmentation: Business Horizons, February, pp. 61-73.

Grinyer P and McKiernan P (1990), Generating Major Change in Stagnating Companies. Strategic Management Journal, 11, pp. 131-146.

Georski P A (1981), Specification and testing the profits-concentration relationship: some experiments for the UK. Economica Vol. 48, pp. 279-288.

Gourvish T R and Wilson R G (2008), The British Brewing Industry 1830-1980. Cambridge University Press.

Hall W K (1980), Strategies in a hostile environment. Harvard Business Review September-October, pp. 75-85.

Hallagan W and Joerding W (1983), Polymorphic equilibrium in advertising. The Bell Journal of Economics, Vol. 14, No. 1, pp. 191-2O1.

Hambrick D C (1987), The Top Management Team: Key to strategic success. California management Review, Fall 1987, pp. 88.108.

Hannah L (1983), The Rise of the Corporate Economy. Methuen.

Harrigan K R (1980), Strategies for Declining Industries. Lexington Books.

Harrigan K R (1985), An Application of Clustering for Strategic Group Analysis. Strategic Management Journal, Vol.6, pp. 55-73.

Harrigan K R (1985), Strategic Flexibility: A Management Guide for Changing Times. Lexington Books.

Harrigan K R and Porter M E (1983), End-game strategies for declining industries. Harvard Business Review, July-August, pp. 111-12O.

Hatten K J and Hatten M L (1985), Some empirical insights for strategic marketeers: the case of beer. Ed. Thomas and Gardner, Strategic Marketing and Management, John Wiley and Sons.

Hatten K J and Hatten M L (1987), Strategic groups, asymmetrical mobility barriers and contestability. Strategic Management Journal, Vol. 8, pp. 329-342.

Hatten K L and Schendel D E (1977), Heterogeneity within an industry: firm conduct within the U.S. brewing industry, 1952-1977. Journal of Industrial Economics, Vol. 26, No. 2, pp. 97-113.

Hatten K L, Schendel D E and Cooper A (1978), A strategic model of the U.S. brewing industry: 1952-1971: Academy of Management Journal, 21, pp.592-610.

Hayek F A (1945), The use of knowledge in society. American Economic Review 35: 519-530.

Hill C W L (1988), Differentiation versus Low Cost or Differentiation and Low Cost: A Contingency Framework, Academy of Management Review, Vol. 13, No.3, pp. 401-412.

Hinkle D (1965), The Change of Personal Construct Implications. Unpublished PhD.

Thesis, Ohio State University.

Hirschey M, Pappas J L and Whigham D (1995), Managerial Economics. The Dryden Press, European Edition.

Hirshleifer J (1999), There are many pathways to cooperation, Journal of Bioeconomics 1: 73-93.

Hofer C W (1989), Strategies for business turnarounds. Ed. Fahey L, The Strategic Planning Management Reader, Prentice Hall.

Hofer C W and Schendel D E (1978), Strategy Formulation: Analytical Concepts. West Publishing Company, S E Paul, Minnesota.

Holstead G (1980), Motivation, Leadership and Organisation: Do American Theories apply abroad? Organizational Dynamics, Summer, pp. 42-63.

Holterman (1973), Structure and economic performance in UK manufacturing industry. Journal of Industrial Economics, Vol. 21, pp. 119–139.

Hout, Porter and Rudden (1982), How global companies win out. Harvard Business Review, September-October, pp. 98-1O8.

Huff A S (1982), Industry influences on strategy reformulation: Strategic Management Journal, 3, pp. 119-131.

Huff A S (1990), Mapping Strategic Thought, Wiley, Chichester.

Hunt M S (1972), Competition in the Major Home Appliance Industry, 1960-1970. Unpublished PhD thesis, Harvard University.

Johnson G (1987), Strategic Change and the Management Process. Basil Blackwell.

Johnson G (1992), Managing Strategic Change – Strategy, Culture and Action. Long Range Planning, 25, 1, pp. 28-36.

Johnson G and Thomas H (1987), The industry context of strategy, structure and performance: The U.K. brewing industry. Strategic Management Journal, 8, pp. 343-361.

Johnson P (1985), British Industry: An Economic Introduction. Blackwell.

Karnani A (1984), Generic competitive strategies - an analytical approach. Strategic Management Journal, Vol. 5, pp. 367-38O.

Kelly G A (1955), The Psychology of Personal Constructs. Norton. New York: Vols. 1&2.

Key Note Report (1995), Breweries and the Beer Market: A market sector overview. Key Note Publications.

Key Note Report (1998), Breweries and the Beer Market: An Industry Report. Key Note Publications.

Kim L and Lim Y (1988), Environment, generic strategies, and performance in a rapidly developing country: A taxonomic approach. Academy of Management Journal, Vol.31, No.4, pp. 802-827.

Kumar K R, Thomas H and Fiegenbaum A (1990), Strategic groupings as competitive benchmarks for formulating future competitive strategy: A modelling approach. Managerial Decision Economics, 11, pp. 99-109.

Kwoka J (1979), The effect of market share distribution on industry performance. Review of Economics and Statistics, February pp. 101-109.

Laidler D (1981), Introduction to Microeconomics. Philip Allan.

Lant T K and Mezias S J (1992), An Organizational Learning Model of Convergence and Reorientation. Organizational Science, 3. Pp.47-71.

Lant T K, Milliken F J and Batra B (1992), The role of managerial learning and interpretation in strategic persistence and reorientation. An empirical exploration.

Strategic Management Journal, 13. Pp. 585-608.

Lawless M W, D D Bergh and Wilstead W D (1989), Performance variations among strategic group members: An examination of individual firm capacity. Journal of Management, 15, pp. 649-661.

Lawless M W and Tegarden L F (1991), A test of performance similarity among strategic group members in conforming and non-conforming industry structures. Journal of Management Studies, 28, pp. 645-664.

Lessem R and Sudhanshu P (1997), Managing in Four Worlds: From Competition to Co-creation. Blackwell.

Levy D (1994), Chaos Theory and Strategy Theory, Application and managerial Implications. Strategic Management Journal Vol.15, Summer, pp. 167-178.

Lewis P and Thomas H (1990), The Linkage between strategy, strategic groups, and performance in the U.K. retail grocery industry. Strategic Management Journal, Vol.11, pp. 385-397.

Littlechild S C (1981), Misleading calculations of the social costs of monopoly power. Economic Journal, Vol. 91, pp. 348-363.

Lorenz E N (1963), Deterministic non-periodic Flow. Journal of Atmospheric Sciences, 20. Pp. 130-141.

Mann H M (1966), Seller concentration, barriers to entry and rates of return in thirty industries, 1950-60. Review of Economics and Statistics Vol. 48, pp. 286-296.

Mascarenhas B (1989), Strategic Group Dynamics. Academy of Management Journal, 32, pp. 333-352.

Mascarenhas B and Aaker D D (1989), Mobility barriers and strategic groups. Strategic Management Journal, Vol. 10, No.5, pp. 475-485.

McGee J (1985), Strategic Groups: A Bridge between Industry Structure and Strategic Management. In Thomas H and Gardner D (Eds) Strategic Marketing and Management, Chichester. John Wiley and Sons.

McGee J and Thomas H (1986), Strategic Groups: A useful linkage between industry structure and strategic management. Strategic Management Journal, 7, pp. 141-160.

McGee J and Thomas H (1986a), Strategic Group: Theory, Research and Taxonomy. Strategic Management Journal, Vol.7, pp. 141-160.

McGee J and Thomas H (1986b), Strategic Group Analysis and Strategic Management: Patterns and Trends in Existing Studies. In. McGee J and Thomas H (Eds) Strategic Management Research, Chichester. John Wiley and Sons.

McGee J and Thomas H (1989), Strategic Groups: a Further Comment. Strategic Management Journal Vol. 10, pp. 105-107.

McKenzie R B and Dwight R L (2017), Microeconomics for MBAs: The Economic Way of Thinking for Managers. (3rd ed.) Cambridge University Press.

McKenzie R B and Dwight R L (2017), Microeconomics for MBAs: The Economic Way of Thinking for Managers. (3rd ed.) Cambridge University Press.

McNamee D B and McHugh M (1989), Mapping competitive groups in the clothing industry. Long Range Planning Vol. 22, No. 5, pp. 89–97.

Meyer A D (1982), Adapting to Environmental Jolts. Administrative Science Quarterly. 27, pp. 515-537.

Millar D (1990), The Icarus Paradox: How Excellent Organisations Can Bring About Their Own Downfall. New York, Harper Business.

Miller G A (1956), The Magic number seven, plus or minus two: Some limits to our capacity for processing information. Psychological Review, No.50, pp. 81-97.

Mintzberg H D (1978), Patterns of strategy formation, Management Science, 24, pp. 934948.

Mintzberg H, Ahlstrand B and Lampel J (1998), Strategy Safari. The Free Press, New York.

Mintzberg H and Waters J A (1985), Of Strategies Deliberate and Emergent: Strategic Management Journal, Vol.6, No.3, July- September, pp. 257-273.

Michael C R (1969), Retinal Processing of Visual Images. In, Physiological Psychology : Readings from the Scientific American, (1972) San Francisco, W H Freeman & Co.

Michael C R (1972), Retinal Processing of Visual Images. Scientific American.

Miles R E and Snow C C (1978), Organisational Strategy, Structure and Process. New York. McGraw-Hill.

Montgomery C A and Porter M E (eds) (1991), Strategy: Seeking and Securing Competitive Advantage. Harvard Business Review Books, Boston.

Montgomery and Singh (1984), Diversification strategy and systematic risk. Strategic Management Journal, Vol. 5, pp. 181-191.

Mullins L J (1985), Management and Organisational Behaviour. Pitman.

Murray A I (1988), A contingency view of Porter's generic strategies. Academy of Management Review, Vol. 13, No. 3, pp. 39O-4OO.

Naayer P (1989), Strategic groups: a comment. Strategic Management Journal, Vol. 1O, pp. 1O1-1O3.

Nonaka I (1993), The knowledge – Creating Company. Harvard Business Review, JulyAugust.

Nonaka I and Takeuchi H (1995), The knowledge – Creating Company: How the Japanese Companies Create the Dynamics of Innovation. Oxford University Press, New York.

Narayanan V K (1989), How the broader environment can shape industry elements. Ed. Fahey L The Strategic Planning Management Reader, Prentice Hall.

Newman H H (1978), Strategic groups and the structure-performance relationship. Review of Economics and Statistics, Vol. 6O, August, pp. 417-427

Nohria N and Garcia-Pont C (1991), Global strategic linkages and industry structure. Strategic Management Journal, 12(Special Issue), pp. 105-124

Norufis M J (1986), SPSS/PC+, SPSS INC.

Ohmae K (1982), The Mind of the Strategist. Penguin.

Ohmae K (1989), Managing in a borderless world. Harvard Business Review May - June, pp. 152-161.

Oliver G (1986), Marketing Today. Prentice-Hall.

Olson M (1971), The Logic of Collective Action: Public Goods and the Theory of Groups. Cambridge, MA: Harvard University Press.

Oster S (1982), Intra industry structure and the ease of strategic change. Review of Economics and Statistics, Vol. 64, No.3. pp. 376–384.

Ouchi W G (1982), Theory Z: How the American Business can meet the Japanese Challenge. New York, Avon Books.

Pascale R T (1990), Managing on the Edge: How successful Companies use Conflict to Stay Ahead. Viking Penguin, London.

Payton T H (1986), Towards Compatible Objectives: The Production Marketing Interface. Marketing Intelligence & Planning, Vol.4, No.4. pp. 14-26.

Penrose E T (1980), The growth of the firm. Basil Blackwell.

Peteraf M and Shanley M (1997), A Theory of Strategic Group Identity. Strategic Management Journal, Vol 18, Summer. pp.165-186.

Pettigrew A (1987), Context and Action in the Transformation of the Firm. Journal of Management Studies, 24, pp. 649-670.

Porac J F and Thomas H (1990), Taxonomic mental models in competitor definition. Academy of Management Review, 15, pp. 224-240.

Porac J F, Thomas H and Baden-Fuller C (1989), Competitive groups as cognitive communities: The case of Scottish Knitwear manufacturers. Journal of Management Studies, Vol. 26, No.4, pp. 397-416.

Porac J F, Thomas H and Emme B (1980), Understanding strategists' mental models of competition, In G N Johnson (ed). Business Strategy and Retailing, Wiley, New York and Chichester, pp 59-79.

Porter M E (1974), Consumer behaviour, retailer power and market performance in consumer goods industries. Review of Economics and Statistics, Vol. 56, pp. 419-436.

Porter M E (1976), Interbrand Choice, Strategy and Bilateral Market Power. Harvard University Press, Cambridge MA.

Porter M E (1979), The structure within industries and companies performance. Review of Economics and Statistics, Vol.61, pp. 227-241

Porter M E (1980), Competitive Strategy. Free Press New York.

Porter M E (1983), How competitive forces shape strategy. Ed. Hamermesh R G, Strategic Management. HBR Executive Book Series.

Porter M E (1985), Competitive Advantage. Free Press New York.

Porter M E (1990), The Competitive Advantage of Nations. The Free Press, New York.

Porter M E (1997), Response to Letter to the Editor. Harvard Business Review. March April, pp. 162-163.

Rafferty J (1987), Exit barriers and strategic position in declining markets. Long Range Planning, Vol. 2O No. 2, pp. 86–91.

Rafferty J (1988), Strategic Change Agency and its links to Corporate Culture. Paper presented to the Eighth Annual Strategic Management Society Conference, October, Amsterdam.

Rafferty J (1997), The Synthesis of Economic Organisation and the Management of Change: Intercultural Transferability and the Japanese Paradigm. Wincott Discussion Papers, April, No.4, University of Buckingham.

Rajagopalan N and Spreitzer G M (1996), Toward a Theory of Strategic Change: A Multi-Lens Perspective and Integrative Framework. Academy of Management Review, Vol.22, No.1, pp.48-79.

Rasmusen E (1989), Games and Information. Basil Blackwell.

Reger R K (1990), Managerial Thought Structures and Competitive Positioning, in Huff A.S. (ed), Mapping Strategic Thought. Wiley, Chichester, pp. 71-88.

Reger R K and Huff A S (1993), Strategic Groups: A Cognitive Perspective. Strategic Management Journal. Vol.14, No.2, February, pp. 103-123.

Retail Business (1989), Beer Market Report. Economists Intelligence Unit, No. 374, April.

Ridley M (1996), The Origins Of Virtue. Penguin UK.

Robinson J (1956), The industry and the market. Economic Journal Vol. 56, pp. 36O– 361.

Robock and Simmonds (1989), International Business and Multinational Enterprises. Irwin.

Rubin P H (2002), Darwinian Politics: The Evolutionary Origin of Freedom, New Brunswick, NJ: Rutgers University Press.

Rumelt R (1984), Toward a strategic theory of the firm. In R Lamb (ed.), Competitive Strategy Management, Prentice Hall, Englewood Cliffs, NJ, pp. 556-570.

Schank R C (1982), Dynamic Memory. London, Cambridge University Press.

Schacter D L (1989), Memory, in Posney M.I. (Ed), Foundation of Cognitive Science, Cambridge, Massachusetts.

Schendel D E (1985), Strategic Management and Strategic Marketing: What's strategic about either one? In Strategic Marketing and Management, (eds) Thomas H and Gardner D. John Wiley and Sons.

Schendel D and Patton R (1978), A simultanious equation model of corporate strategy. Management Science, November, pp. 1611-1621.

Schroeder D M (1990), A dynamic perspective on the impact of process innovation upon competitive strategies. Strategic Management Journal, 11, pp. 25-41.

Schwenk C R (1984), Cognitive simplification process in strategic decision-making. Strategic Management Journal 5, pp. 111-128.

Senge P M (1990), The Fifth Discipline: The Art and Practice of The Learning Organization. Century Business, London.

Shipley D D (1985), Marketing objectives in UK and US manufacturing companies. European Journal of Marketing Vol. 19, No. 3, pp. 48-55.

Smith A (1937), Wealth of Nations. Modern Library ed. New York.

Smith K G and Grimm C M (1987), Environmental Variation, Strategic Change and Firm Performance: A Study of Railroad deregulation. Strategic Management Journal, 8 (1), pp. 363-376.

Snow C C and Hambrick D C (1980), Measuring organisational strategies: Some Theoretical and Methodological Problems. Academy of Management Review, Vol.5, pp. 527-538.

Spender J C (1989), Industry Recipes: An Enquiry into the Nature and Sources of Managerial Judgement. Basil Blackwell.

Stacey R D (1993), Strategic Management and Organisational Dynamics. Pitman Publishing, London.

Stigler G J (1968), The Organization of Industry. Richard D Irwin.

Stubbart C I (1989), Managerial Cognition: A Missing Link in Strategic Managerial Research. Journal of Management Studies, Vol. 24, No.4, pp. 325-347.

Sun Zu and Sun Bin (1995), The Art of War. Rusong W and Xianlin W (eds), People's China publishing House, Beijing.

Sudharshan D H and Fiegenbaum A (1991), Assessing mobility barriers in dynamic strategic groups analysis. Journal of Management Studies, 28, pp. 429-438.

Thomas P and Gardner B (1985), Strategic Marketing and Management. John Wiley and Sons.

Thomas H and Venkatraman N (1988), Research on strategic groups: Process and prognosis. Journal of Management Studies, 25, pp. 537-555.

Thompcson E P (1991), Customs in Common. Merlin Press Limited.

Tushman M L and Romainelli E (1985), Organizational evolution: A metamorphosis model of convergence and reorientation. In Cummings L and Straw B (eds), Research in Organisational Behaviour. Vol.7, pp. 171-229 JAI Press.

Utton M A (1970), Industrial Concentration. Penguin.

Utton M A (1982), Domestic concentration and international trade. Oxford Economic Papers, Vol. 34, pp. 479-497.

Uyterhoven R E H, Ackerman W R and Rosenblum W J (1977), Strategy & Organisation, Richard D Irwin inc.

Ward J (1963), Hierarchical groupings to optimize an objective function. Journal of the American Statistical Association, 58, pp. 236-244.

Webb K and Dawson P (1991), Measure for Measure: Strategic Change in an Electronic Instrument Corporation. Journal of Management Studies, 28, pp. 191-206.

Weber M (1964), The Theory of Social and Economic Organisation. Collier McMillan.

Weick K E (1965), The Social Psychology of Organizing. Addison-Wesley. Reading, MA,

Wernerfelt B (2016), Adaptation, Specialization and the Theory of the Firm: Foundations of the Resource-Based View. Cambridge University Press.

Whipp R, Rosenfeld R and Pettigrew A (1989), Culture and Competitiveness: Evidence from two mature U.K. industries. Journal of Management Studies, 26, pp. 561-585.

Williams J R (1985), Organizational impact of product market choice. ed. Thomas and Gardner, Strategic Marketing and Management. John Wiley and Sons.

Zajac E J and Shortell S M (1989), Changing Generic Strategies: Likelihood, Direction and Performance Implications. Strategic Management Journal, 10, pp. 413-429.

INDEX

221